Withdrawn

SALADIN

SALADIN

The Sultan Who Vanquished the
Crusaders and Built an Islamic Empire

JOHN MAN

DA CAPO PRESS
A Member of the Perseus Books Group

Typeset in Sabon by Falcon Oast Graphic Art Ltd.

Cataloging-in-Publication data for this book is available from the Library of Congress.

ISBN: 978-0-306-82487-6 (hardcover)
ISBN: 978-0-306-82488-3 (e-book)

Published by Da Capo Press
A Member of the Perseus Books Group
www.dacapopress.com

Da Capo Press books are available at special discounts for bulk purchases in the U.S. by corporations, institutions, and other organizations. For more information, please contact the Special Markets Department at the Perseus Books Group, 2300 Chestnut Street, Suite 200, Philadelphia, PA 19103, or call (800) 810-4145, ext. 5000, or e-mail special.markets@perseusbooks.com.

10 9 8 7 6 5 4 3 2 1

Contents

List of Illustrations and Maps

List of maps

Preface

The Once and Future King

ASK ANYONE IN THE EASTERN MEDITERRANEAN TO NAME their greatest hero and the answer you will get is almost certainly 'Saladin'. All across Europe and America, if you ask for one *Arabic* hero, the answer, after a pause for thought, will probably be the same. One in a million might say that, strictly speaking, he wasn't Arabic but Kurdish. But you get the point. Kurds, Arabs, Iranians, Turks, north Africans, Jews and Europeans of all nationalities, and many Americans with Middle Eastern connections, think Saladin is one of the greatest leaders of all time, with virtues to match his achievements.

History supports them, up to a point. But there is more at

work than history. Saladin is a fantasy hero as well as a real one. He embodies dreams and wishes, like Arthur, though rather better because so much more is known of him. Take one theme of his life story, which is like the plot of a good-guy v. bad-guy movie. Saladin himself is, of course, the good guy. Against him is set a baddie with such archetypical faults that he sounds like a caricature. His name was Reynald, and he came to the Holy Land for fame and fortune, which he found by doing terrible things. He caught the eye of a princess and took control of her city. He wrung cash from a prelate by torturing him and leaving him naked in the burning sun to be food for insects. He used that money to invade and ruin a beautiful and peaceful island. A spell in prison made him even more fanatical, greedy and bloodthirsty. By the time Saladin came up against him, Reynald was the grim master of the grimmest of Crusader castles. He ignored truces and insulted those who remonstrated. Saladin was so appalled by his behaviour that he set aside his usual magnanimity and swore he would kill Reynald with his own hands. Finally, after a famous victory, he did so, taking off his head with one blow of his sword. Insult, vengeance, retribution: these are themes that have driven great storylines from the ancient Greeks to Hollywood.

There's Hollywood in another strand of Saladin's story too. In the battle following the one in which Saladin slew Reynald, the Crusaders bore aloft their greatest treasure, which they called the True Cross. In fact, it was a wooden fragment set in a gold-and-silver cross. This object had its own back-story, which totally convinced the Crusaders of its authenticity. It was for them what Alfred Hitchcock called the McGuffin, the object of power that everyone wants, and which therefore drives the plot. It may have 'real' power (as the Ark does in *Raiders of the Lost Ark*) or it may not, just as long as it is desired. The True Cross was an object of both desire and power. For Christians, it was more than a *symbol* of why they were crusading; it was the very reason why. It was, to them, the actual thing upon which Christ was crucified, or part of it. It had the power to work miracles, a talisman that would confound all enemies, confer victory, and keep Jerusalem in Christian hands for ever and ever amen, until Christ returned in glory.

Well, they lost the battle to Saladin, and they lost Jerusalem, and they lost the True Cross – enough, one might think, to demonize Saladin in their eyes. And yet Christians admired him, not simply because he was in fact admirable, but because his fine qualities were explained and magnified, with a convoluted logic, which ran as follows:

Christians are good, and must prevail in the end because God is on our side. But in this case Saladin prevailed. This must be because we are not good enough Christians, so God is punishing us. Saladin is his instrument. Therefore, in this instance, Saladin is close to God and is to be seen as a closet Christian, and therefore admirable, an embodiment of Christian virtues, the perfect knight.

How to separate out the strands of fact and fantasy is one object of this book. Another is to see why down the centuries Saladin has remained a hero, and remains one still.

The quick answer is that there are many similarities between then and now.

Now, as then, the Muslim world is divided by the great Sunni–Shia schism; now, as then, sects multiply; now, as then, Arabs are hungry for some way to heal the split; now, as then, they are eager to confront and confound the challenge from without – then the Crusaders, now the USA, working through its proxy, Israel, and its other allies, its armed forces, its companies. There is a hunger for simpler problems and a solution as simple as 'Liberate Jerusalem!' One cry remains the same: 'Jihad!' – though it was simpler then, because the enemy was not a distant and indestructible superpower but was on the spot, occupying cities and castles, with finite forces, which could be vanquished with the right leadership.

Another echo from the past is the habit of taking hostages. The circumstances in Iraq and (as I write) Syria are often remarkably similar, even more so recently. Not long ago, announcing the taking of a hostage and the terms for his – almost always his – release took a simple call on the victim's mobile phone. But today mobile phones are easily traced, revealing hiding places and summoning drones. Kidnappers have resorted to medieval means: handwritten demands, go-betweens and in one case . . . well, a source who advises on kidnap-and-ransom cases told me the story. An Iraqi businessman was taken hostage. Soon after, his family received a large crate. It contained homing pigeons, along with instructions: tape $100 to the legs of each pigeon, and release it. When the last pigeon was released, so was the prisoner. Any Muslim leader in the twelfth century would have understood, because carrier-pigeons were the equivalents of email servers, linking in hours even the most distant of friends and enemies.

Today, as then, the main focal point is Damascus, the home town of both Assad and Saladin. Today, warring factions make it impossible even to imagine a solution. In Saladin's day, the problems were similar. Even if he had expelled all crusading

Christians, Muslim divisions would have remained. The underlying difference between then and now is leadership. Saladin was a genius, able briefly to focus Islamic energy on the tasks of unity and jihad. He was the best his people could have hoped for, and a role model for any leader working for a better tomorrow.

A Note on Dating

Since this book is initially for western readers, I use AD/ BC, increasingly called the Common Era (CE) or Before the Common Era (BCE). The Muslim calendar has a different system. Its base-year is the Hijira (also spelled Hijra and Hegira), the year of Muhammad's flight from Mecca to Medina. In theory all AD dates can be transferred into AH (After Hijira). But it is not straightforward. The two systems overlap and the relationship between them in the early years of Islam is still disputed. The base-year of 1 AH runs for a year, roughly from the spring of 622. By convention, Saladin's birth was in 532 AH, which ran for a year from September 1137.

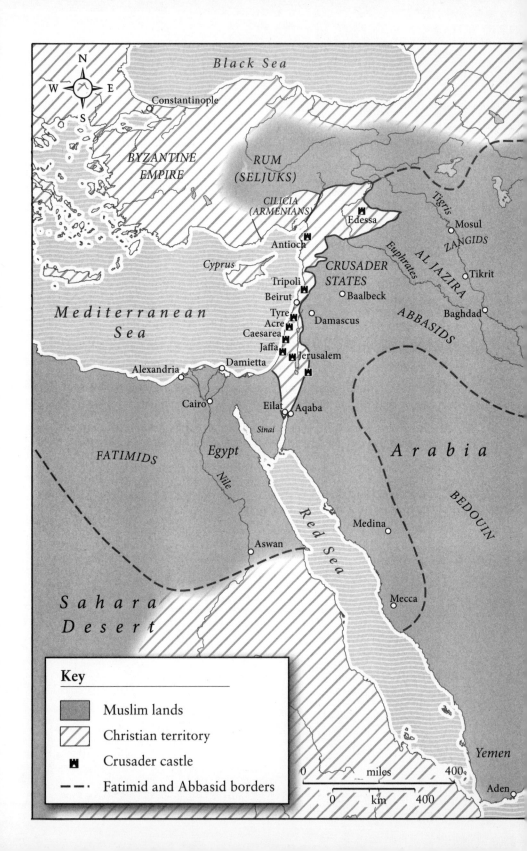

Key

▨	Muslim lands
▨	Christian territory
🏰	Crusader castle
− − −	Fatimid and Abbasid borders

The World of Young Ṣaladin c.1140

Crusader (Frankish) States 1186

Caspian Sea

Persian Gulf

COUNTY OF EDESSA

oHarran

Antioch o

o Aleppo

Rakka

Latakia o

PRINCIPALITY OF ANTIOCH

Tortosa

o Hama

Tripoli

o Homs

COUNTY OF TRIPOLI

Beirut

Sidon

Damascus

Tyre

Acre

Caesarea

KINGDOM OF JERUSALEM

Jaffa

Ascalon

Jerusalem

Gaza

OUTREJOURDAIN

Sinai

Arabia

Eilat

Aqaba

1

A World in Conflict

BAALBEK, LEBANON, 900 YEARS AGO WAS A WONDERFUL PLACE and a wonderful time for a curious boy. So much life. Such mysteries.

The Temple of Jupiter, with fifty-four columns, each of them 63 feet high, looked like the work of titans, but this Roman glory stood on massive monoliths which are today, as they were then, the world's greatest hewn stones. Weighing up to 1,000 tonnes each – twenty times the weight of the megaliths of Stonehenge – they hark back to some ancient culture whose people had somehow managed to cut and shift them. Who made them? How did they move them? No one knew then, no one knows now.

Other ruins recalled construction and destruction by Macedonians, Greeks, Romans, Arabs and the earth itself. This is a region of earthquakes, which ruined buildings and buried ruins. But Baalbek was a phoenix, endlessly renewed by its people and by nature. Standing half a mile high, its crisp, clean air smelled of orchards and gardens. It was at the centre of the Islamic world, almost on the frontier between Islam's two rival Arabic empires, Abbasid and Fatimid, almost equidistant from their two ancient capitals, Baghdad and Cairo. What a mixture of security and apprehension the young Saladin would have breathed – the security of his religion set against the region's unending wars, power struggles, rebellions and assassinations, all this mayhem made worse in living memory by a new set of invaders, alien in creed and culture.

Saladin – little Yusuf (Joseph) as he was then – was not born in Baalbek. He was brought there by his father, Ayyub (Job) al-Din,[1] for reasons we will get to in due course. So it was in Baalbek, during his unrecorded childhood, that Saladin began to learn something of the world into which he had been born.

Islam, despite all its diversity and violence, was united by religion and culture. At its heart was the Quran, which distilled and stimulated a language at a crucial moment in its evolution. Muslim scholars from the Hindu Kush to southern Spain all worshipped the same god, honoured the same prophet, shared Arabic as a lingua franca, and inherited the same astonishingly rich intellectual mantle. All Islam shared

---

[1] To give them their full names, Yusuf al-Din ibn Ayyub and Ayyub Najm al-Din ibn Shadhi ibn Shadhi.

the same economic strength, with trade linking north Africa, Europe, Russia, the Middle East, India and China. Since Islam accepted the enslavement of non-Muslims, all benefited from a lucrative trade in slaves, whether African, Turkish, Indian or Slav. Arab coins found their way north as far as Finland, and Muslim merchants wrote cheques honoured by banks in major cities. One trader had a warehouse on the Volga, another near Bukhara in present-day Uzbekistan and a third in Gujarat, India.

Fuelled by staggering wealth, medieval Islam hungered for learning and inspired brilliant scholarship. Paper displaced papyrus, bookshops thrived, libraries graced the homes of the rich. At the end of the ninth century, according to the geographer al-Ya'qubi, one street in Damascus had a hundred bookshops. Since Arabic was the language of divine revelation, the written word was venerated and calligraphy became an art form valued above painting. Medieval Islam, assured of its superiority, was innovative and curious. The Arabs, looking back to the Greeks for the foundations of science and philosophy, translated Greek classics en masse (a strand of scholarship that would eventually feed into Europe's Renaissance in the fifteenth century). Many other languages and creeds – Persian, Sanskrit and Syriac, Christianity, Judaism and Zoroastrianism – also formed part of this rich amalgam.

One consequence of Islamic scholarship and self-assurance was its tolerance. This was not a world of inward-looking fundamentalism. True, Jews and Christians were seen as benighted, the Jews for believing that divine revelation had stopped with the Hebrew prophets, the Christians for abandoning monotheism, believing that God was not one but a Trinity. Yet Judaism and Christianity were seen as stepping-stones from barbarism to revelation and Islam. All three were 'Peoples of the Book', namely what Christians know as the Old Testament.

The arts flourished. Urbanized literati patronized the ornate and elegant creations of poets. Historians recorded and honoured Islamic achievements. Though Islam discouraged (and later banned) human likenesses in art, there was nothing to inhibit design and architecture. Wonderful domed mosques arose, pre-dating Italian Renaissance domes by centuries. Potters tried to match Chinese porcelain (they failed, but they created lustrous, wonderfully decorated glazes). Stuccoed and frescoed palaces set an ornate style emulated throughout Islam.

Science also blossomed. It was not seen as a threat to Islam. How could it be, seeing as all Creation reflected the glory of Allah? Indeed, the late-tenth-century bibliographer ibn al-Nadim said that Aristotle had appeared to him in a dream and assured him there was no conflict between reason and religion. Thousands of scientific works were translated from Persian, Sanskrit and – most notably – Greek. 'Arabic' numerals, derived from Indian ones, provided a far more powerful mathematical tool than any previous system, as Europe later discovered. Though Arab scientists remained convinced that gold could be produced by the transformation of metals, their rigorous search for the 'philosopher's stone' that would cause this to happen created the bridge between alchemy (*al-kimiya*, 'transmutation') and modern chemistry. Muslim travellers wrote reports of China, Europe and much of Africa. European languages, enriched by translations from Arabic into Latin, still contain many other tributes to Arab scientific predominance: zero (from *sifr*, 'empty'), algebra (*al-jebr*, 'integration'), star-names such as Betelgeuse (from *bayt al-jawza*, 'the house of the twins') and Altair ('the flyer'), zenith, nadir, azimuth.

Among the great centres, Baghdad was the greatest. With its roots in the wealth of ancient Persia, the city was a magnet for traders, scholars and artists from as far afield as Spain and northern India. By 1000, it had become one of the largest cities in the world, equalling Constantinople – 1,200,000, about the same size as London in 1800 – with wealth to match. One caliph greeted a Byzantine ruler with a pageant of 160,000 cavalrymen and 100 lions. The city's wharves harboured vessels bringing porcelain from China, silk, musk and ivory from east Africa, spices and pearls from Malaya, Russian slaves, wax and furs.

To the east lay a subdivision of Islam that was not Arabic, but Persian and Turkish. Its centres were the ancient oasis cities of Samarkand, Bukhara, Merv and Gurganj (later Urgench), all worthy if lesser counterparts to Baghdad. Once, for a long century (874–999), this region had been independent. Looking back to their eighth-century Persian ancestor Saman Khudat, the Samanids had thrown out their Arab overlords and built their own brand of Islam, spreading east into Afghanistan, holding off the Arabs to the west and, for a while, the Turks, who ended Samanid rule in 999. All four cities were trade emporia linking east and west, China and Islam, their exports including soap, sulphur, silks, sable, leatherware and ornamental arms. Watermelons packed in snow were couriered westwards from the foothills of the Tien Shan to Baghdad. Paper from Samarkand was in demand all over the Muslim world. Caravans the size of small armies – one numbered 5,000 men and 3,000 horses and camels – ranged back and forth to eastern Europe, trading silks, copper bowls and jewellery for furs, amber and sheep skins. From China came pottery and spices, in exchange for glass and horses, of which China could never get enough.

Bukhara, the old Samanid capital, with a population of 300,000, almost rivalled Baghdad itself. Its scholars and poets, writing in both Arabic and Persian, made it the 'dome of Islam in the east', in a common epithet. Its royal library, with 45,000 volumes, had a suite of rooms, each devoted to a different discipline. In the words of an eleventh-century anthologist, al-Tha'alabi, it was the 'focus of splendour, the shrine of empire, the meeting-place of the most unique intellects of the age'. Perhaps the greatest of the greats was the philosopher-physician ibn Sina, known in Europe by the Spanish version of his name, Avicenna (980–1037), who poured out over 200 books, most famously his medical encyclopedia, *Canons of Medicine*, which when translated into Latin became Europe's pre-eminent medical textbook for five centuries.

So, in theory, all were united under Allah, the Prophet, and his divinely inspired words, the Quran. All owed allegiance to God's earthly representative, the caliph, a sort of Muslim equivalent of the Pope.

In theory.

In practice, Islam had been divided against itself almost from the start. The main division was the split between Sunni and Shi'ite. One doctrinal source was the *sunnah*, the deeds and sayings of both the Prophet and his successors, whereas those who belonged to the Shi'a (party) of Ali, claimed that authority derived from Muhammad's descendants through his son-in-law Ali. Sunnis, for whom the Quran is the intermediary between God and mankind, established their caliphate first in Damascus then in Baghdad. Shi'ites proclaimed their 'leader in prayer', the imam, as their intermediary with God (though one Shia branch also set up its own rival caliph in Cairo, a development which demands a more detailed look a few paragraphs further on). Shi'ites claimed that from Ali's descendants a divinely appointed imam would emerge as Mahdi, 'the guided one'. Since there was no obvious Mahdi, Shi'ites came to believe that he was being hidden by God. The notion of the 'hidden imam' became a central tenet of Shi'ism, one that inspired numerous pretenders and a very strange sub-sect, as we shall see shortly.

By 1000, the Islamic world, created as one imperial river by the Arabs, had divided into a delta of five major streams and an uncounted number of minor ones. The Sunni–Shia split remained as the prime division, ever more confused by dynasties and sects and sub-sects and rebellions and tribal feuds and family squabbles that formed and re-formed frontiers from India to the Pyrenees. A time-lapse map of the region would seethe like colonies of cells under a microscope, breeding, growing, absorbing, vanishing. Unnumbered thousands died fighting for some orthodoxy or heresy, for this or that dynasty, for their own beloved and soon-to-be forgotten caliph or sultan or emir.

When Saladin was young, the Shia–Sunni split had a political dimension, focused on Cairo and Baghdad, each with its own caliph, each certain of its own rectitude, each determined to destroy the other. Egypt was ruled by Shi'ites claiming descent from the Prophet's daughter Fatima and her husband, Ali; Baghdad by Sunnis who looked back to the Prophet's uncle, Abbas. Fatimid and Abbasid: the two empires met in what is today northern Lebanon, with both running up against the southern borders of Christendom's eastern section, Byzantium. The cities where Saladin grew up under Abbasid rule were near the point where the three rival Muslim empires had once converged.

By the time of Saladin's birth in around 1137–8 (uncertain because of the inexact relationship between the western and Muslim calendars; see note on p.xiii) the days of Abbasid glory were over, undermined by luxury, broken up by petty chiefdoms, torn apart by Crusaders (on which more later), shattered by the Turks drifting slowly westwards towards the land now named after them. As they migrated, the Seljuk Turks, named after their tenth-century sultan, converted to Sunni Islam and paid lip-service to the impotent caliph in Baghdad. But they followed their own agenda and were unreliable allies.

So all Arabs, Shi'ite and Sunni alike, recalled a golden age, singing of what was once achieved in the name of Islam, dreaming of a future when unity and prosperity would return.

One element in this unstable mixture is worth explaining at length because of the subject's fame, sheer oddity and malign influence, especially on Saladin himself, who was almost murdered twice by them.

This was the group known as the Assassins, whose story is rooted deep in Shi'ite Islam. They claimed that Ismail, the disinherited son of the Sixth Imam, represented the true line of authority from Muhammad. Ismail's followers claimed that he had been succeeded by 'hidden imams'. When the Turks swept into the Islamic world from the Asian heartland around the year 1000, they turned on Shi'ites, including the Ismailis, who responded by forming a network of underground cells, with extraordinary consequences. In the second half of the eleventh century, a man named Hassan i-Sabbah, newly converted to Ismailism, decided to wage his own war for Ismailism and its 'hidden imam' in the heart of Turkish territory. He spotted the perfect base: a formidable castle, Alamut, 6,000 feet up in the Elburz mountains south of the Caspian. Here he set about asserting his own peculiar version of Ismailism, based on the premise that Nizar, the heir to the Fatimid state murdered in 1097, would produce the Mahdi who would magically reappear to save Islam from impurity and its Turkish invaders. The fact that Nizar had no designated heir was a problem quickly solved. The line was merely declared 'hidden' and one of them would reappear in due course. Meanwhile, Hassan named himself Nizar's deputy and champion. Technically, his followers were Nizaris, an offshoot of the Ismailis, an offshoot of the Shi'ites – a sect of a sect of a sect. This 'New Preaching' (as Hassan called it) appealed strongly to the poor and dis-possessed, who were happy to devote themselves to a cause in absolute and unthinking obedience. Hassan sent them out in ones and twos and threes to kill with knife or sword whatever Arab, Turk, sultan, emir, priest, vizier or general seemed to him to deserve death, whether Sunni or Shia. These were, of course, the original Assassins.

It is a puzzling term. The European word in various spell-ings derives from the Arabic *hashish*, Indian hemp, *Cannabis sativa*. Some people referred to the Nizaris as *hashishiyya* (or a Persian equivalent) – hashish-users – and that was the term picked up by the Crusaders in the twelfth century when they heard of them in Syria. So everyone assumed that's what they were, hashish being their secret drug of choice to relax them before going off to stab some high official and perhaps meet their own death. By the early nineteenth century, it was a conventional wisdom and is still widely believed today. But it was not so. Hashish was well known, not a Nizari secret; and no Nizari source mentions it. More likely, the term was an insult applied to this despised and feared group.

Other hilltop castles fell to Hassan, giving him an impregnable power-base from which to launch his malign campaign against anyone whom he judged to stand in his way. He never again left Alamut, where for thirty-five years he instructed, inspired and organized his followers, who, like today's suicide bombers, embraced death as martyrdom, knowing they would be rewarded by an after-life in Paradise. Rulers everywhere lived in fear. They wore armour under their robes, remained locked indoors, ordered special protection, dared not condemn, but kept a panic-stricken silence. Terror spawned counter-terror, with other echoes of modernity – random accusations, round-ups, imprisonments and deaths in custody. Nothing worked. Alamut remained impregnable, while the Assassins' ideology became ever more eccentric, eventually proclaiming them free of all laws but their own. Naturally, mainstream Muslims looked on all this with horror, and condemned the Assassins as heretics.

There was more, however, to the Assassins than duplicity, violence and heresy. They were, after all, asserting what they believed was a truth about God's will. Truth can always do with extra help, in the form of reason and science. Surprisingly, Ismaili imams were lovers of objective as well as esoteric knowledge. They built a famous library. Scholars were welcomed, one being the famous astronomer and theologian Nasir al-Din Tusi, who lived in Alamut for many years.

Alamut was not their only base. They had metastasized, like some sort of cancer. Soon after Hassan captured Alamut, his agents began to spread the word in Syria. From 1103, the Persian-based Assassins had an Arabic branch, an enclave centred on a castle almost as formidable as Alamut – Masyaf, in Syria, 45 kilometres from the Mediterranean. From here, they sent agents to kill Turks, Crusaders (with whom on occasion they also collaborated) and any Muslim leader, Sunni or Shia, who offended them. Their most redoubtable leader, Rashid al-Din Sinan, became known to Crusaders as 'the Old Man of the Mountain', after the massif in which he was based. To Sunni and Shia alike, Sinan was as vile as Hassan. In the words of the Spanish traveller and poet ibn Jubayr, he led 'a sect which swerved from Islam and vested divinity in a man. The prophet was a devil in disguise named Sinan, who deceived them with falsehoods and chimeras embellished for them to act upon. He bewitched them with these black arts, so that they took him as a god and worshipped him.' Later, the term was applied vaguely to any Assassin leader.

In 1256, a century after Saladin's death, the Assassins were destroyed by Islam's next and greatest scourge, the Mongols. In 1273 the Syrian Assassins were cowed by the sultan of Egypt, Baybars, and that was the end of the real Assassins (though the Nizaris endured, flourishing today under their imam, the Aga Khan).

In 1096, just forty years before Saladin's birth, there had come into this united, disunited world a new, alien element: the Crusaders.

Saladin would not have known, for no Muslim could have known, of the original seed or why it had fallen on such rich soil. It had been tossed by the Pope in 1095. Urban II was supposedly head of a super-state, Christendom, which in theory included most of Europe and also Rome's so-called eastern empire in Constantinople, made into Rome's successor by its founder Constantine. But Urban had severe problems. Firstly, he had just received a plea for help from Constantinople: the Seljuk Turks were advancing into the world of Islam and had, seventeen years before, taken the revered city of Nicaea, in Anatolia, present-day eastern Turkey, famous as a Christian centre for almost 800 years, since the great council of 325 that formalized what Christians were supposed to believe by stating the tenets in the Nicene Creed. Nicaea, the one-time symbol of Christian unity, was a mere 70 kilometres from Constantinople, so the barbarians who had swarmed through the city's sturdy Roman walls were already inside the outer bulwarks of Christendom. Secondly, Christendom was not united at all, but divided between Rome and Constantinople, who were at loggerheads over a point of doctrine that sounds bizarre to non-Christians: since God was a Trinity – Father, Son and Holy Spirit – did the Spirit proceed 'from the Father' (as the Orthodox east said) or 'from the Father and the Son' (as Rome claimed)? The so-called Filioque ('and the Son') Clause had been part of the western Creed since 1020. Bizarre perhaps, but so fundamental that Pope and Patriarch could never make up (and never have). Thirdly, the Pope's own backyard, western Europe, was in disarray, France in particular. Pope rivalled emperor, baron fought baron, ordinary people suffered. Urban's solution was that of many leaders seeking to unite unruly subjects: a foreign war and a cause that sounded noble.

His chance came at a gathering of French leaders in

Clermont, south-west France, in November 1095. 'Let those who have been accustomed unjustly to wage private warfare against the faithful now go against the infidels,' he told a crowd of 300 bishops, knights and assorted lay people;[2] 'let those who have been fighting against their brothers and relatives now fight in a proper way against the barbarians.'

His words fell on fertile soil. The once-backward region of Europe, which had fallen into barbarism after the end of the Roman Empire 700 years before, was beginning a slow revival. Charlemagne had kick-started the political process in 800 by making himself ruler of an incipient European state, the Holy Roman Empire. But there was also a revolution of another sort brewing. With metal-bladed ox-ploughs and crop rotation, farmers produced better harvests. With more food, couples had more and healthier children. Mercifully, there were no major plagues. The population grew, and spread into the badlands of eastern Europe. The Vikings, who had once nibbled at Europe's flanks, had settled. So had the Hungarians, the last of the barbarian invaders. In the south-west, the tide of Islam that had flowed over Spain and into France had been dammed and turned back. By the time of Urban's appeal, the people of Europe faced a future that was rosier, or at least less dismal, than their past. They could afford foreign adventure.

They loved the idea. Urban's speech was, in the words of one historian, 'probably the most effective speech in all history'.[3] The crowd roared its approval and scattered to spread the message, summarized in a catchphrase, '*Deus vult!*' ('God wills it!'). Their focus was Jerusalem, where Christ had

[2] According to one version of the speech by the chronicler Fulcher of Chartres in *Gesta Francorum Jerusalem Expugnantium*.
[3] Philip Hitti, *A History of the Arabs*, p. 636.

preached and (they believed) worked miracles and been cruci-fied and risen from the dead. Somewhere in the Church of the Holy Sepulchre lay a piece of the True Cross, which would surely have miraculous powers. The city had been in Turkish hands for 450 years. The time had come to take it back.

And they did, with extreme violence, because, in the words of the historian John Roberts, there would be oppor-tunities for looting unavailable in Europe; 'they could spoil the pagans with clear consciences'. By the spring of 1097, hundreds of knights leading a rabble of some 30,000 met in Constantinople. They were mainly French, or Franks as they were known – Franj as the Muslims called them – though there was little sense of nationhood to unite Normans, Provençals, Angevins and Flemings. Despite a scattering of Italians and Hungarians, 'Franks' became a catch-all term for the Crusaders. The only war aims were vague: take the Holy Land, convert the heathen, seize Jerusalem. And then? No one said. A few leaders were high-minded, some saw a chance to grab territory, many were romantics and adventurers, and most no more than rough peasants happy to escape a harsh life or ruffians eager for loot. All, though, could *claim* to be high-minded, displaying the Cross as the symbol of Christianity. This was what came to be called the First Crusade, the first of eight campaigns to the Holy Land over the next two cen-turies. Most failed, some were disastrous, but this first one did indeed achieve its aims, so is sometimes called a success, if extreme and unprovoked aggression can ever be classified as such.

There followed the recapture of the new Turkish capital, Nicaea, today the little town of Iznik. The siege involved an aspect of warfare that would soon have significance for

Saladin. The Crusader army was simply not strong enough to overwhelm Nicaea's immense walls or batter down its gates. The Byzantine emperor, Alexios Komnenos, knew this, because he had seen the army and knew the walls: 5 kilometres around, 10 metres high, 100 towers. It would of course be wonderful if the town could be retaken for Christianity, pushing back the Turkish and Islamic frontier. But how to do this, without throwing soldiers uselessly against the city's walls? What the Crusaders needed was heavy artillery. The emperor happened to be a great military leader, aged forty-three, at the height of his powers, eager to recapture borderlands in present-day Turkey lost to the Seljuk Turks. War is often the necessity that mothers invention, and in this case Alexios was the father. He knew as much as anyone about heavy artillery in the form of trebuchets, the machines that could sling rocks astonishing distances. He had commissioned several of these devices for his army. They were of various types, all referred to as 'city-takers', and they will take centre stage in due course. Alexios was a designer as well as a commander. He created machines that broke new ground, literally and figuratively. His daughter Anna wrote of his new city-takers and their effect in the siege of Nicaea: 'most of them were not old-fashioned according to the conventional designs for such machines, but followed ideas he had devised himself and which amazed everyone.' Possibly these devices were the prototypes of the so-called counterweight trebuchets, whose specifications dwarfed earlier machines: 10-tonne counterweights, lever-arms 15 metres long, projectiles weighing over 100 kilograms, ranges of 200 metres. They cracked Nicaea open like a hammer on a nut, though Alexios took care to seize control of the town before the Crusaders had a chance to loot it. Alexios's machines, which had so 'amazed everyone', changed warfare from then on. The improved versions would have dramatic effects when, eighty years later, Saladin got the power to command them.

On the Crusaders went: a pitched battle, a five-month advance across Turkey, an eight-month siege of Antioch (where by happy chance a mystic named Peter Bartholomew, guided by St Andrew, found a chunk of iron which he declared to be the Holy Lance that had pierced the side of Christ), and more sieges, including the taking of Ma'arat, 80 kilometres south-east of Antioch, in today's Syria. It was winter, the end of 1098, with food in short supply, so, according to a chronicler, the French 'boiled pagan adults in cooking pots; they impaled children on spits and devoured them grilled.' An exaggeration? If the source had been Arabic, perhaps; but this was a Frank, Ralph of Caen, speaking.[4] Another French chronicler, Albert of Aix, confirmed it: 'Not only did our troops not shrink from eating dead Turks and Saracens; they also ate dogs.'

What could Muslims do? Not much. There was no hope of a united response, whether from Islam as a whole or from local princes. Every leader, Sunni or Shia, wondered if the new arrivals might perhaps be of use against their Islamic rivals. Every town was on its own, and the only way to survive was to flee or to fawn: 'Kiss any arm you cannot break', in the words of a popular proverb. Delegates arrived bringing gifts of gold, jewellery and horses, hoping to bribe the 'Franj' either to become an ally or to move on in peace.

So the Franks advanced, with almost no opposition, to the

---

[4] Or Radulph, as he is also known; in *Gesta Tancredi*, quoted in Amin Maalouf, *The Crusades Through Arab Eyes*, as is Albert of Aix.

walls of Jerusalem, which they assaulted for a month with two siege-towers and fourteen stone-throwing catapults. In mid-July 1099, they took the city, with terrible consequences for the place they claimed to venerate. In an outpouring of xenophobia and greed, all suffered – Muslims, Jews, Orthodox Christians. The Crusaders sacked the Dome of the Rock (sometimes wrongly called the Mosque of Umar, the second successor of the Prophet). They expelled from the Holy Sepulchre all eastern Christians – Greeks, Georgians, Armenians, Copts and Syrians – who had shared the place for centuries. There followed the indiscriminate slaughter of thousands, perhaps tens of thousands, of men, women and children. 'Some of the pagans were mercifully beheaded,' wrote the chronicler Raymond d'Aguilers. 'Others pierced by arrows plunged from towers, and yet others, tortured for a long time, were burned to death in searing flames. Piles of heads, hands and feet lay in the houses and streets, and indeed there was a running to and fro of men and knights over the corpses.' The mob of Crusaders, apparently berserk with bloodlust, burned the main synagogue around a mass of Jews hoping for sanctuary. Afterwards, Muslim survivors were forced to drag the bodies outside the walls, where they made piles 'as big as houses'.

In early August, the newly appointed Patriarch of Jerusalem, Arnulf, made the discovery that all Christians wanted. Arnulf needed a coup of some sort. He and others had been doubtful about the previous 'discovery' of the Holy Lance in Antioch. Peter had countered the doubters with more visions, and finally with an offer to undergo an ordeal by fire, the idea being that if he was telling the truth, the fire would not touch him. The flames did what flames do. Scorched almost to death, and then mobbed by a crowd, Peter said Christ himself had actually protected him and blamed the crowd for his burns. He died twelve days later. After that, the Holy Lance lost its holiness, leaving the Crusaders without a talisman. The only one that really mattered now was the True Cross, which supposedly lay somewhere in the Holy Sepulchre, of which Arnulf was the guardian. Only the Greek Orthodox priests knew where it was, and they weren't telling. Arnulf had them tortured until they did. The True Cross, as it was called – though it was in fact a piece of wood embedded in a gold-and-silver cross – became the most sacred relic of the Christian Holy Land. It was their object of power, to be displayed at the head of armies as if it were some sort of secret weapon.

No one seems to have known what was supposed to happen next. Most Crusaders trickled homewards, but many stayed, as soldiers helping to subdue other cities and as citizens of four 'Latin' statelets: Edessa, Antioch and Jerusalem, plus Jerusalem's semi-independent offshoot, Tripoli. So by 1110 the four colonies controlled the coastal bits of present-day Turkey, Syria, Lebanon, Jordan and Israel by means of thirty-six formidable castles, which dominated the ports and trade routes.

Turks or Arabs at first saw the Crusaders as animals, drunk on a brew of religious zeal, bloodlust, xenophobia and greed. Devout Muslims demanded holy war, jihad. 'Do you not owe an obligation to God and Islam?' an anonymous poet begged the reluctant sultans.[5] 'Respond to God! Woe to you! Respond!' But hatred and despair achieved nothing, because emotion was not focused by leadership. Despite overwhelming

[5] Carole Hillenbrand, *The Crusades: Islamic Perspectives*, p.70.

numbers and several counter-attacks, nothing worked, for many reasons – bad luck, treachery, lack of courage, lack of leadership – the main one being that, frankly, most Muslim leaders had better things to do fighting each other. Better a Christian than a heretic, better a Christian buffer state than a rival Muslim neighbour. 'The sultans did not agree among themselves,' wrote the historian Ali ibn al-Athir, 'and it was for this reason that the Franj were able to seize control.'

The response, when it came, was not a holy war, more an unholy peace. Both sides accommodated. The Franks employed locals, introduced a form of feudalism that promoted mutual responsibilities, adopted the local dress and cuisine, and married into local families. Each side sought alliance with the other, each mini-state squabbled with others, each had its disputes over succession. Much changed superficially, and nothing changed fundamentally. By the time of Saladin's birth in 1137–8, almost forty years after the loss of Jerusalem, hatred of the Franks had been diluted by both complacency – since many ordinary Arabs preferred the Franks to their own grasping and unreliable leaders – and a growing belief that no great leader would arise to heal Muslim rivalries and drive the Franks into the sea.

2

A Teenager in Damascus

WHAT BROUGHT ONE-YEAR-OLD YUSUF – SALADIN AS HE would become – to Baalbek?

He was born in Tikrit, in present-day Iraq, now famous as the birthplace of Saddam Hussein. His father Ayyub was there because his father, a Kurd from Armenia, had sought a better life in Baghdad, the capital of the decaying Abbasid Empire, now under new Turkish rulers, the Seljuks. Ayyub's father was appointed governor of Tikrit, a position inherited by Ayyub, who was therefore governor when, in the 1130s, civil war broke out between the Seljuks.One of the participants was a bristly bearded, heavy-drinking, brutal and erratic Turk named Imad al-Din ('Pillar of the Faith')

Zangi,[6] who had won the governorship of Aleppo and Mosul (today's northern Iraq and northern Syria) in earlier, more stable times. He was more than the sum of his faults, also being austere, immensely tough, a leader who identified with his state, and a strict disciplinarian who knew how to win respect from ordinary soldiers. He was not interested in luxury. When he arrived at a city, he would disdain its palaces and sleep outside the city walls in a tent. No wonder one chronicler, al-Athir, overlooked his faults and called him 'the gift of divine providence to the Muslims'. He would become a vital link in the chain of events leading to Saladin's rise.

Character is not always destiny, but it was in the case of Zangi and Ayyub. In 1132, Zangi fought and lost a battle near Tikrit. Wounded, he needed help to get back to his power-base in Aleppo. Ayyub might have stuck with his masters in Baghdad and handed Zangi over. But he didn't. Perhaps it was his innate generosity, perhaps some political insight that guided him, for he was, in the chronicler Baha al-Din ibn Shaddad's words, an 'honourable, generous and good man'. In any event, he treated Zangi's wounds and ferried him and his army to safety across the river Tigris, allowing him to set himself up in Aleppo.

We still need to know why Ayyub left Tikrit. Ayyub had a brother named Shirkuh (Asad al-Din Shirkuh), a fine soldier but rather quick-tempered, who killed a man in a quarrel. As a target for the enraged family, he had to get out, fast. Ayyub backed him and the two fled together, with their families. Tradition has it that they left on the very night of Saladin's birth on some unrecorded day in 532 AH (September 1137–

---

[6] Or Zengi. As usual, transcriptions vary.

September 1138). The following year, with the two brothers by his side, Zangi, eager to extend his power-base, added to Baalbek's ruins by bombarding the city with fourteen giant catapults. He promised to spare the garrison if they surrendered, then broke his word by crucifying thirty-seven of them. Whatever his faults, though, Zangi was not one to forget a generous action. He made Ayyub the town's governor and Shirkuh an army officer in Aleppo, where he rose rapidly to become Zangi's top general.

Meanwhile, what of the new alien menace, the Crusaders? Zangi was the only one willing to confront them. Over almost two decades, he had several minor successes and in 1144 a major one, with consequences far beyond the world of Islam.

Edessa (today's Urfa, in Turkey), whose 10,000 inhabitants were mostly Armenian Orthodox Christians, had been in Frankish hands for half a century. It lay in a steep valley, with its walls running between hills. Its ruler was Joscelin II, who was notorious for his ugliness – short, with a big nose and bulging eyes – and lack of military skills. Towards the end of 1144, he took a small force on a raid along the Euphrates, opening a route to Edessa. Zangi, eager to expand his empire into Christian lands, took advantage of this and led his army to besiege the city. Since the only occupants were (as the Syrian bishop Abu'l-Faraj put it) 'shoemakers, weavers, silk merchants, tailors and priests', the city's most senior officials were three bishops – Frankish, Armenian and Abu'l-Faraj himself. Zangi was keen to get a surrender before Joscelin returned. His troops began to undermine the walls. Joscelin, having discovered the situation, had no intention of tangling with Zangi's superior force until he got more help from some other Christian state, Antioch or

Jerusalem. In several letters, Zangi repeated his message to the dithering bishops: 'O, unfortunate people! You can see that all hope is lost. What do you want? What can you still expect? Have pity on yourselves, your women and your homes! Act now, that your city may not be devastated and emptied of its inhabitants!' No help came for Joscelin, or from him to his city. Zangi's sappers continued their work, removing all the foundations of the north wall and replacing them with immense quantities of wood doused with inflammable animal fat, sulphur and naphtha. The fire started, smoke blanketed the city, the wall collapsed, the Turks fought their way in over the rubble and began to kill. Over 5,000 died, says Abu'l-Faraj (though all figures should be seen as approximate, and were often exaggerated to serve the agendas of the writers). The women and children fled to an upper citadel, only to find the door barred, because the Frankish bishop had ordered the guards to open it only to him in person. In the panic, many were trampled to death. 'It was a lamentable and horrifying spectacle: about 5,000 people, perhaps more, died atrociously, twisted, suffocating, pressed together in a single compact mass.' Zangi intervened personally to stop the killing, and sent a message to Abu'l-Faraj, offering peace in exchange for the city. 'You know very well that this city was a thriving metropolis during the 200 years that the Arabs governed it. Today, the Franj have occupied it for just 50 years, and already they have ruined it.' There was no choice, and Zangi was free to assert his will. While the Syrians and Armenians – the original residents – were allowed to return to their homes,

> everything was taken from the Franj: gold, silver, holy vases, chalices, patens, ornamented crucifixes, and great quantities

of jewels. The priests, nobles and notables were taken aside, stripped of their robes, and led away in chains to Aleppo. Of the rest, the artisans were identified, and Zangi kept them as prisoners, setting each to work at his craft. All the other Franj, about 100 men, were executed.

News of the victory took the Arab world by storm, proving that the enemy could be beaten, inspiring talk of the re-conquest of Jerusalem. Zangi was the hero of the hour, being granted a string of titles by the caliph in Baghdad: victorious king, ornament of Islam, and many more. There would also be interesting consequences when the news reached Europe.

But Zangi had no time to do more, because two years later he was killed by one of his own slaves. He was the fifth of Aleppo's rulers in thirty-two years to die by violence, but unlike the previous four there was no political motive. According to one account – there were several – he was besieging a fortress, Qal'at Jabr,[7] in September 1146. He awoke from a drunken sleep to see the slave, a eunuch named Yarankash, snatching a surreptitious glass of wine. Zangi angrily swore he would punish him the next day, and went back to sleep. To avoid punishment, Yarankash stabbed his master and fled to safety. But Zangi was not dead. An aide found him, and reported, 'when he saw me the atabeg [ruler] thought I had come to finish him off, and with a gesture of his finger, he asked for the coup de grâce. Choked with emotion, I fell to my knees and said to him, "Master, who did this

---

[7] The ruins of pink bricks jut up from a rocky hillock which is now a peninsula in a vast reservoir on the Euphrates, finished in 1974 and named Lake Assad after Syria's then ruler.

to you?" But he was unable to answer, and gave up his soul, may God have mercy on him.'

At once, Zangi's main rival – Unar, who had just appointed himself the new boss of Damascus – took advantage and besieged Baalbek. Ayyub, still officially the city's governor, had no choice but to hand it over in exchange for a lesser position as administrator of some villages near Damascus. It was to Damascus, therefore, that Yusuf now moved with his family, at the age of nine, and there that he spent his teenage years.

Of Zangi's three sons, the youngest one was the star. The oldest, Sayf al-Din, inherited the eastern half of Zangi's realm, centred on Mosul (basically today's northern Iraq), which would one day be inherited by the middle son, Qutb. That left the western half (northern Syria) and its capital Aleppo to the brilliant and very appealing Nur al-Din.

Nur al-Din ('Light of Religion') had the piety, reserve and sense of justice that made him a natural leader. He had his father's positive qualities – austerity, courage, statesmanship – but none of his cruelty and lack of scruples. He looked the part as well. At twenty-nine, he was, in al-Athir's pen-portrait, 'a tall, swarthy man with a beard but no moustache, a fine forehead and a pleasant appearance enhanced by beautiful, melting eyes.' The father got his way with fear; the third son with intelligence, high-mindedness and patience. In terms of today's leadership theory, he was an exponent of 'soft power'. Al-Athir said that, of all Islam's rulers, excluding of course the first caliphs,[8] 'I have found no man as virtuous and just as Nur al-Din.'

---

[8] Who were traditionally above criticism.

So it was Nur al-Din who took on the role of holy warrior, aiming to finish his father's work, building a Sunni state that would confront the Franks, retake Jerusalem and crush the European infidels. To do this he became a master of propaganda, employing several hundred scholars to produce poems, letters and books to sway public opinion. He knew the publicity value of his own personality, carefully spreading stories about himself as the fount and origin of the qualities he admired: austerity, low taxes, dedication to Islam, generosity, charity. Ibn al-Athir tells one of these stories:

> Nur al-Din's wife once complained that she did not have enough money to provide adequately for his needs. He had assigned her three shops which he owned in Homs; these generated about 20 dinars a year. When she found that this was not enough, he retorted: 'I have nothing else. With all the money I command, I am but the treasurer of the Muslims, and I have no intention of betraying them, nor of casting myself into hell on your account.'

He bought his own food and clothing rather than relying on servants, respected Islamic law without being a fanatic, and often risked his life in battle, always carrying two bows. There was no denying his commitment or his effectiveness. His first major action was to nip in the bud a Christian attempt to retake Edessa, a move that prompted the city's governor to give Nur al-Din his daughter in marriage. He was a worthy predecessor, even a role model, for the young man who would become his protégé, Saladin.

The connection was close, for when Nur al-Din arrived in Aleppo to assume his share of his father's estate in

September 1146 he brought with him Saladin's uncle, Shirkuh.

Damascus was the first Islamic capital outside Saudi Arabia, taken over by the Prophet's successors in the seventh century to secure Islam's frontier with Christian Byzantium. It is not an obvious place for a capital – not central, not on a great river, no access to the coast. But nature and the weight of history made up for its lack of strategic advantages.

Close by the city, to the north, reared the angular 1,100-metre peak of Mount Qasiyoun, where Abraham had been born, in a cave which now lay beneath a mosque – so the Andalusian traveller ibn Jubayr reported anyway. It was also on this mountain that Cain killed his brother Abel, an event recalled then and now by the so-called Cave of Blood. Prophets used to climb the mountain to make their ascent to heaven. On the horizon to the south-west was the snow-capped ridge of Mount Hermon, Syria's highest point at 2,814 metres, and also the site of the highest shrine of the ancient world.

Damascus's immediate surroundings were a joy, in contrast to the desolation further out. Whether you approached from the north and west, following the gorge where the Barada river, the city's lifeblood, tumbled from the forbidding Anti-Lebanon mountains and fanned out into seven branches; or from the south, across a lava wilderness and the cores of dead volcanoes; or from the east across a monochrome desert – from all directions you were relieved to reach a huge oasis, the Ghouta, which encircled the city with villages, rivers, canals, orchards and fields. Damascus was always famous for its water-supply. In the Bible, when Naaman is told by the prophet Elisha to bathe in the Jordan to heal his leprosy, he replies angrily, 'Are not the rivers of Damascus better than all the waters of Israel?'[9] According to ibn Jubayr, the greenery was 'like a halo round the moon', or, as the historian Philip Hitti puts it, the city was 'set like a pearl in the emerald girdle of its gardens'.

A pearl is an apt image. To modern eyes, the city was tiny, an oblong a mere 2 kilometres long and one across. It was its compactness that made it so appealing, with its canals, houses of wood and mud-brick, close-packed alleyways and markets, and crowds pressing through the eight gates in the strong walls.

At its heart stood the superb Umayyad Mosque (or Great Mosque), which is still one of the wonders of the city, and of all Islam. The 15-hectare rectangle had been a place of pagan worship for 1,000 years, then in succession a Roman temple and a Christian cathedral dedicated to John the Baptist, making it a perfect site for the eighth-century sultan al-Walid to proclaim the dominance of Islam over all other religions. His creation is still the fourth in holiness after Mecca, Medina and Jerusalem. Employing a multinational work-force of 12,000, al-Walid rebuilt the whole thing, creating three naves, a transept, a vast courtyard, colonnades, arches and a great dome, all decorated with mosaics in gold and – in ibn Jubayr's words – 'all kinds of remarkable colours in the pattern of plants throwing out branches and arranged amongst the gold stones with the most wonderful of exquisite work that it is impossible to describe, and that dazzles the eye with its brightness and lustre.' Ibn Jubayr often says he was

---

[9] Well, no, they weren't actually. He did as he was told, bathed instead in the river Jordan, and was cured (II Kings, 5.12–14).

overwhelmed by this or that glory, claiming to be speech-
less, incapable or incompetent. He lacks words for what he
sees, and then lacks words to describe his own inadequacy.
Here, praise is heightened by self-denigration: overwhelming,
awe-inspiring, miraculously executed, so grand as to beggar
description, words cannot express, etc., etc. But in this case,
he had good reason for awe and humility. In the vestibule a
fountain spouted water like silver wands. The portico contained a unique clock of twelve doors, each of which opened
in turn to mark the hour, the action being dependent on two
brass falcons which dropped balls into bowls, while out of
sight an attendant collected the balls and put them back
where they came from. Each door had a perforated disc above
it, and at night a lamp shone through each in turn, being
moved from disc to disc by a water-powered mechanism. A
shrine to John the Baptist, which supposedly contained his
head, was the focus of special worship, since he is honoured
in Islam as well as in Christianity. Ibn Jubayr was particularly
struck by the main dome. With a party of other travellers, he
mounted stairs to the roof and, 'nearly carried away by giddi-
ness', circled the lead-covered dome on a platform – eighty
paces around, about three-quarters the size of the dome of St
Paul's. He then climbed inside the dome through a narrow
entrance, to find that it was a *double* dome, 'a spectacle that
sends the senses reeling', the inner one being of wood bound
with iron, with windows into the interior through which the
men on the floor far below seemed as small as boys.

When Saladin came to Damascus with his father in the
mid-twelfth century, its glory days as an imperial capital were
long gone. Islam had been made anarchic by rival dynasties,
and the capital was now Baghdad. The Umayyad Mosque

had been ruined by fire in 1069. But now the former capital was being resurrected by the Seljuks. A thousand scholars, teaching in two dozen *madrasas*, drew students from across the Islamic world. Religious students were sure of a good reception. 'The door of the East is open, so enter it in peace, industrious youth,' urged ibn Jubayr, 'and seize the chance of undistracted study and seclusion before a wife and children cling to you and you gnash your teeth in regret at the time you lost.' The Umayyad Mosque had been restored, complete with dome and golden mosaics. Other mosques provided help for travelling priests at public expense: 'the needy stranger, so long as he has come for righteous purposes, will be cared for without being caused to blush.' A superb hospital had been built some fifty years before, and a second would be built while he was there. They provided some of the best medical care in all Eurasia. Doctors made their rounds every morning, prescribing medicines and advising on diets, while officials kept records of patients, treatments and costs.

Ibn Jubayr was much impressed by the good manners of the citizens, though he found their cordiality a bit over the top. They walked with their hands folded behind their backs, in a show of humility and modesty, but shook hands with each other most warmly after prayers They

address each other as Lord or Sir, and use the expressions 'Your servant' and 'Your excellency'. When one meets another, instead of giving the ordinary greeting, he says respectfully, 'Here is your slave', or 'Here is your servant at your service' . . . Their style of salutation is either a deep bow or a protestation, and you will see their necks in play, lifting and lowering, stretching and contracting . . . What odd people! If they treat each other in this way, reaching such an extravagance of epithets in their common intercourse, how do they address their sultans?

Many thought the place a paradise, or at least a reflection of the Quran's words: 'As for those that fear the Lord, they shall dwell in lofty chambers set about with running streams.'[10] There was a story told of Muhammad according to which he hesitated at the gates of Damascus because, he said, he wanted to enter Paradise only once. 'By Allah,' wrote ibn Jubayr, echoing the anecdote, 'they spoke truth who said: "If Paradise is on the earth, then Damascus without a doubt is in it".'

Yet now, during Saladin's teenage years, this was a paradise under threat from its own factions. There was, anyway, distrust between the city's Turkish rulers and the Arabic population. The Assassins held power for a few years in the 1120s. Nervous of their unpopularity, they did a deal with the king of Jerusalem, agreeing that they would hand over the city in exchange for a new base, Tyre. This would have antagonized the many Arab refugees from the Crusader states. Hearing of the plot, a new emir turned on the Assassins and had them killed or expelled. Ten years later, a young, greedy and oppressive sultan named Ismail, having survived an assassination attempt, began killing all suspected opponents, thus increasing hatred against him and feeding his own paranoia. In his crazed state, he decided to hand Damascus over to Zangi in exchange for protection. Ismail's own

[10] Surah 39:20.

mother, Zumurrud, put an end to the scheme by having him murdered and handing the throne to another son, who was in his turn murdered in unexplained circumstances. Zangi's ambitions received a boost when the same Zumurrud agreed to marry him, mainly so that he could come and avenge the murder of her second son. Damascus, it seemed, would fall into his lap. But no: a new leader, Mu'in al-Din Unar, held his own by threatening to approach the Franks for help, which would in effect have made Damascus a Frankish protectorate. Zangi held back. And so, for a while, Damascus retained its precarious independence.

If the recapture of Edessa in 1144 had a powerful impact on Muslims, its impact on Christians was many times greater. The four Crusader states wrote demanding help from the French king, the Pope and the emperor of what would soon become the German-dominated Holy Roman Empire. As in the build-up to the First Crusade, each had good reason to respond. Louis VII, taking advantage of a population boom, was keen to unite his knights in a grand escapade; and France, after all, had been the driving force behind the First Crusade. The German emperor, Conrad III, was struggling to impose himself on his still-to-be-unified lands. And the new Pope, Eugenius III, needed a show of authority to overawe opponents trying to expel him. It was he who once again threw the mantle of religion over the venture, promising to pardon the sins of Crusaders and have anyone who died while campaigning declared a martyr.

He was eloquently backed by his friend, Bernard of Clairvaux, future saint and greatest orator of his day, so riveting that he was nicknamed 'the Mellifluous Doctor'. He was at his most persuasive in Vézelay, north-east France, one of northern Europe's greatest religious crossroads because it had what were claimed to be the bones of Mary Magdalene. For almost a century, since the Pope had confirmed that the bones were genuine, Vézelay's superb hilltop abbey had drawn pilgrims from far afield, to adore the relics and to set off on the long road to the Spanish holy city of Santiago de Compostela. At Easter 1146 there gathered in Vézelay an immense crowd, including the French king, Louis VII, and his beautiful twenty-two-year-old wife, Eleanor, Duchess of Aquitaine – a province one-third the size of all France. Queen since the age of fifteen, she was already an icon, with another sixty years ahead of her, during which she would divorce Louis and marry England's king, Henry II, making Aquitaine English.[11] On a wooden platform built in a field, they knelt to hear Bernard bless the new Crusade. 'Hasten then to expiate your sins by victories over the Infidels,' he said. 'Cursed be he who does not stain his sword with blood.' They heard, and – to cries of 'To Jerusalem! To Jerusalem!' – vowed to take the Cross. And Bernard moved on to Cologne to preach the same message to Conrad, with equal success.

Again, word spread across Europe that there would be transport, food, loot and women, all available with a clear conscience for those who survived, and the certainty of a place in Heaven for those who didn't. How many responded to the call? Some medieval historians suggest 140,000, while Edward Gibbon, the great eighteenth-century historian of Rome's decline and fall, proposed 400,000; both of which

[11] Which explains some oddities about modern Aquitaine, e.g. why the people of Pau still like fox-hunting.

are nowadays dismissed as ludicrous. Frankly, no one knows how many. Or rather, as the Arab chronicler al-Athir put it, *Allahu 'aalim* ('God alone knows'). Tens of thousands, certainly.

It all started well enough, in several different columns under the charismatic Bernard and two kings, Louis VII (plus Eleanor with a retinue of 300 chambermaids) and Conrad III. They were still in Europe when things began to go wrong. In early September 1147, the Germans were approaching Constantinople when they unwisely made camp between two dry river beds, which by chance flooded, drowning some of them and washing away many of their supplies. Arriving exhausted in Constantinople, they seemed more like vagabonds than soldiers. Meanwhile, the French were approaching overland and a Sicilian fleet was raiding Byzantine forts. The Byzantine emperor, Manuel I, decided to try to move the westerners along as fast as possible.

The Seljuks, well informed this time, set up roadblocks and ambushes. German and French leaders dithered. Armies divided, some taking coast roads, some heading inland, some travelling by boat.

Inland, halfway across the grasslands of what is today central Turkey, Conrad's columns ran out of food and became targets for Turkish freebooters operating in Byzantine territory. Conrad decided on a retreat, which degenerated into a rout. Stragglers were picked off by Turkish arrows. Conrad himself was wounded. The survivors regrouped in Constantinople.

The newly arrived French set off along the coast, slowed by mountains and rivers, as well as lack of food and skirmishing Turks, and then, to cap it all, by winter weather. When the column – cavalry in front, guarding the baggage, with the king in the rearguard – came to the Byzantine–Seljuk frontier at Honaz, disaster struck. Ahead was a grim landscape of forested valleys and bare hills, surging like a wrestler's muscles and dominated by the great snowy shoulder of what was then Mount Cadmus and is now Mount Honaz. The road led over a 1,200-metre pass a few kilometres to the south of the mountain. Climbing it, the rearguard, commanded by the king, held back in defence, while the vanguard – among them Queen Eleanor – disobeyed orders and pulled away. This left the baggage-train toiling upwards, stretched out over several kilometres, defended front and rear but fatally vulnerable from the sides. The Turks – tough riders and good horseback archers – tore into the Crusaders. Louis, who had dressed as a common soldier, escaped only by climbing a cliff and hiding until it was safe. As the survivors straggled onwards, the Turks drove flocks ahead of the French, stripping the ice-bound countryside of the little pasture that remained. At the coast, Louis divided his army, sending some by land, some by sea to Antioch.

In Antioch, scandal compounded disaster. Eleanor was already fed up with her weak, ineffectual husband, with his bad decisions and his inability to maintain discipline. Coward, she could have said, without the guts to wear royal robes in battle; while he could well have blamed her for slowing progress with her baggage and army of servants. There was a fearful row; rumours of an affair between Eleanor and her admired uncle, Antioch's ruler, Raymond; and disagreements over what should happen now.

Meanwhile, back in Constantinople, Conrad and his German force had recovered, thanks to much-delayed help from the Byzantine emperor, Manuel. His ships carried them south, into storms, which sank several and scattered the rest along the Palestinian coast. Conrad himself, his wounds healed, managed to reach Jerusalem. Here, at a meeting in April with Jerusalem's king, Baldwin II, and its Patriarch, Fulcher, the three made a decision: to forget the original war aim, which was to retake Edessa, and instead assault Damascus. Why? No one knows for sure. Perhaps it was simply a greater prize. In any event, it was disastrous. King Louis, arriving in Antioch with the survivors of his horrible march across Turkey, insisted on a time-wasting round of religious rituals. It was not until June that the leaders could all meet and agree the new strategy – time enough for Unar in Damascus to prepare the city's defences, stock up with food and send for reinforcements.

In July 1148 – the height of summer – the crusading forces gathered in Tiberias, on the Sea of Galilee, making an army of perhaps some 50,000 (though, as ever, very few figures are reliable), along with camels for the baggage and cattle which would be butchered to supply meat. Having reached the orchards and fields outside Damascus, the westerners seized land on either side of the Barada river. Muslim reinforcements poured in, peasants and warriors, Arabs, Turks and Kurds, villagers and townsmen, foot-soldiers and cavalry, and forced the Christians back. For three days the two sides skirmished, each losing men. Saladin, aged only eleven, would not have fought, but surely watched, and suffered, for one of those who died in action was his elder brother, Shahanshah.

Things were not going well for the Crusaders. On the third day, a bearded priest decided to inspire them by displaying crosses as if they were bits of the True Cross. He hung a cross round his neck, took two more in either hand, hung a fourth round the neck of a donkey and rode, Christ-like, to one of the gates, where he told the assembled army, 'The Messiah has promised me that today I will wipe out this city.' This was tempting fate. The gate opened, a Muslim force charged out, and one of the warriors 'reached the priest, who was fighting in the front line, struck his head from his body and killed his ass too'.[12]

More Muslim troops were on their way, led by Zangi's sons, Sayf and Nur al-Din. And Nur al-Din, remember, had a fine army, commanded by Saladin's uncle, Shirkuh, who had trained an elite guard of 500 emancipated Turkish slaves. Short, fat, one-eyed, heavy-drinking – Shirkuh might have been no more than a caricature, a sort of medieval Slobodan Milošević; but he was also hard-fighting and utterly fearless, and happy to eat with his troops. His men adored him. The Crusaders, drained by the heat, knew they were in trouble, at risk of being caught between the city walls and an over-whelming force. They either had to pull back, or make an immediate assault – and succeed. They wasted a day probing the southern suburbs, where a large market and a cemetery provided open ground clear of gardens and orchards. But there was no source of food there, and no water except a polluted canal. Deciding that failure was better than death, the commanders ordered a retreat. Inspired by the sight, Muslim cavalry harassed them, swooping in with bows and swords, leaving uncounted corpses rotting in the countryside. 'The air was poisoned by the exhalations of these bodies,' wrote one eyewitness, 'to the extent that in

---

[12] Francesco Gabrieli, *Arab Historians of the Crusades*, p. 63.

much of the land it was impossible to breathe.'[13]

For the westerners there was nothing left but to scurry home, having achieved precisely nothing. Not that this dampened enthusiasm for crusading, which remained for western Christendom a divinely ordained duty. The disaster of the Second Crusade was quickly dismissed as the fault of local Christians for their disunity, or of Eleanor for her ungodly affair with her uncle, or of Bernard for backing the Crusade in the first place, or of the Byzantine emperor for failing to engage. Besides, said some, it was not all bad. Had not the Pope promised salvation to the dead? Had not sins been forgiven and souls saved? Only a few wondered whether God was on their side after all. All in all, the whole thing was best forgotten.

Behind them the Crusaders left Unar and Nur al-Din skirmishing with local Christians, extending their reach into Tripoli and Antioch, the city of Eleanor's uncle. Nur al-Din, with Shirkuh and his well-trained army, beat Raymond in battle. Shirkuh is said to have personally killed him – quite possible, given his temper and violent habits. In any event, he cut off Raymond's head and right hand and, as tradition demanded, sent them to the caliph in Baghdad in a silver box. Unar died a year later, leaving Damascus a fruit waiting to be plucked by Nur al-Din, always ambitious for Muslim unity on his own terms. He planned to take the city without a fight, a strategy that would stretch out over the next five years.

In June 1149, he surrounded the city, yet offered reassurance. 'I have not pitched camp here in order to make war against

[13] Abu Shama, *Book of the Two Gardens*, excerpted in *Receuil des historiens*, pp. 58–9.

you or to lay siege,' he wrote to its leaders. 'Only the many complaints of the Muslims have induced me to act in this way, for the peasants have been despoiled of their goods and separated from their children by the Franj, and they have no one to defend them.' Only in this way could he be sure that the citizens of Damascus would trust him and not call for help from the Franks. It worked, or at least began to. From then on his name was mentioned in Friday prayers along with the caliph and the sultan, proof of his popularity.

A year later, in 1150, he returned, and urged the new ruler, a callow teenager called Abaq, to join him: 'If you come over to my side with the army of Damascus, if we help each other to wage the jihad, my wish will be fulfilled.' The boy-ruler held out, all the while maintaining links with the Franks as potential allies. Nur al-Din bided his time for a couple of years, preferring subversion to war, cultivating contacts inside Damascus, building distrust between governor and governed, especially the military officers. This was delicate work. The main go-between was none other than Ayyub, the discreet saviour and aide of Nur al-Din's father. Saladin, by now fifteen, must have been aware of living in a world of intrigue.

The crisis came to a head four years later when Nur al-Din allowed Damascus's ruler, Abaq, to know that plots were being hatched against him. This was a high-risk and cynical tactic, but it worked. Abaq panicked and executed some of the prime suspects – some of whom must surely have been groomed by Ayyub and Nur al-Din – thereby guaranteeing his own isolation. So when Nur al-Din tightened the screws and intercepted Damascus's food supplies, threatening starvation, it was easy to spread rumours that the real culprits were Abaq and his Frankish friends.

When Nur al-Din's army, still under the command of Ayyub's brother Shirkuh, came to the walls of Damascus on 25 April 1154, someone threw down a rope. Within minutes, a few of Nur al-Din's men were on the battlements shouting, 'Ya Mansur!' ('Victorious One!'). A sapper ran unopposed to the east gate and broke the locks. The gate swung open and troops flooded in, bearing Nur al-Din, to the cheers of citizens grateful to be saved from famine and the Franks. He followed up with wagonloads of food and tax cuts. Generous in victory, Nur al-Din let Abaq and his family go, granting them fiefdoms in Homs.

The more thoughtful citizens would have been delighted that the two great cities of Syria, Aleppo and Damascus, were at last united under a ruler who was young (thirty-seven), magnanimous to his fellow-Muslims and determined to take on the Franks. None would have dreamed that he was the one who would open the way to even wider unity and even greater victory under an even greater commander, who was at the time a sixteen-year-old awaiting his chance to shine.

3

Into Egypt

SALADIN WOULD HAVE HAD A CHANCE SOMETIME OR OTHER. He was, after all, one remove from the leadership – twice over, in fact, since his father, the discreet politician Ayyub, was Nur al-Din's top aide and his uncle Shirkuh was the emir's temperamental but highly effective army commander. Very little is known about Saladin's early years. Since his biographers were Muslim, they record only a few snippets about his religious education, which suggest a tight-knit, loving family. 'Brought up in his father's bosom,' wrote Baha al-Din in his biography of Saladin, 'and nourished on the lofty principles which his father set before him, he soon showed signs of the good fortune that was always to accompany him.' Everything pointed to a career in Syria, the focus of two Crusades, many battles and much inter-group rivalry over the previous half-century. In fact, by the mid-twelfth century the region had settled. Nur al-Din's kingdom, the Seljuk Turks, the Byzantines in Constantinople, the Crusader states – all were like wary predators, eyeing each other, but none seeing an opening.

While waiting for Saladin to emerge from the shadows, let us recall how close all the antagonists and protagonists in his story were, and how much they knew about each other. Turks, Arabs and Europeans were enemies and rivals, but also allies, trading partners and friends, often all these things in quick succession.

Information flew between them, literally, because all major cities were linked by pigeon-post. This gets only passing mention in Arab sources, possibly because it was so routine as to be unworthy of comment. It would have started a long, unrecorded time – perhaps centuries – before, with pigeons being kept for food, as we keep chickens. Over the years, people noticed that they were able to find their way home from very far away (modern fanciers race their pigeons for up to 1,600 kilometres). Pigeons can fly for up to twelve hours at 100 kilometres per hour, for three days, resting at night. All leaders, civilian and military, would have kept pigeons ready to send to distant cities or take into battle.

The historian al-Maqrizi recorded one very non-routine use of homing pigeons. In the late tenth century, the fifth Fatimid caliph al-Aziz loved the cherries of Baalbek. As a treat, his vizier – in effect, prime minister – arranged for 600 homing pigeons to be sent off from Baalbek to Cairo, each carrying a silk bag attached to either leg, with a single cherry inside each bag. The pigeons had 600 kilometres to fly. If they left in the morning, al-Aziz could have had fresh cherries for dessert that evening, with enough left over for his many guests.

Others took note, and were impressed. Sir John Mandeville mentions pigeons in his fourteenth-century book of *Travels*. This was a compendium of travellers' tales, with a heavy emphasis on *tales*. 'Sir John' never existed; he was (probably, possibly) a Flemish physician, perhaps a traveller himself, but also a fantasist and shameless plagiarist. He wrote in French, but many much-corrupted translations of the lost original gave the work international popularity. From somewhere – perhaps during his own travels in the Holy Land – 'Sir John' heard about the pigeon-post. As an early and rather cumbersome translation puts it:

> In that country and other countries beyond they have a custom, when they shall use war, and when men hold siege about city or castle, and they within dare not send out messengers with letter from lord to lord for to ask succour, they make their letters and bind them to the neck of a culver [an obsolete word for a pigeon, perhaps from the Latin *columba*], and let the culver flee. And the culvers be so taught, that they flee with those letters to the very place that men would send them to. For the culvers be nourished in those places where they be sent to.

Consider: for this system to work at all, every major town must have trained its teams of pigeons, which would have been divided among every other major town. How many towns the size of Baalbek or larger would have been part of the pigeon-postal system? Shall we say twenty? The 600 cherry-carriers were raised and trained in Cairo, their home base, then transferred by horse or camel to Baalbek, along with (say) a few dozen more which would have been kept for official business. But Baalbek would have had pigeons delivered from all the other nineteen cities as well, and constantly redelivered after each mission. And as breeders know today, you need redundancy.[14] Not all pigeons are equally talented: the good ones lead the bad. Nor is there a guarantee that any one pigeon will survive severe weather or predators. Over 160 kilometres, 95 per cent survive; but over several hundred kilometres you expect to lose about 50–80 per cent of them. Of al-Aziz's 600 cherry-carriers, perhaps only 300 made it. To be sure of a message getting through long distance, you had to copy the same message three or more times and attach it to that many different birds. There must have been a whole specialist industry of dovecote builders, breeders, trainers, transporters and supervisors – hundreds of people to look after tens of thousands of pigeons.

But pigeons were not the only links. Officials acted as ambassadors, rulers linked families by marrying off their sons and daughters, pilgrims went from mosque to mosque, slaves were bought and sold, prisoners were taken, and ransomed, and exchanged. Here, for instance, is the Samuel Pepys of his time, the Syrian Usamah ibn Munqidh, recording how he freed some captives, or rather paid to turn them from prisoners into slaves. This was in 1139–40, during one of several visits he made to Acre during a truce between the Christians in Jerusalem and the Muslims in Damascus (this

[14] Many thanks to Jim Savage for his guidance on the subject of today's homing pigeons. See his website www.homingpigeon.co.uk.

is from Philip Hitti's translation, which I have modernized):

> During these visits, the Franks used to bring before me their captives so that I might buy them off . . . Once a devil of a Frank named William Jiba set out in his vessel for a piratical raid, and captured a vessel in which were north African pilgrims numbering about 400 souls, men and women. Now some of these north Africans would be brought to me by their [new] owners, and I would buy from among them those whom I could buy. One of the captives was a young man who would salute and sit without uttering a word. I inquired about him and was told that he was an ascetic owned by a tanner.
>
> So I said to the tanner, 'How much will you sell this one for?'
>
> The tanner replied, 'By the truth of my religion, I will only sell him together with this old man, and will do so for the same price I paid for them, namely 43 dinars.' I bought them both, and a few others for my own use. I also bought for the Emir Mu'in al-Din [his patron in Damascus] a few others costing 120 dinars. I paid the money I had with me, and offered a bond for the balance.

Note the routine nature of the exchange, the ease of operating in a Christian base, the low-level philanthropy – the captives were going from bondage to servitude – and the fact that Usamah could, in effect, write a cheque. Despite the regular violence, the economy was stable. In another later visit to Jerusalem, he tries to negotiate the purchase of thirty-eight remaining captives:

> I rode to Jiba's home (may Allah's curse be upon him!) and said, 'Will you sell me ten of the captives?'

'By my religion,' he replied, 'I'll only sell them all together.'

'I haven't got the price of them all on me,' I replied. 'I could buy some now, and buy the rest another time.'

'I will only sell them all together,' he repeated.

So I left. But Allah decreed and they fled away that very night, all of them. The inhabitants of the villages of Acre being all Muslims, whenever a captive came to them they would hide him and see that he got into Muslim territory. That accursed one sought his runaways, but succeeded in capturing none.

For Saladin, opportunity came from a new and unexpected quarter – from the south, from Egypt.

For two centuries, Egypt had gone its own way, having followed Islam's other sectarian channel, the Shi'ite branch. Since they claimed to be descendants of the Prophet's daughter Fatima, they were known by their dynastic name as Fatimids. From the Fatimids sprang the Ismailis, followers of their eighth-century figurehead, Ismail. They predicted the return of Ismail's son Muhammad as their messiah, the Mahdi. And, as we have seen, from the Ismailis sprang their most extreme manifestation, the Assassins. Whatever the names, all were Shi'ites, all opposed, often violently, to the Sunni Abbasids, based in Baghdad, and their Turkish conquerors and their breakaways, like Zangi and now Nur al-Din.

From their accession in 973, the Fatimids thrived for some two centuries. Cairo became a centre of art, architecture and scholarship. The first Fatimid caliph of the new Cairo, Jawhar al-Siqilli (the Sicilian), founded al-Azhar ('The Bright', one of Fatima's titles), destined to become the world's most important Islamic university. By Saladin's day, however, the Fatimids were in decline. They had just lost their last eastern outpost, Ascalon (Ashkelon today, on the coast, 60 kilometres from Jerusalem) to the Franks. Of fifteen Fatimid viziers, fourteen had died violently: hanged, beheaded, stabbed, crucified, poisoned and lynched. In fact, it was accepted that the only way to become vizier was to murder one's predecessor.

So it was, of course, yet more seizures of power that had started the most recent trouble. The man responsible was an Egyptian vizier named Shawar. Having murdered his way to office, he almost became a victim himself. His army commander, Dirgham, threw a banquet for seventy senior officers, among them Shawar, then set his own private guard loose and killed the lot, except for Shawar, who somehow escaped and, in early 1163, appeared at Nur al-Din's court in Damascus asking for help. The emir hesitated. Sending an army to Egypt would mean crossing Frankish territory and stepping into the murky and dangerous waters of Fatimid politics.

But there was another factor to reckon with: the Franks, in the form of Amalric, the new king of Jerusalem, who would emerge as one of the three dominant personalities of the decade, besides Shawar himself and his commander, Shirkuh. The three powers – Franks, Egyptians and Syrians – would be circling and scrapping for the next four years, trying to secure the prize, Egypt.

Amalric – Amaury to the French, Morri to the Arabs – had inherited Ascalon, part of Jerusalem since 1153, and also the well-established ambition of Jerusalem's rulers to take over Egypt, which would provide an almost unlimited flow of wealth and secure the Holy Land for Christianity until the Day of Judgement. For Amalric, a gangling figure with a nervous stutter, which he tended to cover with loud and lengthy fits of laughter, the conquest of Egypt had become an obsession. He could possibly make it a reality, given that Egypt was in chaos and that he commanded the key border town of Ascalon. He had already tried it once, in the autumn of 1162, but his troops had been stopped by floods at Bilbeis, a port on a branch of the Nile 50 kilometres north-east of Cairo. Clearly, he would soon try again. Nur al-Din could not allow the Franks such an extension to their kingdom. He had to get there first and seize control. So, yes, he would help Shawar back into power – in exchange for one-third of his grain revenues. In brief, Shawar was expected to become a puppet, and to pay for the privilege. Shawar wanted to lead. Nur al-Din, of course, would not hear of it, so on 15 April 1164 the two set out as joint leaders of 10,000 cavalry.

This was the first big campaign in which Saladin participated, and the first time he steps on to the world stage. He was well connected, destined for high office, but that's about all we can say about him, for as the modern historians Malcolm Lyons and D. E. P. Jackson remark, 'for the first 26 years of his life we have no picture of him at all.'[15] Sources disagree on the nature of his involvement in the campaign. Some say he was part of it, some not. He himself never claimed to be present. But it seems he was, firstly because some sources mention him at crucial phases of the campaign and secondly because he would soon be given command, which suggests that he had acquired experience somehow. It's likely that he

---

[15] Lyons and Jackson, *Saladin*, p. 9.

was his uncle's aide-de-camp. Perhaps he later suppressed this information, because it was not the most successful of episodes to begin his rise to power.

They faced a long, hard journey from Damascus, as much of it at the gallop as possible to evade Frank attacks: down the Jordan for 220 kilometres – that was the easy bit – then on for another 250 kilometres past the Dead Sea and southwards, to avoid crossing Crusader territory on the coast. Covering almost 100 kilometres a day, they followed the present-day border between Israel and Jordan through dunes, salt-pans, gravel plains and jagged, eroded hills – grim country, but a good time to cross it. Oases and springtime streams kept the horses well watered and the goatskin water-bags full. They were needed, for from Aqaba westwards ranged the wastes of Sinai for another 250 kilometres, until at last, after the final 110 kilometres, they reached their first target, Bilbeis.

This was an extraordinary achievement. Sources say that they left on 15 April and arrived outside Bilbeis on 24 April. That's 830 kilometres in nine days. Is this possible? Endurance competitions today race individual horses over 160 kilometres in a day, for which the current record is just under six hours at a speed of 25 kph. Horses have been raced over 300 miles (480 kilometres) in five days. In the Mongol Derby, perhaps the world's toughest horserace, the winner covers 1,000 kilometres in eight days – but needs a change of mount every 40 kilometres, twenty-five in all. Shirkuh's expeditionary force supposedly covered 100 kilometres a day at, say, 10 kph for close to ten hours per day for nine days – which is inconceivable without way-stations and fresh horses. Did they take spare horses along with them? And there's not much pasture south of the Dead Sea, and none at all in Sinai.

Did they bring fodder? We have no idea, because the sources do not say.

Having somehow completed the epic gallop, Nur al-Din's army seized Bilbeis, advanced to Cairo and four days later took the city, killing Shawar's rival and replacing him in his old position as vizier. The Shia caliph, al-Adid, a boy of thirteen, was helpless. At this point, Shawar turned from Nur al-Din's puppet into puppet-master, with all Egypt as his stage. He wanted Shirkuh and his army out. To accomplish this, he sent for help from, of all people, Amalric, king of Jerusalem, Nur al-Din's old enemy. Shawar promised cash. Amalric, happy to have a second chance at gaining a foothold in Egypt, started at once from Ascalon on the 300-kilometre, month-long march, setting off a series of moves and counter-moves as all three parties jockeyed for advantage. Shirkuh pulled out of Cairo, back to Bilbeis, where (according to one source, the historian ibn Abi Tayy[16]) Saladin was put in charge of organizing stores. There followed a three-month siege by the Frankish–Fatimid allies. In response, back in Syria, Nur al-Din seized a Frankish fortress near Antioch and captured Antioch's ruler. In case the news did not make the point strongly enough, he sent a sack full of Frankish heads to Shirkuh with instructions to display them on the ramparts of Bilbeis to 'strike fear into the infidels'. That was enough for the two outsiders. Both the Frankish and Turkish armies declared a truce and agreed to withdraw simultaneously.

But this was not peace. Nur al-Din would never forgive Shawar's duplicity and would continue eyeing Egypt, and

---

[16] A Shi'ite from Aleppo, he favoured Saladin, perhaps because Saladin treated Aleppine Shi'ites well. His work is lost, but quoted by Abu Shama.

Shawar knew it. So it was no surprise that Shawar again sought an alliance with Amalric, nor that Nur al-Din again planned a pre-emptive strike to take Egypt. Nur al-Din's move came in January 1167. Seldom does history repeat itself so exactly: the same alliance, the same armies, the same routes.

Though this time Shirkuh sprang a surprise. The Franks and Egyptians commanded Cairo so, rather than challenge them directly, Shirkuh circled south of the city, then west, crossing the Nile in small boats. In the city, Amalric, knowing how unreliable Shawar was, cemented the shaky alliance by insisting on meeting the aloof sultan himself, now sixteen, who, in an immensely impressive ceremony conducted in the opulent heart of his palace – armed guards, marble columns, pools, tame gazelles, mazes of corridors, bejewelled curtains – promised his support 'in good faith and without fraud', all sealed with an *ungloved handshake*, a precedent utterly shocking to courtiers used to their ruler's untouchability. Who could doubt the strength of such a bond?

But the two armies – Shirkuh's and Amalric's Frankish–Egyptian alliance – were divided by the Nile. Time passed. Amalric started to build a pontoon bridge across the river. More Crusaders arrived to join him. No reinforcements came to help Shirkuh. If this went on for another day, Shirkuh would face overwhelming odds and inevitable defeat.

There was only one possible tactic. Shirkuh had to draw his enemy away from Cairo before it was too late. He led his army – all mounted – southwards on the west bank, in apparent flight. The Frankish–Egyptian cavalry duly followed, leaving the foot-soldiers behind. A week and 250 kilometres from Cairo, near al-Ashmunein, Shirkuh chose to make a stand at a spot where a gentle rise led between two hills, close to the valley holding the Bahr Yusuf canal, made around 2000 BC to channel water from the Nile to the Fayum depression to the north. This time – on 19 March – Saladin had his chance. Though sources are unclear about how the battle unfolded, a likely version is that Shirkuh gave Saladin command of the centre, ordering him to fall back when Amalric's heavy horses charged. Saladin obeyed orders, retreating uphill, drawing the cumbersome Frankish cavalry onwards, until the two Syrian wings – Turkish archers on small nimble horses, Bedouin on camels – galloped in from behind the two hills. The result was a draw. But at least Saladin had shown his mettle as a commander, and Shirkuh had avoided defeat.

But avoiding defeat is not victory. He needed something more. While Shawar and Amalric trailed back to Cairo, Shirkuh led his horsemen across the desert, 130 kilometres north-west of Cairo, to Alexandria, the pre-Islamic capital named after its founder, Alexander the Great, 1,500 years before. In Saladin's day it was still famous for its offshore lighthouse, built soon after the city's foundation on the island of Pharos.[17] Actually, it wasn't quite an island: a viaduct led to it across the bay, creating a sheltered harbour. Its inter-locking masonry, towering up to some 130 metres, made the lighthouse one of the seven wonders of the ancient world. Ibn Jubayr, the traveller from Spain, took a guided tour and gasped at the baffling scale of its interior, 'with stairways and entrances and numerous apartments so that he who penetrates and wanders through its passages may be lost'. In Saladin's day it was not what it had been, because earthquakes

---

[17] . . . which gave its name to the Greek (*pharos*) and French (*phare*) words for 'lighthouse'.

had begun to shake its stones. It would last another 200 years before it was reduced to rubble, leaving solid foundations on which a fifteenth-century fortress now stands.

Shirkuh made for Alexandria because he was sure of a good reception from a city incensed that their vizier had invited the Franks into Islam. He was right. Alexandria opened its gates.

But Alexandria relied mainly on the Nile for its supplies. So Amalric and Shawar set up blockades. Patrols barred the river and the approach roads. Eventually, the city would starve, long before which its citizens would turn on Shirkuh. His response was to split his forces. One half he led away from the city southwards, avoiding roads and rivers, seeking reinforcements. The other half he left in the city under Saladin. In this game of move and counter-move, Shawar's plan was to start an all-out siege, cutting orchards for wood to build siege-towers and catapults that would soon reduce Alexandria's walls to rubble.

Saladin was in trouble. His garrison was small, his communications cut, his supplies blocked. All he had going for him was the support of the townspeople, and that would not last long. For a while he kept them on side, spending his own money to do so, but after three months more and more Alexandrians were being driven away by hunger and drawn out by Shawar's promises of tax relief. Saladin's only hope was that Shirkuh would come to his rescue.

Shirkuh, though, was not in good shape. He had been 650 kilometres south, to the great bend of the Nile, where he acquired a few more Bedouin, some cash and some supplies, but nothing that would allow him to take Cairo or relieve Alexandria. Once more, the forces were evenly balanced.

Again, all outcomes looked bad, at least for the Muslims. For Shawar, defeating Saladin would be almost as bad as not defeating him, because it would leave the Franks in a dominant position, with Shirkuh roaming and ravaging at will, but with no chance of victory. Amalric had become anxious about leaving his homeland undefended. It was a deadlock, with peace as the least bad option for everyone. At Shirkuh's suggestion, all agreed to stop fighting. The catapults were burned, prisoners were exchanged, the Syrians and the Franks left, and Shawar retook Alexandria. Nothing had been decided, no one defeated.

But Saladin had had a good little war, commanding with success in the field, directing the defences of a siege, which ended without bloodshed. As a reward, Nur al-Din granted him two villages near Aleppo. As the historian Imad al-Din said, 'he thought he had everything for which he could wish.'

His uncle, on the other hand, had for the second time planned an invasion, avoided defeat only by improvisation, and then been forced out, leaving Egypt in the hands of the brutal, erratic Shawar, and the main enemy – the Franks – as strong as ever. Nur al-Din knew failure when he saw it. 'You have exerted yourself twice,' he supposedly told his general, 'but have not achieved what you sought.' While Shirkuh was given nothing more than the command of Homs, on the border with Abbasid lands, Saladin would have been the rising star, in line for high command when his master felt ready to make another attempt on Egypt. *Would have been*, but wasn't quite yet. Nur al-Din was in no hurry, because the return of his troops allowed him to focus on his restive northern frontier (in

fact on Qal'at Jabr, the fortress being besieged by Zangi
when he was killed almost twenty years before); and
Saladin's time was happily taken up with his two little
estates.

His next chance came a year later, in autumn 1168, thanks
to the Byzantine emperor Manuel. He sent an embassy to
Amalric in Jerusalem to say he was unhappy with Egypt's
'weakling' rulers. It was ripe for a takeover. Nur al-Din
would make a move sooner or later. Manuel suggested that
he and Amalric forestall Nur al-Din by launching a joint
attack. Amalric moved fast, without waiting for Manuel. In
early November he was at Bilbeis, which was commanded
by Shawar's son, Tayy, who sent a contemptuous message
to Amalric: 'Do you think Bilbeis is a piece of cheese for the
eating?'

To which Amalric replied, 'Yes, it's cheese, and Cairo is
the butter,' and, as if in pique, ordered a brutal assault, with
totally unnecessary violence. He swallowed the city up in a
day; captured Tayy (and ransomed him later); burned houses;
and killed thousands. Nothing could have served Nur al-Din
better than this brutal act, for nothing could have so starkly
laid bare to Egyptians the uselessness of the luxury-loving,
easy-going Fatimids, the brutality of the Crusaders and by
contrast the strength and reliability of the Syrians, represented at that moment by Shirkuh, headed by his master, Nur
al-Din, and in the not-too-distant future by his successor,
Saladin.

Having unwittingly secured failure for himself, Amalric
moved on to the main course, Cairo. At which point Shawar
also ensured his own failure. To stop Amalric taking the

unwalled suburb of Fustat (old Cairo), Shawar torched it – part of his own capital – creating fires that burned for almost two months, forcing residents to flee to the new part of Cairo previously reserved for the caliph and the army. He then offered Amalric cash to pay him off, but asked for time to raise it. Amalric pulled back northwards, 20 kilometres outside Cairo, to wait for it.

All this had spurred Nur al-Din to action. He summoned Shirkuh, handed over 200,000 dinars, promised more, and told him to raise an army. Shirkuh, of course, wanted Saladin as his aide. Saladin was not keen, having seen what war meant, especially the pain of others and his own personal loss (for the income from two villages did not support an officer for long):

> I answered that I was not prepared to forget the suffering endured in Alexandria. My uncle then said to Nur al-Din: 'It is absolutely necessary that Yussuf go with me.' And Nur al-Din repeated his orders. I tried to explain the state of financial embarrassment in which I found myself. He ordered that money be given to me and I had to go, like a man being led off to his death.

The piratical Shirkuh was eager for more action. Certainly he was serving Nur al-Din; but he was also keen to further his own interests. Here was another chance to eject first Amalric, then Shawar, and – assured of popular support by the disastrous actions of both men – to take over as Egyptian vizier, in effect making himself Egypt's ruler. In the words of Lyons and Jackson, 'when he left Syria, he and his force can better be seen as independent adventurers looking for fortune than as a detachment of the Syrian army on a foreign campaign.'[18]

It all went his way. By mid-December news of his approach with at least 7,000 cavalry and tens of thousands of foot-soldiers drove Amalric first into Bilbeis and then, when he saw he had no hope of victory, into all-out retreat, taking 12,000 Muslim prisoners with him to guarantee his safety, plus an immense sum, perhaps as much as 2 million dinars, as well as 100,000 dinars as a ransom for Tayy. The road to Cairo was open. Its people greeted Shirkuh as a liberator. In early January, he had an audience with the now nineteen-year-old caliph al-Adid, who welcomed him as the saviour of Egypt, implying that Shawar's days were numbered. Better stability under the Syrians than chaos under Shawar.

Except that Shawar was still at large, still vizier. Possibly, he would have made peace, and accepted a lesser role under Shirkuh in exchange for sanctuary, which was why – according to some sources – he rode into the Syrian camp one foggy day. In the absence of Shirkuh, Saladin and a fellow-officer arrested Shawar – the leader who was both former enemy and potential ally against the Franks. Or perhaps Saladin arrested him on the streets of Cairo. Either way, for a brief while Saladin was his warder as 'one messenger after another came from the caliph's palace to demand Shawar's head.' Wealth could not save him; nor would popular opinion, since his cruelty had set him beyond the pale; nor would the caliph, because he was a notorious turncoat and had failed militarily; nor would Shirkuh, for as Saladin said, 'while Shawar holds power, we have no authority.' As

[18] Lyons and Jackson, *Saladin*, Chapter 1.

often with ex-leaders, the new ones saw him as the embodiment of evil. Execution was justified and necessary and, in
the Egyptian tradition, his head was sent off to the caliph.
Soon afterwards Shirkuh – dressed in a white turban stitched
with gold and a scarlet-lined robe, bearing a sword encrusted
with jewels – was made vizier by al-Adid, thus changing
from army commander to the official ruler of Egypt, but
also a servant of two masters, the caliph al-Adid next door
and Nur al-Din in Baghdad – and in theory three masters,
if you include Nur al-Din's nominal boss, the other caliph,
al-Mustadi in Baghdad. At his side, as his executive officer,
was Saladin.

The changeover to a tubby, one-eyed foreigner was not
popular, but Shirkuh knew how to manage that problem. Out
in the streets of Cairo, he was surrounded by a surly mob,
which might have turned nasty had not Shirkuh redirected
their anger towards their former vizier, who had, after all,
burned them out of house and home. 'I now speak with the
authority of your caliph,' he said. 'Go and ransack Shawar's
palace!' With a programme of reconstruction, the refugees
were persuaded to leave royal Cairo and return to their
burned-out suburbs.

Back in Syria, Nur al-Din was not completely happy. Yes,
the conquest of Egypt was good news, to be proclaimed and
celebrated in public. It fulfilled a long-term ambition, and it
kept the Franks out. In private, however, it was a different
matter. Shirkuh was supposed to be Nur al-Din's servant, but
he had made himself Egypt's vizier. They both owed nominal
allegiance to a caliph, which made them of equal rank. But
Shirkuh had switched caliphs, from Baghdad's to Cairo's,
from Sunni to Shia. Was he perhaps more interested in serving

his own interests than those of Nur al-Din? Would he turn on the caliph himself and make himself into an emperor, in control of church, state and army?

As things worked out, such worries were needless, because three months after taking office Shirkuh fell ill, several times, probably because of his penchant for rich foods and underlying ill-health. Short, red-faced, burly, he was probably heading for a heart attack or stroke. One night, after another heavy meal, he took a hot bath, suffered some sort of a seizure, and died.

After three days of official mourning, Egypt's caliph and his aides decided they could not wait for a decision from Damascus and set about electing a successor. There were several possibilities, none of them perfect, none of them agreed by all. As army commander, the obvious compromise candidate was Shirkuh's aide and nephew, Saladin. He had experience, and being of a Kurdish family he would be accepted by one of the largest military groups. Almost all Syrian officers supported him. But as an administrator? He was young, he had no local power-base, and his only experience was as executive for his uncle – all of which was to his advantage, because for the caliph, who would have to confirm Saladin's appointment as vizier, inexperience, youth and weakness were excellent qualifications: he would surely be easy to control.

So at the end of March 1169, Egypt fell into Saladin's lap. Was he hungry for it? Ambitious? Well, a display of ambition was not the fashion for a twelfth-century Muslim leader aspiring to greatness. Saladin had his father as a role model: the image of discretion and generosity. He had seen the opposite in his rough-cut uncle, a man of military ambition, but limited ability. There were standards to uphold. One accepted office with humility when it was thrust into one's seemingly reluctant hands. One was wary of expressing anything as crude as ambition. But without ambition no one becomes a leader, at least not a great one. With Saladin, ambition was subject to his larger skills, as commander, diplomat, Muslim and now administrator.

Dressed as his uncle had been, in white turban, scarlet-lined robe and jewelled sword, he was confirmed as vizier by al-Adid. In flowery words composed by one of Saladin's advisers, al-Adid spelled out his new vizier's duty to wage holy war: 'As for the jihad, thou art the nursling of its milk and the child of its bosom. Gird up therefore the shanks of spears to meet it and to plunge on its service into the sea of sword-points.' A chestnut mare with a pearl-studded saddle carried Saladin back to his official residence. At the age of thirty-one, he had, more by luck than judgement, become the recipient of many titles: Very Illustrious Lord, Sultan of the Armies, Friend of the Community, Glory of the Dynasty and, most notably, for he would keep the title until his death, al-Malik al-Nasir, the Victorious King.

He was ready to start what he considered to be his life's work: holy war against the Franks, fair governance, and submission to the caliph, all three goals to be pursued with honour.

4

Building a Power-base

HOLY WAR AND GOOD GOVERNANCE WERE ALL WELL AND good in theory, but in practice hard. Saladin was serving three masters and two versions of Islam – his Sunni boss Nur al-Din in Damascus and through him the Sunni caliph, al-Mustadi, in Baghdad, and Egypt's Shia Fatimid caliph al-Adid. In Egypt, true, many of the people were Sunnis, and therefore happy to be free of an oppressive Shia vizier, but several sub-groups were unhappy – officials resentful of his takeover, Christian Armenians and, most significantly, a 50,000-strong army of blacks, Nubians in the far south, who were loyal to Cairo's caliph but had no love for the new foreign ruler. These were notorious troublemakers, 'insolent and violent' as one source called them, something like the sectarian militiamen of Northern Ireland during the Troubles; 'they thought all white men were pieces of fat and that all black men were coals', ready to grill their opponents. Like most Islamic rulers, Saladin was at risk of rebellion and assassination. His strategy was to build a good, loyal army; acquire a devious and effective secret service; and proceed slowly, with great care.

In the palace, one of the controllers of the vizier's secretariat was a eunuch named Mutamin al-Khalifa, who took against the way Syrians were being given land under the new regime. Around him clustered a group of Egyptian officials who felt the same way. To turn the clock back – to throw the Syrians out and restore local rule – they turned to the old standby, Amalric and his Franks in Jerusalem. A letter was dictated to a Jewish scribe, then sealed into the soles of a pair of shoes and handed to a courier, who disguised himself as a poor traveller and set off for Jerusalem. He had reached Bilbeis when one of Saladin's informants happened to spot the suspicious figure who, although dressed in rags, was carrying a new pair of shoes. The man was arrested, his nice new shoes sliced open, the letter discovered, and the Jewish scribe identified. With the right sort of persuasion, the Jew fingered the treacherous eunuch. In these circumstances, efficient secret agents do not pounce immediately. Arrests or murders within the palace might have had incendiary consequences. So they waited until Mutamin went out of town to visit his estates. There, where the crime could be put down as a robbery gone wrong, Mutamin met a nasty end.

This story, told by Imad al-Din, may or may not be true.

But it points to a problem: opponents in Cairo would have looked to Jerusalem for help; and if the Christians had responded, Saladin would have had to march his army northwards to confront them; and that would have left Cairo open to an uprising. Best forestall any such danger by any means, fair or foul.

Another way Saladin secured his position was by surrounding himself with trusted aides, mainly family members – two nephews, an uncle and three of his brothers, the eldest of whom, Turanshah, was on hand when, immediately after Mutamin's murder became known, the Nubian contingents in the army went on the rampage. There followed a number of street fights, which ended with Turanshah burning their houses and chasing them out of town, after which they never again challenged Saladin's authority.

The next to confront him was the Byzantine emperor Manuel in alliance with Amalric, in a way that highlighted just how much the Egyptian navy had been weakened by the loss to the Crusaders of the Syrian ports – the outer belt of Egypt's naval defences. For the last twenty years, Crusader, Norman and Byzantine ships had been raiding virtually at will. Now, at the end of October 1170, a fleet of some 150–200 galleys, sixty of them with doors in their sterns through which horses could be loaded, arrived at the port of Damietta, a few kilometres inland on one of the Nile's branches. But before Amalric's force could join them, Saladin ordered reinforcements to the city, where the Syrians blocked the river by slinging a chain across it. Nur al-Din sent more troops, the caliph in Baghdad sent cash. By the time the Franks arrived, the Byzantines were low on food, unable to supply themselves and furious with their allies for the delay.

All they could do was batter the newly strengthened walls with catapults. Then the rains came, turning the Byzantine camp into a quagmire. After six weeks, the Byzantines sued for peace, which Saladin granted on the understanding that the Franks would burn their catapults. In mid-December the Byzantine fleet sailed away and the Franks left for home. Once again, Saladin and his Syrian invaders had saved Egypt from invasion by the Christians.

Saladin was now secure; the more so when early the following year his father, Ayyub, joined him. Other family members followed, and with their help he was able to build his army. He had some 5,000 Kurdish cavalrymen, under their own officers. He had inherited from Shirkuh a force of 500 mamluks (former slaves), to which he added another 500 to form his own personal guard. He ordered the building of new ships to strengthen the navy and safeguard the coast. He dispersed those local units that he had beaten, some 40,000 of them – Egyptians, Armenian archers, the unruly Nubians – being sent off to man the frontiers in Yemen and north Africa.

But securing his power had political implications for Saladin. It made him increasingly independent of Nur al-Din back in Damascus, and Nur al-Din was worried that his protégé might have ambitions beyond his station. He would have done something to reassert his authority, except that in June 1169 northern Syria was struck by the worst earthquake in living memory. Baalbek, Homs, Hama, Aleppo – these, though not Damascus, were turned to rubble. Muslims and Christians alike wondered what they had done to deserve it. Both sides agreed that it was some sort of divine judgement; both decided it was best not to risk further retribution by making any wrong move; both stopped fighting to recover their dead and repair the damage.

That bought Saladin three months' grace. Then in September another reprieve: Nur al-Din's brother, Qutb, chief of Mosul, died. Rumours of a plot pointed to Qutb's administrator, a Christian. There were complicated implications for the family, because Nur's daughter was married to Qutb's son, Imad, who had been named as heir but then, in some family wrangle, rejected for his brother, Sayf. In a swirl of military actions and negotiations, Nur took matters into his own hands, seized Mosul and settled it on Sayf, giving Imad only a small town, thus inadvertently causing animosity between the brothers.

Meanwhile, Saladin was free to expand his power-base, putting his father in control of Alexandria and Damietta and his elder brother, Turanshah, in charge of the upper Nile. He also took steps to prove his Islamic credentials by taking up the cause of holy war. This took the form of a raid into Amalric's territory with some 8,400 cavalry – half his army, but still a force that outnumbered Amalric's four to one. Amalric retreated and wisely refused to retaliate, so other than proving Saladin's willingness to engage in jihad, the raid accomplished nothing.

But a second one did. The aim was to retake the castle of Eilat – Ayla as it is in Arabic – which had been seized by the Franks over fifty years before. It sat on a lump of rock jutting up from the sea 12 kilometres from the head of the Gulf of Aqaba, some 250 metres off the Sinai coast. Set on its rocky spine, called Île de Graye by the Franks, it had been built to guard pilgrims en route to St Catherine's monastery in Sinai, but it could sustain only a small garrison because it had no water supply of its own, relying on a source from the mainland. Today, its coral reefs make it popular with divers. Back then, with the unification of Syria and Egypt, it was suddenly worth attention, because it was on the main road between Damascus and Cairo, and one day, possibly, its little garrison might pose a threat. That's why Saladin decided to take it out.

It was an easy victory. On the last day of 1170, having dismantled a few ships and packed them on camels for the desert approach, Saladin's force crossed the few metres of sea and landed on the island's rocky shore. One look was enough. The castle surrendered without a fight.

It was now 1171. Saladin continued to consolidate. He visited Alexandria, where he ordered stronger fortifications. He reversed many of the legal and administrative moves by which the former Shia leaders had dominated their mainly Sunni population. He fired Egypt's Shia judges and replaced them with Sunni ones. He founded two Sunni law schools. He favoured Sunni bureaucrats, making one of them, Qadi al-Fadil, his top civil servant – in fact, the very man who had composed the ringing words read out by the caliph at Saladin's investiture as vizier.

A major obstacle to his rise remained: Cairo's caliph, al-Adid, the main pillar of Shia influence and the most notable – if only nominal – remnant of Fatimid/Shia power. He had already lost all his troops in battle. Of course, Baghdad's caliph and Nur al-Din wanted him out. The most significant step would be to have Baghdad's caliph included in Cairo's Friday noon prayer, the public *khutba* (address) in which the imam prays for the head of state. In politics, words are actions. If the top cleric blesses a new head of state, that's pretty much the end of the old one.

But Saladin was smart enough to bide his time. There was no point making himself an even more obvious target for assassins loyal to the local caliph. Weeks passed. Saladin played for time. His secret police made rebellious emirs vanish. He paid private visits to the caliph, treating him as a friend, while also confiscating his possessions, including the horses on which he had once made public appearances. The caliph, still only twenty, must have seen his days were numbered. Perhaps it was too much to bear, because in late August he fell ill.

The tenth of September 1171 was the first Friday in the new year of 567, according to the Muslim calendar. Saladin took the decisive step and ordered Cairo's caliph to be replaced by that of Baghdad. Sources disagree on exactly how it happened. In one version, a Persian emir mounted the main pulpit ahead of the local preacher and read out the new names. In another, Saladin gave the order through his father, who threatened to kill the preacher if he did not replace the old names with the new in his prayers. The preacher half-complied, by omitting al-Adid's name without actually naming the Abbasid caliph, al-Mustadi, because (he said) he didn't know all the titles – but he added he would insert them the following week.

However it happened, it certainly did happen, and everyone knew it. There was a risk of rebellion, because the caliph, though a political cipher, claimed descent from the Prophet and was head of a dynasty that had ruled for 200 years. The following day Saladin countered the possibility of a threat with a huge display of military might, a march-past through the streets of Cairo by 147 units, each of which had between 70 and 200 men, almost 90 per cent of his army, which now numbered some 16,000. These were formidable men – mounted archers by the thousand, lightly armoured but fast-moving; catapult teams hauling their vast machines; sappers who knew about undermining walls; men who could build siege-towers; loose-robed Bedouin on camels – all out to impress the crowds. 'Those who saw this review,' wrote Saladin's right-hand man, Qadi al-Fadil, 'thought that no king of Islam had ever possessed an army to match this.' If the *khutba* had inspired opposition, the march-past killed it.

And anyway, two days later the caliph died. Rumours flew, of course: he had been poisoned, or poisoned himself, or was murdered, or committed suicide. But in fact he had been ill for weeks. Did Saladin play a role in the young man's death? If he did, it was indirect, as one story suggests:[19] 'If I had known he was going to die,' he said to Qadi al-Fadil, 'I would not have crushed him by removing his name from the *khutba*.' To which his chief administrator replied, 'If he had known you would have kept his name on the *khutba*, he would not have died.'

Fortunately for Saladin, the circumstances allowed him to act the respectful, generous sultan, as he now became, accompanying the caliph's body to the grave, looking after his children and giving the surviving family members their own quarters, though separating them to prevent them producing a new generation, but very obviously *not* executing them, which is what most new rulers would have done; while also *not* announcing a successor, in the knowledge that the next Friday's *khutba* would include the name of Baghdad's caliph,

---

[19] The ultimate source is ibn Abi Tayy, a Shia living in Aleppo, whose works are lost, but who is much quoted by Abu Shama.

al-Mustadi. Like any king or caesar, Saladin proclaimed his new-found power by minting coins with the Baghdad caliph's head on one side, his own as sultan on the other.

It all worked perfectly, with no hint of trouble.

Saladin's takeover as virtual dictator of Egypt marked the start of a revolution, what would now be called a 'peace dividend'. Cairo's suburb of Fustat, burned by Shawar, was restored. Building up the army, with weapons, siege-engines, horses and camels, and the navy all demanded skilled labour and a boost in trade. Saladin sent off an expedition westwards along the coast, looking for lumber, bases and recruits (it reached Tunisia, and was away for sixteen years). Buildings taken over from the Fatimid government became hospitals, covered markets, jails and colleges. Estates (*iqtas*) seized from Fatimid officials were handed over to Saladin's men, and raised taxes. He encouraged – in fact enforced – almsgiving, which was after all one of the five Pillars of Islam, but at the same time he abolished an unpopular tax on merchants, traders, artisans and manufacturers, to widespread applause. The economy grew, and so did foreign trade, even with Europeans – notably Italians, mostly from Pisa, who in their main enclave in Alexandria built their own offices, houses and a bathhouse. European goods were vital, in particular for the growing army and navy – chemicals, fabrics, lumber, iron and pitch. Peace also allowed trade goods to flow in from the east – spices, perfumes, dyes and cloth. Christians and Jews, though kept in their places by petty restrictions on their religious practices, were still valued for their administrative and business skills.

And, occasionally, their genius. The most famous Jewish

intellectual of his age, Maimonides[20] – philosopher, astronomer, theologian, physician – found sanctuary in Cairo. Faced with the extreme anti-Semitism of the Arab rulers in his native Spain, he chose exile over forced conversion or death, and settled in Fustat in about 1168. After his brother David drowned on his way to India, taking the family fortune with him, Maimonides focused on the most lucrative of his many skills, and became physician first to the vizier Qadi al-Fadil, then to Saladin himself, a virtual guarantee of Saladin's lasting tolerance.

With his economy flourishing, power in his hands, and all Fatimid property his for the taking, it was not hard for Saladin to raise 60,000 dinars, which he handed over to Nur al-Din as proof of his loyalty. Nur al-Din was not much reassured. He wanted not the occasional lump sum, but regular payments on which he could count when planning holy war. After all, Saladin now commanded the wealth of Egypt. What was that worth? Nur al-Din decided to send in his auditors to find out and set up, as it were, a standing order. There seemed a distinct possibility that Saladin's boss and role model might turn out to be his nemesis. 'Knife cuts and needle pricks', that's how Saladin described Nur al-Din's actions. Seething but compliant, he opened his books, explaining how expensive it was to administer his realm and guard it against anti-Islamic Crusaders and pro-Fatimid subversives.

As it happened, a plot was discovered even as the accounting went on. Former Fatimid officials, Armenians, Nubians, Amalric, the Assassins, the Crusaders – they were all in on it,

---

[20] Abu Imran Musa ibn-Maymun in Arabic, Mosheh ben-Maimon in Hebrew.

according to Saladin's agents. The conspirators were caught before completing their plans and were crucified, the crosses being set up in key public places as evidence of the dangers faced by the state and a warning to future dissidents.

Nur al-Din had cause for concern. Saladin had begun to empire-build on his own account.[21] In Yemen, a local chief had ambitions to restore the old regime. In response, Saladin sent his older brother, Turanshah, south to Aden, the port that was a gateway to Africa and the east, to impose Syrian rule. Military forays to secure the frontier went off to Libya and Arabia, displaying Saladin's military might. Clearly he had the resources to fight Nur al-Din, if it came to that.

But it didn't, because, as the physician and chronicler al-Athir put it, 'there came a command from God that he [Nur al-Din] could not disobey.' On 6 May 1174, in Damascus, Nur al-Din was playing polo when he lost his temper and had some sort of fit. He lingered for another few days, when al-Athir and a team of other doctors were called to his bedside. The chronicler – and one of Saladin's top administrators – Baha al-Din ibn Shaddad says he was suffering from quinsy, an extreme form of tonsillitis that blocks the throat:

> We found him lying in a small room in the citadel in Damascus, in the clutches of an attack of angina and even then at the point of death – he could not even speak loudly enough to be heard. When we entered the room and I saw the condition he was in I said, 'You should not have waited until you were as ill as this to call us. You should be moved at once into a

---

[21] At the end of July (1173), Saladin's father, Ayyub, injured himself falling off his horse, and ten days later he was dead.

large, well-lit room. In an illness such as this it is important.'

We gathered round to examine him, and blood-letting was advised.

Then he spoke: 'You would not bleed a man of sixty.'

And he refused to be treated. So we tried other specifics, but they did him no good, and he grew worse, and died.

So ended the life of a man who would have been the light of his age, at least for Sunnis, if he had not been outshone by Saladin.

A panegyric by the thirteenth-century historian Abu Shama summarizes Nur al-Din's virtues, as seen by a Sunni:[22]

He took the lead in everything that was good about his age. He re-established order everywhere, thanks to his even-handedness, his courage, and the universal respect he inspired, which he did despite serious setbacks and extended disasters. In the lands he conquered, he found the resources necessary to continue Holy War, so that he made it easy for his successors to continue the same course. In Aleppo, he established orthodoxy, abolished impious novelties which heretics had introduced into the call to prayer, and eradicated the Shi'ite heresy. He endowed the city with colleges and pious foundations and caused justice to flourish. Having finally conquered Damascus, he re-established order, surrounded the city with ramparts, built colleges and mosques, repaired roads and enlarged markets. He punished those who used wine severely. In war, he distinguished himself by his firmness, by his use of the bow and by the vigour of his swordsmanship . . . His

---

[22] In *Book of the Two Gardens*, by which he means the two dynasties of Nur al-Din and Saladin.

script was fine. He took pleasure in reading religious books, and followed the traditions of the Prophet. Passionate in his determination to do good, he was restrained in the pleasures of the table and the harem, moderate in spending and simple in his tastes.

His death left a power vacuum in Syrian politics that his eleven-year-old son could not possibly fill.

5

Back to Syria, and a Dead-end

NO, NUR AL-DIN'S ELEVEN-YEAR-OLD SON, AL-SALIH, COULD not fill the void left by his father's death. But Saladin could, because he could now see before him a grand vision. He could unite Egypt and Syria as a firm foundation for holy war against the Christian invaders. Egypt was too far away to assault Jerusalem. He needed to be back in Syria.

To rule Syria, he would need patience and a good deal of luck, for there were other contenders: Nur al-Din's two nephews, Sayf in Mosul and his scorned elder brother, Imad. But neither had the power to seize all Syria, and as rivals they would never cooperate. In Damascus and Aleppo, officials and top families jockeyed for influence. Over the border, the

Frankish leader Amalric saw a chance to regain lost ground for Jerusalem, but he had dysentery and died in mid-July. This was a sign of God's favour, as far as Saladin was concerned: Jerusalem was left in the shaky hands of Amalric's thirteen-year-old son Baldwin IV, removing the threat of invasion for a while. Alliances formed and re-formed, plot countered plot, until al-Salih's regent, the eunuch Gumushtegin, based in Aleppo, emerged as the front-runner and Saladin's top opponent.

Saladin's best weapon, as often, was masterly inactivity. He had a big stick, in the form of the Egyptian army, but in the tradition of Nur al-Din he preferred soft speech to force. He wrote some very careful letters, one to little al-Salih, calling his father's death 'an earthquake shock' that deprived Islam of her Alexander; and another to the leaders of Damascus. He would serve them if asked, if it served a nobler cause – that of Islam: 'In the interests of Islam and its people we put first and foremost whatever will combine and unite them in one purpose.' That meant remaining loyal to Nur al-Din's will. Unity and loyalty – those were the necessities.

Good for him that he did nothing precipitate, because in July 1174 came a Christian invasion led by William II, the Norman king of Sicily. These Normans were the descendants of the Norsemen – the Vikings – who had raided their way around the coast of Europe into the Mediterranean; so pillage was in their blood. They had, perforce, come to terms with their Arab and Christian neighbours, and had themselves adopted Christianity. But they made unreliable allies. In this case, they had planned an assault on Alexandria with those other raiders, Jerusalem's Crusaders under Amalric. The whole operation was a disaster for William, for many reasons. The Normans didn't know that Amalric had just died; nor that Manuel of Constantinople had warned Saladin of a Norman invasion (Manuel and William having quarrelled because Manuel had offered his daughter in marriage, then withdrawn the offer); nor that Saladin was near enough to be told of the landing by pigeon-post, which brought the news from Alexandria in a few hours. After bombarding the walls of Alexandria for three days, the Normans learned of Saladin's imminent arrival and fled – giving Saladin a propaganda coup, allowing him to claim to be the right man to deal with outside threats to Islam.

Saladin still made no move, delayed for two more months first by a campaign to crush another pro-Fatimid revolt in the south, and then by his concern for legitimacy. Ideally he wanted the support of the caliph in Baghdad. But then out of the blue Damascus gave him the backing he needed. By popular request, the governor asked him to take over the city.

He set off, leaving Egypt in the competent hands of his brother al-Adil, and confident of success because he carried with him large sums of money to convince others to join him, there being nothing quite so convincing as cash. He was so confident that he brought only 700 cavalry, sure that others would join him en route. They did, by the hundred, so that his journey turned into a triumph. As his secretary al-Fadil said, he spent the wealth of Egypt on the conquest of Syria, and so, in Saladin's own words, 'we dawned on the people like light in the darkness.'

He entered Damascus at the end of November. As with all effective leaders, he knew the benefit of symbolic gestures. He prayed in the great Umayyad Mosque, then went on to his father's old house, where he had lived as a teenager, a statement that he was retaking what was rightfully his. But the key was cash – some from Cairo, some from the city treasury; he re-opened the markets, cancelled an unpopular tax, took no revenge on officials resentful at their loss of power, and insisted, once again, that he was in the service of Nur al-Din. All this, he said, was in the noble cause of holy war and the retaking of Jerusalem, nothing at all to do with greed or personal ambition, perish the thought. He himself would be the guardian of his former master's young son, to 'direct his affairs and set straight what had gone awry'.

But Damascus was not all Syria. In Mosul, Edessa, Aleppo, Hama, Baalbek and Homs there were those who accused Saladin of treason and a lust for power. He marched to each in turn, with an army swollen by new recruits to over 7,000 horsemen and uncounted infantry. Most places surrendered at the mere sight of his force (though in Homs the citadel remained untaken for another three months, when it was battered into submission by catapults). Aleppo, his main target, proved a tougher nut. It was under its emir, Gumushtegin, regent to Nur al-Din's heir, eleven-year-old al-Salih. The boy was brought out to address the crowds and won them over by appealing for protection, even breaking down in tears in the middle of his speech.

While outside the walls, Saladin had a lucky escape. This was in January 1175, and as he wrote in a letter to his nephew Farrukh-Shah, they were camping in tents that did not keep out the winter rain, with fires that did not keep out the cold. Gumushtegin, fearing a long siege, had written to the head of the Assassins, Sinan, promising riches if he could arrange

for Saladin's murder. Sinan had reasons of his own to elimi-
nate Saladin – the anti-Shi'ite, the would-be unifier of Islam
under the Sunnis, the man who had re-introduced the name
of the hated Abbasid caliph into the Friday prayers. A group
of thirteen managed to infiltrate the camp, but were recognized by an officer, who by chance owned a castle close to the
Assassins' main base. The officer, Khumartegin, challenged
them. In the fight that followed, he and several others died,
including all the Assassins. Be on guard, Saladin told his
nephew, day and night, at rest or travelling, and employ only
those of guaranteed loyalty, for 'the knives have been distributed' and money paid to the Assassins. Saladin, unhurt, never
forgot his debt to Khumartegin; fourteen years later, he gave
a newly conquered fortress to the officer's son.[23]

Aleppo and Mosul, the capitals of Zangi's divided empire,
remained independent under Nur al-Din's two nephews, Qutb
and Sayf. Skirmish followed skirmish. Negotiations between
Turks, Arabs and Franks continued. Fortresses were seized,
then returned in temporary peace settlements. Carrier-pigeons
flew back and forth with offers and counter-offers. All this
whipped up a froth of events without any firm conclusion,
until on 13 April 1175 Saladin met Sayf and Gumushtegin,
briefly united in an uncertain alliance, 8 kilometres north of
Hama, near a hill with a double summit called the Horns of
Hama. What happened next was so fast that no details of the
battle exist. Indeed, it was hardly a battle. Perhaps there had
been bribery, or treachery, or just a failure of nerve. Anyway,

---

[23] Gumushtegin, prime mover in this plot, came to a bad end. Al-Salih, Nur
al-Din's young heir, had him arrested in 1177. He was hung by his feet outside his fortress, plunged into vinegar and lime, squeezed between planks and
strangled with a bow string.

the Zangid troops simply fled in a cloud of dust. As Saladin wrote, he broke the enemy like glass, without the loss of a single life.

That suited him perfectly. The key element in Saladin's campaign was his forbearance. Since he was aiming to unite Syria with a view to wider unity, his current enemies would one day be his allies, so he was careful never to be vindictive, holding back his troops from indiscriminate slaughter, sparing fugitives and the wounded, releasing prisoners, employing soldiers who wished to defect. The Aleppans asked for peace, and Saladin agreed. Better restraint than a long and bloody assault.

A month later, the caliph al-Mustadi himself acknowledged Saladin as master of almost the whole region – the rest of Syria, Egypt, the Mahgreb (most of the rest of north Africa), Nubia, western Arabia, Palestine – everywhere except al-Salih's domain around Baghdad. Not that the caliph, though nominal head of all Islam, really controlled such a vast territory. As Hitti writes, he 'gave away what was in reality not his to give, but what was flattering to him not to refuse'.[24] Saladin, blessed by Islam's highest religious authority, kitted out with black flags and honorific robes, now had the legitimacy he needed. All he had to do was get everyone else to acknowledge him.

He consolidated his rule in Damascus for almost a year. His third brother, al-Adil, came to support him from Egypt, another (Turanshah) from Yemen. An uneasy peace held the three main players – Saladin in Damascus, Qutb in Aleppo and Sayf in Mosul – in check. In early 1176, Sayf moved,

[24] Philip Hitti, *History of the Arabs*, p. 646.

marching from Mosul towards Aleppo. Saladin countered, completing his move with an exhausting two-day advance to a hill named Tell Sultan (Tall as-Sultan), 37 kilometres south-west of Aleppo. Sayf's staff advised an immediate attack, but Sayf shrugged: 'Why should we fight that outsider right now? Tomorrow morning we will get all of them anyhow.' A mistake. Perhaps the scouts had underestimated Saladin's reinforcements, out of sight behind Tell Sultan. Next morning, an uncoordinated charge by Sayf's army gave Saladin his chance. He led a counter-charge, scattered the opposition and drove the Aleppo–Mosul troops from their camp, which Saladin's men found to be 'more like a tavern, with all its wines, guitars, lutes, bands, singers and singing girls', plus a collection of doves, nightingales and parrots. Again, Saladin was magnanimous in victory. He returned most of the treasure, allowed his enemies to seek sanctuary in Aleppo, 'naked, bare-foot and impoverished'. He told Sayf to go back to playing with his birds; they would help him avoid dangerous situations in the future. Captured enemy officers were treated politely, then freed. It was like a duel between friendly rivals, with Saladin careful not to deal a knock-out blow in the certainty that one day his rivals would be his allies in the true battle still to come, the jihad against the Franks.

Unwilling to undertake an all-out assault on Aleppo, Saladin set about strangling the city by tightening the noose on outlying defences and communications. May 1176 found him besieging Azaz, a castle on an artificial mound 35 kilometres north of Aleppo, when again the Assassins tried to get him. Four of them, disguised as bodyguards – a serious breach of security – attacked him while he was watching the action, but, as often with extremists, it was a high-risk venture that virtually guaranteed their own deaths. Saladin was wearing armour and a helmet at the time, and his guards were close by. One of the assailants managed to throw Saladin to the ground and wound him on the cheek before a guard seized the blade of the knife, cutting his fingers to the bone. Another officer killed the Assassin, with the knife still held by both men. Two of the Assassins fell to other officers. The fourth escaped, only to be pursued and cut to pieces in the surrounding camp. It was only a scratch, Saladin wrote to a brother, 'with some few drops of blood, nothing to cause distress', but the affair left him so shaken that he had his tent surrounded by a fence and took to sleeping in a wooden tower.

This was too close for comfort. Several leaders, both Muslim and Christian, had fallen victim to the Assassins, and several had had narrow escapes (including Nur al-Din). To allow such people to operate was to risk disaster.

Azaz fell a month later, and Saladin closed in on Aleppo, crammed with refugees who had fled Saladin's troops following the battle of Tell Sultan. But the city was clearly not going to surrender. Expenses built, and the troops were restless. After two weeks, the two sides started peace talks, exchanging proposals, blaming each other for delay, hypocrisy and other sorts of small-scale bad behaviour. The long and the short of it was that Saladin's generous treatment of his opponents had done nothing to undermine support for al-Salih. At the end of July, Saladin called off the siege. All the rivals agreed a peace treaty. Saladin dropped his claim to become al-Salih's guardian, handed back Azaz, agreed that all of northern Syria would belong to al-Salih, and turned to the greater threat: the Assassins in their Syrian enclave.

The Assassins had been in the area since the 1130s, acquiring eight fortresses in all, one of which was the tenth-century Byzantine castle of Masyaf – stronghold of the Assassin leader Sinan – built on top of a rocky pinnacle. Today, it is a tourist attraction, or was before civil war broke out in 2012. It is a formidable-looking place, a 170-metre-long oval of walls, towers and barbicans, springing from a core of rock. Inside, it is a maze of rooms, stairways and tunnels on two overlapping levels that circle the hill and a third that caps it. For invaders, it would have been a nightmare, because stairs and corridors divide and swoop and double back, blunting attacks and making places for defenders to hide and counter-attack. One room has a 'murder-hole' cut through the ceiling, so that defenders can shoot down on to attackers breaking in below. Hewn out of the rocky foundations are three inter-linked water cisterns that could hold some 400,000 litres, enough to sustain 1,000 people for six months. All of this, and more, is revealed in a detailed guide funded by today's phil-anthropic Ismaili leader, the Aga Khan,[25] whose foundation was busy restoring the castle before the present troubles.

Perhaps Saladin knew some of the details from spies, in which case he must have seen he would be in for a long siege. Catapults started to batter down the walls, but would never have blasted open the warren of rooms quarried from the rock beneath. On the other hand, Sinan was surrounded. If the siege was long enough, he would run out of food and water. But if he was forced to capitulate, who knew what

[25] Haytham Hasan, *The Citadel of Masyaf.*

terrible revenge these fanatics might unleash in years to come?

In brief: yet another stalemate. Both sides needed a way out. Within days, discussions were opened through one of Saladin's uncles, Shihab al-Din (one source says Sinan threatened him with death if he didn't initiate talks). How it happened and what was agreed, no one knows. But all sources agree that the siege had been going on for only a week when there was a truce, which lasted. For seventeen years, the Assassins left Saladin alone to beat first his Muslim foes then the Christians. And that allowed Saladin to leave Sinan free to plan other assassinations from the castle that could never have been taken in the first place.

A secret accord? Possibly. Anyway, it was a quick and pragmatic outcome, because Saladin was now able to secure what Nur al-Din had won. In Damascus, to which he returned for just twelve days, he married Nur al-Din's widow, Ismat (not little al-Salih's mother, who was a concubine), and gave his sister Rabia to Ismat's brother, forging two links between his family and Nur al-Din's, and very obviously claiming his legacy. Ismat was fortyish, and his fifth wife, and the match was purely political, but it turned out well. There would be no children – in any case he already had at least seven children from various other wives and concubines – but she was a generous-hearted woman to whom Saladin remained attached for the rest of his life.

Officially, he was still al-Malik, the King. But from now on his supporters started calling him Sultan Salah al-Din – 'Righteousness of the Faith' – giving us the name by which he would soon be famous: Saladin. But really the previous two years had not given him what he had hoped for: Nur's inheritance. Southern Syria was not enough. He had spent the whole time scrapping with his co-religionists and no time at all fighting his real enemies, the Franks. The money he had brought with him from Cairo had been spent, his high hopes reduced to dust – literally, for to cap it all, the rains failed, threatening his men with drought. He could do nothing more in Syria.

So at the end of October he made the twelve-day journey back to Cairo, where he would spend the next year, until the end of 1177. There, flush once again with taxes raised locally, he busied himself with projects to strengthen his own fiefdom. His major undertaking was to enclose two separate town-ships, Cairo and its suburb Fustat, behind one wall, a vast project that would take thirty years to complete. Secondly, he added to the defences of Damietta, Tanis and Alexandria. And thirdly, he started a crash programme to expand his fleet to sixty galleys and twenty transports, back to its strength under the Fatimids. There were also non-military projects: a law college in Alexandria; the abolition of a toll paid by pilgrims crossing the Red Sea on their way to Mecca, with due compensation paid to Mecca itself for loss of income – an astute PR move that made him popular all along the pilgrim routes, and also made him in effect Mecca's patron. Both civilian and military projects served his overarching mission – to take Aleppo at last, bring all Syria under his rule and finally unify Syria and Egypt under Sunni rule, and then, as he wrote to his brother Turanshah in Syria, 'Our only object in this life . . . is to fight against the infidels.'

Little did he know that Aleppo was so nervous of his advances that they had approached their supposed enemies, the Crusaders, for help. As a sweetener, the Aleppans had agreed to release a number of Frankish prisoners, among them the man who would become Saladin's most bitter enemy. He had just emerged from sixteen years in prison and had offered his fiercely anti-Muslim services to Jerusalem's young and sickly king.

6

Enter the Villain

THE VILLAIN IN QUESTION IS REYNALD, WHOSE STORY IS SO interwoven with Saladin's that we have to go back over twenty years, relating events which explain why Saladin despised him. If Saladin is our chivalric and generous hero, Reynald is the opposite, his appalling behaviour making a background against which Saladin's virtues stand out more clearly.

He called himself 'de Châtillon'. There are thirty-three Châtillons in France. Scholars used to argue about which one Reynald[26] came from. Now most agree that he was from one

---

[26] His name had various spellings in different languages: Renaud, Rainalt, Reginald. The Muslims called him 'Brins Arnat', a corruption of Prince Renaud.

of no great significance on the river Loing, a tributary of the Seine in the middle of France. Nothing else is known of his early years, except that he arrived with the Second Crusade in 1147, when he was in his early twenties, apparently hungry for loot, blood and power. As far as Muslims were concerned, he was a nasty piece of work, the worst of Crusaders, as al-Athir called him: 'one of the greatest and wickedest of the Franks, the most hostile to the Muslims and the most dangerous of them.' Also, as we shall see, he was brutal, deceitful, vengeful and shameless, quite capable of grovelling in the face of a superior one moment and stabbing him in the back the next.

Yet there must have been something more to him. Few villains are irredeemably monstrous. A later chapter will look at an adventure that suggests he was as much swashbuckler as thug. His biographer, Gustave Schlumberger, a Frenchman writing in the 1890s, spoke of him as a hero: 'One of the boldest and one of the most extraordinary warriors of the Crusades, one of those iron men of the east . . . who would have figured among the demi-gods if he had been born in ancient times.' There's a hint of admiration in the Muslim judgement, a hint of disapproval in the Christian praise. He was, no doubt, a man who radiated danger. He must also have had piratical charm, because soon after his arrival he won the affection of the twenty-six-year-old princess of Antioch, Constance.

Antioch was in Christian eyes second only to Jerusalem itself in wealth, size, strength and significance – St Peter its first Patriarch, St Paul a citizen. Once upon a time it had been Asia's greatest city. Earthquakes and the Arab conquest had reduced it; but it still had its vast Roman and Byzantine walls, which ran from the Orontes river in a crenellated semicircle up and along the ridge of Mount Silpius, climbing peaks and leaping valleys like a miniature Great Wall of China. Four hundred towers ranged away on either side of a citadel, which looked down on the city 330 metres below. Inside the walls, the city – single-storey houses forming garden-courtyards, churches, monasteries, bazaars and pasture land – covered a plain 4 kilometres across. As Schlumberger puts it, the nearby port of St Symeon (today's Samandaq) was the gateway through which poured 'a picturesque and gaudy mixture of people' who turned Antioch into a seething commercial centre. Any invader from the north had to take Antioch and its surrounding territory if he hoped to move on southwards.

Having seized it from the Turks in 1098, its Christian rulers owed vague allegiance to the Byzantine emperor, Manuel, since it was on his southern frontier. But they also depended on the Christian king in Jerusalem, for reasons of faith and family. How these relationships worked out depended on unpredictable changes in the balance between half a dozen powers great and small, with a myriad twists and turns. Our guides through this historical labyrinth are the personalities, starting with Constance.

It is a truth universally acknowledged that a princess without a husband must be in need of a prince – acknowledged not by the princess, perhaps, but certainly by those with the power to choose the husband, for without a husband there can no heirs, so the kingdom is at risk. Constance had been ruler-in-name of Antioch since the age of four, when her father, Bohemond, lost his head in battle to the sword of Shirkuh, Saladin's uncle. The little princess grew up under the regency of her mother's father, Baldwin II, king of Jerusalem, and his successor Fulk, much to the distress of her mother, Alice, who had spent much of her life scheming to take over Antioch, and failing. After four years, Baldwin found Constance, now aged eight, a suitable, compliant husband, Raymond, the twenty-two-year-old prince of Aquitaine. Raymond was a legend for his bravery, good looks, charm and strength: they said he could crush a stirrup with one hand (which seems a silly way to prove one's strength; a horseshoe, maybe, but why a stirrup?). Nine years later, at the age of seventeen, Constance bore the first of her three children, a son, named Bohemond after his grandfather. After fourteen years of marriage, Raymond was killed, leaving Constance a widow at twenty-two, under the thumbs of Baldwin III as official regent, her mother and the city's Patriarch, Radulph, but in effect uncrowned queen of the city. Constance liked her independence, and refused three potential husbands. Four years later, into this power vacuum stepped our anti-hero, Reynald.

No one knows how he came to her attention, because he had been taking part in the siege of the city of Ascalon, an event that is worth a diversion. Ascalon was a formidable semicircle of inner and outer walls, towers and gateways, which had escaped capture in the First Crusade and would be vital if the Christians were to invade Egypt. Every now and then in history, some great city becomes a strategic doorway that must be kept locked or forced open, held or taken. When Kublai Khan advanced on southern China in 1268, Xiangyang was such a city. So was Verdun in the First World War, Stalingrad in the Second World War. For the Crusaders and the Muslims, Ascalon was one. It was a very tough nut: no port, no safe haven for invaders; lots of wells and cisterns for fresh water; four gates, squatting over mazes of little streets; and resupplied with arms, fresh troops and food four times a year by the Egyptians.

In mid-January 1153, an immense army gathered on the sandy fields outside the walls to begin a siege that would last seven months. The leaders were the top men of their time: the Patriarch of Jerusalem, archbishops from Caesarea, Nazareth and Tyre, bishops, abbots, princes and Knights Hospitaller and Templar,[27] all inspired by the presence of the True Cross. The Christians, camped in tents and well supplied by markets with meat, cannibalized ships to make catapults and sheds under which they could re-landscape embankments. Among their machines was a huge siege-tower. Reynald was there as a mercenary – 'he served the king for pay', as the chronicler William of Tyre puts it.

William described events as if he had been present, though as a twenty-three-year-old studying in Europe he played no role in the action:

> Volleys of mighty rocks hurled from the casting machines threatened to weaken the walls and towers and to over-throw from their very foundations the houses within the city. Great was the slaughter which resulted. With their bows and arrows, the soldiers in the moveable tower also wrought great destruction not only on the defenders who were resisting them from the top of the towers and walls, but also on those who were forced by necessity to move about the city.

[27] The Hospitallers, also known as the Knights of St John, were named after the hospital in Jerusalem founded in 1023 to care for pilgrims. The Templars, founded in 1129, were a sort of police force to protect pilgrims on the way from the coast to Jerusalem. Both became highly effective, freebooting, well-financed groups of fighters.

So the inhabitants decided that the tower had to be destroyed, come what may. A special operations team risked their lives filling the space between the walls and the tower with wood, enough to make a massive bonfire, on to which they poured 'pitch, oil and other liquids provocative of fire, anything which would make a fiercer flame'. But fate, luck, chance – God, if you happened to be Christian – was against them. An off-sea gale sprang up and drove the flames away from the tower on to the wall, igniting the wooden beams set into the masonry. That section of the wall collapsed in a heap of smoking rubble. Christian soldiers rushed to clamber in, intent not only on victory, but also booty, which was for most of them the only reason they were fighting. Self-interest ruled supreme. First into the breach were the Templars, forty of them, determined to make the city theirs, for ever and a day. They set guards on the breach to stop anyone else entering, and so lost what had been gained. The inhabitants, seeing that only a few had entered, took heart, attacked, killed the intruders and then sealed the breach with fallen beams and stone blocks. Luckily for them, the collapse had thrown rubble against the siege-tower, weakening it so much that no one dared use it. The city was saved, and the citizens took a grisly delight in their escape. As William relates, 'the enemy, for our undoing, suspended the bodies of our slain by ropes from the ramparts of the wall, and, with taunting words and gestures, gave vent to the joy which they felt.'

What was to be done? King and prelates conferred. Some were for giving up; others argued that all the costs and deaths must not be in vain, that God was with them, that those who sought would find. After three days of argument, this was the faction that won. Trumpets called for renewed attack. And, somehow, it worked. William does not say exactly how, falling back on clichés about slaughter, confusion, injuries and woe, but the result was a truce, an exchange of bodies, burials and then, at last, the arrival of a delegation seeking terms. Two days later, on 22 August, the Muslim citizens filed out, and Ascalon was in the hands of the triumphant Christians. In procession behind the True Cross, they turned the main Islamic shrine into the Cathedral of St Paul.

Reynald was not there to see victory. He had returned to Antioch, 320 kilometres and ten days' journey northwards, for in spring 1153, not long after the start of the seven-month siege, Constance decided to marry him. Baldwin III, king of Jerusalem and her guardian, agreed, thinking that at last Antioch would have a lord, who would at least take from him the task of defending the city. The marriage took place in secret, because Antioch's top families, including the local Patriarch, disapproved of their princess, the most powerful woman in the Latin states, marrying an ordinary knight, a mere mercenary with a disreputable background.

The Byzantine emperor, Manuel, was not asked for his approval in advance, although he was Antioch's nominal suzerain. But he would give it, he said, and add a reward in cash, if Reynald would act as enforcer against an Armenian warlord called Thoros (or Theodore), who lived by raiding the empire's Christian subjects from his castle deep in the Taurus mountains in what is today southern Turkey. Armenia was a Christian enclave, but surrounded by Turkish-held territory, so Manuel was helpless. Reynald was happy to oblige, since it gave him a chance to extend his power-base and do what he did best, which was to fight. He was a man who never felt the touch of coloured silk, as one source put it, only chain-mail and leather. In 1156, he headed north, got to what was then Alexandretta and is now Iskanderun, fought Thoros, and either won a brilliant victory or was forced into shameful retreat, depending on which of the two sources one believes. In any event, Thoros survived and fled back into his mountain fastness, while Reynald claimed his cash reward. Manuel, however, refused to pay, sticking to the letter of the agreement and pointing out that Thoros's castle remained untaken.

Reynald, furious, decided to take what he claimed was rightfully his, with the help of his old enemy, Thoros, who now, suddenly, became his ally. There was an ideal target lying 100 kilometres off the coast – the island of Cyprus, a useful naval base for Rome since the first century and part of the Byzantine Empire for the last 700 years. Cyprus, 'whose name excites the ideas of elegance and pleasure',[28] was a jewel, well protected from the wars that had been ravaging the mainland for as long as anyone could remember. With its ancient forests and hard-working farmers, it was rich in fruit and copper and well-endowed churches. And since the emperor's armies were employed fighting off challenges on the mainland, Cyprus had few defences. No enemies threatened it. No one dreamed that destruction would come not from an enemy but from a treacherous imperial vassal. For Reynald, it was a plum ripe for the picking. His only problem was that he needed to fund an invasion force, and he didn't have the cash.

His answer lay to hand, in the form of Antioch's old,

[28] Edward Gibbon, *Decline and Fall of the Roman Empire*, Chapter 60.

influential and wealthy Patriarch, Amaury (Amalric in a different version of his name, though not to be confused with the king of Jerusalem). The story is told by two historians, William of Tyre and John Kinnamos, who differ slightly in detail. First, Reynald asked the Patriarch for money, but was refused, not surprisingly, because the Patriarch considered Reynald an upstart and said so, loudly. According to William of Tyre, he 'often expressed himself rather freely, both in public and in private, about Renaud [Reynald] and his doings.' Amaury was also rather free in other ways, with 'somewhat licentious habits', as William puts it. Reynald decided on a vicious revenge. He had Amaury seized, stripped, beaten, and then, 'since summer was at its height, anointing his wounds with honey, he left him to be burnt by the sun. So wasps, bees, flies and other blood-drinking insects settled on his entirely naked body and sucked his blood. At this the man gave way, offering to yield all his wealth to [Reynald].' That is John Kinnamos's version. William is less dramatic. The old man is imprisoned, but not beaten, before being exposed to the midday sun, and only his head is smeared with honey. But it's still an appalling act, for which Reynald is reprimanded by the king of Jerusalem. Both writers mention that Reynald tried to make amends, either by reclothing the Patriarch and leading him through the streets on horseback, or by returning at least some of the goods he had seized. Amaury was not going to risk more torture. He fled to Jerusalem.[29]

Whatever the details, Reynald now had enough money

[29] This account seems to me the best way of making a narrative of a series of events – Thoros's revolt, Reynald's role, torturing the prelate, raiding Cyprus. Sources disagree – the order of events is not always clear; but no interpretation exonerates Reynald.

to raid Cyprus, along with his new ally, Thoros. Their force utterly overwhelmed the defenders, under the leadership of a nephew of Emperor Manuel. No one recorded the details of this swift and brutal assault, so generalities will have to do. Over three weeks, his soldiers destroyed cities, wrecked fortresses, cut off the hands, feet, noses and/or ears of the more fortunate inhabitants, broke into monasteries and nunneries, stole treasures, 'and shamefully abused nuns and tender maidens. Although the precious vestments and the amount of gold and silver which he carried off were great, yet the loss of these was regarded as nothing in comparison with the violence done to chastity.' Having driven a crowd of leading citizens – prelates, monks, landowners, merchants – down to the shore, the invaders forced them on to the ships. Flush with booty, they headed for home, where Reynald demanded a vast ransom for his hostages, releasing them only when it was paid. Even so, William writes, 'within a short time all the wealth which had been so wickedly acquired was dissipated.'

Reynald could not act like this – torturer, traitor, pirate, thief, rapist, extortionist – and expect to escape punishment from the emperor. John Kinnamos describes what happened next. In the autumn of 1158, Manuel set out on campaign with an immense army to sort out several problems: the rebellious Thoros, Reynald in Antioch, King Baldwin in Jerusalem, the ambitious Nur al-Din, busy trying to extend his rule from Damascus. All threatened to destabilize the emperor's eastern and southern borders. All needed to be controlled, if possible by diplomacy, if not then by force. Only then would he be in a position to confront his real challengers, the Seljuk Turks.

Having failed yet again to catch Thoros – who was warned of the imperial approach by a pilgrim and fled – Manuel set off for Antioch to deal with Reynald, accompanied by an international delegation of envoys from Asia, Syria, Turkey, Armenia and the Crusader states. What was Reynald to do? His senior aide, the archbishop of Latakia in Syria, advised him: eat humble pie on an epic scale. Reynald agreed. He went out to meet the emperor, sending the archbishop on ahead to plead his cause, which the archbishop did persuasively enough to get Reynald a hearing. Lord and vassal met in a town on the ever-shifting frontier, on what is now the Ceyhan river in southern Turkey, spanned then and now by a nine-arched bridge.[30]

Reynald played the penitent as if his life depended on it. Certainly his position as prince of Antioch did. To the astonishment of the assembled diplomats, having put himself centre stage in a rent-a-crowd of pseudo-monks, he 'removed the covering from his head, bared his arms up to his elbows, and going unshod through the city with a multitude of monks, he appeared before the emperor.' In his left hand, he carried a sword by the point, ready for offering as a symbol of submission. The emperor was seated on a dais, surrounded by the ranks of immense, fair-haired Varangian guards,[31] 'tall as palm trees', recruited from descendants of the Scandinavians who had traded and fought their way down the Volga. Reynald prostrated himself far from the imperial tent, as if not daring to approach, while 'the monks who were not monks, unshod,

[30] The river was then the Pyramus, on which stood the city of Mopsuestia, present-day Misis.
[31] Originally, Varangians (from Old Norse *varar*, a pledge) were Swedes recruited for service in Russia. They were employed as imperial bodyguards in Constantinople to avoid the possibility of disloyalty associated with local troops.

with bared heads, approached the emperor. All, bending the knee, wept tears from their eyes and held out their hands.' At first, the emperor refused to acknowledge Reynald, lying in the dirt, but eventually ordered him to advance. 'Moved by his coming in said fashion, he forgave him his offence, while he [Reynald] bound himself with oaths to many things', namely to hand over his citadel and supply soldiers when asked, and to appoint a Greek Patriarch in Antioch – i.e. one of Manuel's men – instead of a Latin one. Having survived with his body and position intact, if not his reputation, Reynald returned to Antioch.

For the emperor, that was one problem solved. Another was Baldwin, king of Jerusalem, who was equally appalled at Manuel's approach and the possibility of losing his kingdom. On the other hand, he had done Manuel no harm and chose to charm his way to peaceful co-existence. It worked well. Manuel befriended the young king, who managed to mediate peace with Thoros. In April 1159, Manuel made a processional entry into Antioch, wearing chain-mail beneath his silks in case of an assassination attempt. He needn't have worried. The people adored him. He paraded on horseback through the narrow streets with Reynald humbly holding his bridle. Even old Amaury was there, ready to forgive Reynald. The Greek Patriarch idea was quietly forgotten. Amaury got his old job back. Friendship reigned supreme.

And after a week of festivities, Manuel decided to leave his enemy Nur al-Din in peace. A show of force was enough. It wasn't worth starting a war to retake Syria when there were far more serious enemies to cope with – conspirators at home and the Turks abroad. Gifts were exchanged, prisoners freed by the thousand, and Manuel headed home.

So there could have been some sort of balance of power in the region. But Reynald could not leave well enough alone. In the autumn of 1160, spies told him that some 150 kilometres northwards, just over the border with the Seljuks, there were farming communities with many flocks. Their pastures were on the Aintab plateau, which rolls between the Taurus mountains and the Euphrates. The peasants were Christian, but that did not bother Reynald. He knew the area, at least by reputation, because ten years before many of the Christians of Edessa had fled across it to Antioch to escape their new Muslim masters, Zangi and his heir, Nur al-Din. Crucially, so his informants said, the farmers and their flocks were unguarded and easy targets. So he set off, with 120 cavalry and 500 eager foot-soldiers, who duly seized all they could.

But it was a set-up. The same informants passed on both the news of Reynald's departure and his target to the governor of Aleppo, Nur al-Din's foster-brother, Majd. A raiding party set off north to ambush Reynald.

Warned of Majd's approach, Reynald and his men argued: should they fight or flee? Reynald, always the headstrong warrior, refused to abandon his stolen cattle, sheep and camels. But the flocks for which he fought were an impossible burden. Reynald's men were outnumbered and he was captured, along with thirty others. He was a valuable catch. All aristocrats were worth keeping, so that the captors could exchange them for some financial or political advantage: a ransom, a city, a captive held by the other side. Shoved on to a camel, his hands tied behind him, Reynald was led off to prison in Aleppo.

There he would remain, while he and his captors awaited payment of an immense ransom, to be negotiated. He had, it seemed, vanished from the earth, leaving Antioch in the hands of its Patriarch, Amaury, and a reputation for violence and treachery.

Only in middle age would he get a chance to indulge both once again. In 1176, finally, after sixteen years, a deal was done, arranged by Damascus's vizier, Gumushtegin. He freed Reynald in a fit of generosity towards the Franks for saving him from Saladin, despite public protests that such a dangerous man should never be released. The cash helped. The more-than-royal ransom paid by the Christians was 120,000 dinars, 380 kilograms of gold coins – about £17 million (or $26 million) at today's prices. Princes had been freed for less. Back then, it was enough to run a large castle for three years.[32]

Saladin was back in far-off Cairo, having recently reached a settlement with the Assassins, totally unaware of what was brewing in his homeland, when Reynald walked out of Aleppo, free at last, but bitter as hell and thirsting for revenge on all Muslims. 'A third and final period of his life was about to begin,' as his biographer Gustave Schlumberger writes, 'more fantastic, stranger and yet more brilliant . . . which would end in its turn in the most dramatic of catastrophes.'

---

[32] Take the immense castle of Saphet (Safed), in northern Israel, 11 kilometres north of the Sea of Galilee. Built by 850 workmen and 400 slaves, the annual running cost came to 40,000 dinars.

7

Defeat and Victory: The Tide on the Turn

OUR HERO WAS NOT ALWAYS A HERO. SOMETIMES HE MADE mistakes, covered up and deceived. One such occasion happened in 1177.

In November of that year, trouble loomed from northern Syria, where Philip, Count of Flanders, landed at Acre, backed by seventy ships sent by Emperor Manuel, apparently threatening an invasion of Egypt. Saladin led some 26,000 troops out of Egypt, both to counter Philip and because Jerusalem itself seemed vulnerable. With the death of its king, Amalric, in 1174 it had been inherited by the thirteen-year-old Baldwin IV, a sickly lad, whose problem was identified by the historian William of Tyre, his tutor. At first, as a nine-year-old, the boy was a pleasure to teach: good-looking, lovable, an excellent horseman, good memory, loved to talk, respectful, keen intellect, well disposed to follow good advice. But then,

> he was playing one day with his companions of noble rank, when they began, as playful boys often do, to pinch each others' arms and hands with their nails. The other boys gave evidence of pain by their outcries, but Baldwin, although his comrades did not spare him, endured it altogether too patiently, as if he felt nothing . . . when I called him and began to inquire what it meant, I discovered that his right arm and hand were partially numb, so that he did not feel pinching or biting in the least. I began to be uneasy . . . physicians were consulted. Repeated fomentations, oil rubs, and even poisonous remedies were employed without result in the attempt to help him. For, as we recognized in the process of time, these were the premonitory symptoms of a most serious and incurable disease which later became plainly apparent. It is impossible to refrain from tears while speaking of this great misfortune. For, as he began to reach years of maturity, it was evident that he was suffering from the terrible disease of leprosy.

No one thought he would amount to anything. But he was a boy of character. As the disease began to eat away at his limbs and face, he emerged as a leader, luckily, because it turned out that Philip of Flanders was more interested in making good marriages for two young cousins than in waging war; he was also keen to indulge in gambling, banquets, baths and drunken debauches, according to William of Tyre. There would be no help against Saladin for Baldwin from that quarter. But there was help nevertheless, from the man who was about to turn a religious war into a deeply personal conflict that will run through our story almost to the end.

Re-enter at this point our anti-hero, Reynald de Châtillon. Emerging from captivity in Aleppo in 1176, he found his wife had died and his two children had been spirited away to Constantinople in preparation for royal marriages. He wasted no time in rebuilding his career. Eager for any action that would give him Muslims to kill, he offered his services to Baldwin the Leper, whose advisers knew exactly how to set him up. If he married a certain young widow, Stephanie (Etiennette), he would become master of her castle, inherited from her husband (Miles de Plancy, assassinated in Acre in 1174).

It was the castle that mattered, not the widow. Kerak (Karak today)[33] had been built thirty years previously, a day's ride east of the Dead Sea inside today's Jordan, commanding a vaguely defined area, Oultrejourdain, Outre- (in modern French) or Trans-Jordan, also known by the Biblical name of Moab. It ran from the Dead Sea for 200 kilometres across the Negev desert to Eilat and the Gulf of Aqaba, even (since there was no border) down to St Catherine's Monastery in the middle of Sinai. All around was desolation: saw-edged mountain ranges, waterless ravines, bare rock, scrub and sand, all

---

[33] It has several spellings, including Crac and Krak. The word derives from the Syriac *karkha*, a town. Not to be confused with the even more impressive Krak des Chevaliers, 200 kilometres to the north, in Syria, just over today's Lebanese border. The French also knew it by the name of its nearby predecessor castle, Montréal, or Mount Royal.

sun-scorched under cloudless skies. But through the desert and past Kerak ran the road south. This crag of a place, with its 80-metre entrance tunnel and walls thick enough to resist the battering of catapults, was the key to the road linking Damascus and Mecca, able to control (that is, raid, rob and tax) camel-trains of traders and pilgrims.

So Reynald was no sooner free than he became a combination of king, warlord and robber-baron, complete with castle, state and income. As Schlumberger puts it, here was an addict of adventure, fighting and pillage, with 'an implacable Islamophobia nurtured by sixteen years of humiliation and torture at the hands of his jailers.' He was the loosest of all loose cannons, just the man to help a leprous teenage king stop Saladin in his tracks.

Baldwin, guided by Reynald, rushed to defend his southern outpost, Ascalon, from Saladin. His 500 knights were just in time to secure the fortress, but such a small body of men would not risk attacking Saladin, who simply ignored Ascalon and marched straight past, on towards Jerusalem. Perhaps unaware that his young and diseased opponent had an extremely dangerous commander, Saladin let his troops remove their armour and scatter across the countryside to pillage the locals. Baldwin sent an urgent message 20 kilometres south to the Knights Templar in Gaza, of whom there were eighty under another dangerous commander, the Grandmaster Odo de St Amand. The Templars were so called because their founder in 1118 had rooms for himself and a few others in a wing of the royal palace, the former al-Aqsa mosque, in Jerusalem's Temple area. The order, led by rich knights, owed allegiance only to the Pope to keep the roads to Jerusalem free of bandits for pilgrims. Their commander,

Grandmaster Odo, or Eudes, was, in the opinion of his fellow Christian William of Tyre, 'a wicked man, haughty and arrogant, in whose nostrils dwelt the spirit of fury, one who neither feared God nor revered man', which makes him sound as loose a cannon as Reynald. In a way he was, because, as a servant of the Pope, he might choose not to answer a cry for help from young Baldwin. This time he did help. On 25 November 1177, a Friday, the two Christian forces, just 375 of them,[34] galloped out of Ascalon along the coast, outflanking Saladin's scattered army.

No one is sure where they found Saladin; somewhere just north of Ascalon, it seems. William of Tyre calls it 'Mons Gisard' (though the spelling varies), and it is often given as 'Mont Gisard', but the name has dropped from use and its location has never been identified. Muslims call the battle after nearby Ramla.

As those of Saladin's force who heard the warning call of trumpets struggled to re-arm and reform, the Christians took heart in the face of overwhelming odds. As Archbishop Albert of Bethlehem held aloft the True Cross, they charged. Usually, Saladin's force would have allowed charging cavalry through and attacked from the sides. But in this case his troops were in no position to do anything much, because they had no line of retreat. They ran. Saladin was hustled away by his bodyguards, identified by yellow silk over their armour. Many, in their haste to escape, threw away their arms, armour and packs, many of which were picked up by their pursuers. 'For 12 miles and more, during this entire

---

[34] According to William of Tyre, but surely a huge underestimation. As a Christian, he may well have understated the Christians' army to emphasize the significance of the 'Life-giving Cross'.

flight, the foe was mercilessly slaughtered,' wrote William, 'nor would any of their number have survived, had not the swift descent of night rescued them.'

It wasn't over. The next few days were bitterly cold. As the Christians headed back to Jerusalem, the Muslim survivors fleeing into Sinai – Saladin among them, on a camel – ran out of water. Many horses died. Lacking guides, the men wandered hopelessly, until Saladin's secretary, camping clear of the battle, hired Bedouin to launch a rescue operation. It took Saladin two weeks to get back to Cairo. All told, some 2,000 Muslims had been killed.

Saladin did what leaders do when handling bad news: he spun events for all he was worth, sending camel-messengers racing ahead to forestall rumours of the catastrophe and to tell Cairo that he was alive and well. Imad al-Din, deputy to his secretary and sometimes called Saladin's chancellor, wasn't fooled. 'I rode out to listen to what they had to say and hear how God had given victory to the Muslims. But I heard them saying "Good news! The Sultan and his family are safe and arriving with spoils" . . . They would not be giving good news of his safety unless there had been a defeat.' Saladin refused to admit any such thing. The Franks had lost many more than the Muslims, he wrote to an unnamed emir. Please read this letter to your officers and tell them to thank God the army was safe. God's grace had guided the survivors through waterless deserts . . . no great name had been lost . . . only beasts had died of thirst . . . the army had re-formed. Saladin went further: 'The people said that it was a defeat, but through the blessing of the Caliphate it was a victory.'

Well, no, it wasn't. It was a catastrophe, and everyone knew it. Within days, the pigeon-post had spread the news across all Egypt. A later scribe recalled a piece of ancient wisdom: that detectable lies should be avoided in reports of defeats.[35] Saladin would have known nothing of the great Chinese strategist Sun Tzu (Sun Zi in pinyin), author of *The Art of War*, but experience had now taught him the truth of the Sun Tzu aphorism: avoid battle unless victory is assured.

How could victory be assured? By focusing not on battles, but on the bases in which they were prepared – the castles.

Refusal to accept defeat is a ploy adopted by leaders devoted to victory against the odds. Sometimes it works, sometimes it doesn't. It worked for Churchill when Hitler dominated most of Europe in 1941, but it didn't work for Hitler after Stalingrad in 1942. One hopes that morality plays a part, but often it doesn't. Stalin rallied his nation in the face of defeat. Genghis Khan took on and destroyed the world of Islam, superior to his in almost every way, because he was able to inspire his people. Are you a brilliant, charismatic leader with once-more-unto-the-breach persistence? Or an egomaniac squandering resources and lives? Time, events and a good dose of hindsight will tell.

In this case, Saladin had both a vision – of Islamic unity to drive out the Crusaders – and the means, in the form of a strong economy, if it could be used properly. He rebuilt, reorganized and replaced lost personnel, equipment and animals. Within four months, he had made good his losses and returned to Syria.

Syria was in disarray. Saladin's brother, Turanshah, was

---

[35] Ahmad al-Qalqashandi (1355/6–1418), quoted in Lyons and Jackson, *Saladin*, p. 126.

making a mess of running Damascus, preferring (in William of Tyre's words) to 'plunge into the sea of his own pleasures' and pay off the Christians rather than fight them. Mosul and Baalbek were under their own warlords. Aleppo was torn by intrigues. Its vizier had been killed by Assassins and his rival, Gumushtegin, accused of complicity, tortured to death. The Franks, spotting signs of weakness, launched an abortive raid on Hama. All of this happened in November 1177, coinciding with Saladin's defeat at Mont Gisard. All in all, as William noted, it was 'a calamitous month', with more bad things to come: the death of Saladin's uncle Shihab al-Din in Hama, and the city of Harim, 60 kilometres west of Aleppo, besieged through the winter, until the Franks were scared away by Saladin's return to northern Syria in March 1178.

For those who like their history presented in clear narrative, the next few years are difficult, because there is no clarity, no narrative leading up to a final, decisive confrontation. After Mont Gisard, Saladin would be very careful about taking on the Christians in open battle. So, as in a football match or a game of chess, everyone knew what they wanted, but there was a lot of groundwork before anything could be achieved. Both sides sought openings that would allow an all-out attack. Little happened, but a few incidents are worth telling for they set the scene for the great battle to come, at Hattin in 1187.

As always, the first problem Saladin faced was establishing his authority over his fellow Muslims before turning on his real enemy, the Franks. In early 1179 a challenge arose in northern Syria in the form of the Turkish sultan of Rum, which occupied what is now eastern Turkey, north of a rather vague frontier with Syria. This Seljuk sultan, Qilij-Arslan, was a Muslim, of course, but he also had claims on bits of Syria, partly because he needed possessions to hand on to his many sons (eleven eventually, though at this stage Qilij was still only twenty-three). Saladin had to get rid of him. Luckily, Saladin was good at choosing lieutenants who were reliable, because many of them were his brothers and cousins and nephews. His closest aide, Taqi al-Din, was the son of Saladin's half-brother. Taqi had been with Saladin in Egypt and had proved his loyalty many times. At the battle of Mont Gisard, he had lost a son. Now Saladin gave him the task of seeing off the Seljuk sultan, which he did with a task-force of 1,000 horsemen, who surprised Qilij and his much larger force and drove them back over the border.

Saladin had based himself in Damascus, his ability to raise more troops limited by famine. Never mind, he wrote to the caliph, the spring of 1180, God willing, would see the capture of Jerusalem. It was a consummation devoutly to be wished, yet endlessly postponed.

Then came one particular siege that marked a turning point. This was another of those places the significance of which leaders were well aware. The undefended site was the only ford over the Jordan between its source and the Sea of Galilee, which made it a key to the grain-rich area north of Lake Tiberias. The area is still a key today, because it is on the western edge of the Golan Heights, seized by Israel in 1948 and deemed crucial to its security. So crucial was the area to the Christians in Jerusalem, and so badly defended, that, as soon as it became known that Saladin had returned from Egypt to Damascus, Baldwin the Leper was approached by the Knights Templar, who as protectors of pilgrims took particular care of the bathing places in the Jordan, including this ford.

It had both strategic and historical importance, for it was the spot where Israel acquired its name. The book of Genesis tells the story (Chapter 32, verses 24–8). The patriarch Jacob, travelling to Canaan, was left alone overnight, 'and there wrestled a man with him, until the breaking of the day.' The unnamed man apparently dislocates Jacob's hip, or as the Authorized Version puts it, 'the hollow of Jacob's thigh was out of joint'. The man asks Jacob's name and then says, 'Thy name shall be no more called Jacob, but Israel', possibly meaning 'El [an ancient name of God] prevails', which is why the man continues, 'for as a prince hast thou power with God and with men, and hast prevailed'. The incident in which Israel gets its name is obviously important, but the Bible offers no help in understanding it. Who is the man? In folklore, he becomes an angel or even a pre-incarnation of Christ. Whatever the explanation, it was here, at this crossing point on the Jordan, that Jacob wrestled, giving the place its name, Jacob's Ford.[36] Now Odo, Grandmaster of the Knights Templar, pressurized the eighteen-year-old King Baldwin to fortify Jacob's Ford by providing it with a castle.

It was not a straightforward decision, because the obvious site for the castle, a hill 3 kilometres from the river, was actually in Muslim territory.

Or was it? What sort of a frontier was this? The question opens up an interesting theoretical point, though in this case the point was also practical. We live today in a world of

[36] Vadum Iacob, as it is in Latin. Other names are Chastellet, Bait al-Ahzan ('House of Grief'), Ateret and Yarda, after a village that vanished when Israel took the area in 1948. I fear another story is waiting to be told.

nation-states with borders that are made real in all sorts of ways, like lines on maps and fences and border controls and passports that allow passage from one side to the other. But before all those things existed, how real were borders? Of course landowners of any kind, from simple farmers to rulers of vast estates, defined their own borders, usually with reference to natural features, like rivers, mountains, rocks and deserts. In modern times, nation-states have often claimed these features as 'natural' frontiers, as if they were God-given. Victor Hugo, French poet and nationalist, did so: 'The Rhine . . . has been accorded a special role by Divine Providence.' Americans did the same: it was their 'manifest destiny' to rule 'from sea to shining sea'.[37] But in Saladin's time, in a world of nomadic herders and civil strife and invasions, there were no nation-states and no borders in the modern sense. There were barriers like Hadrian's Wall and Offa's Dyke, but they were not the same as frontiers or borders. Today's maps neatly demarcate the Kingdom of Jerusalem from Syria, Syria from Rum and Byzantium, but on the ground there was nothing to tell that you had moved from one to another. The Jordan was a possible natural border; except that no one treated it as such. Your sense of identity did not involve loyalty to a nation-state with nicely demarcated borders. If you asked an 'ordinary person', supposing you could find such a creature, 'What is your identity?' the answer would have to refer to a landscape, a religion, a city, a clan, an occupation, a leader.

A castle at Jacob's Ford would in effect *create* a frontier by grabbing land, policing it with a small army and barring

---

[37] Such nonsense. What of the Rhône? And the Rockies? Would not they make 'natural frontiers'? Of course they would; but that did not suit nineteenth-century nationalist agendas.

Saladin from following this route to Jerusalem. Baldwin complied, taking charge in person. Work started in October 1178, in a frantic race against time. Indeed the whole short life of Jacob's Ford was frantic, from conception and creation to occupation and destruction. It would have been the largest castle of its day in the whole eastern Mediterranean, and it might have lasted for centuries. As things turned out, its life was all over in eleven months, perhaps the shortest of any castle ever.

Yet it had a strange after-life, firstly because its sudden death and complete abandonment turned it into a treasure trove for modern archaeologists,[38] headed by Ronnie Ellenblum and his team from the Hebrew University of Jerusalem, who excavated the site in 1997–8; secondly because, by pure chance, it sits right on a tectonic fault-line, and in 1202 an earthquake split it down the middle. This event has nothing to do with Saladin, but geologists love it, because the earth-quake shifted most of Arabia north, taking one half of the castle with it, by an amount exactly revealed by the offset in the walls – 1.6 metres. This allows them to explain the forces involved[39] (7.6 on the Richter scale). Today, archaeologists and geologists have revealed startling details about the way the earth shifts beneath it, and about those who fought and died there in 1178–9.

[38] Summarized in Ronnie Ellenblum, *Crusader Castles and Modern Histories*.
[39] It is on a fault-line that is part of the Dead Sea Transform, a complex of faults that makes the whole region look like a cracked mirror on geological maps. It is hard to analyse, so for geologists Vadum Iacob is treasure. 'Deformation of a human habitat by transform-related shear has not been previously documented' (Ellenblum et al., *Geology*, April 1998). Another quake in 1759 added 0.5 metres to the sideways shift. Details online at vadumiacob.huji.ac.il, which has a full bibliography.

It was obvious to the king and his engineers when they arrived on site that the 1,500 workers might not be able to complete the castle – inner wall, outer wall, gates, moat – in time to defend themselves against Saladin. Their priority was security, which they needed as fast as possible. So the first task for the carpenters and stonecutters (at least 100 being Muslim captives) was to build from the inside outwards, starting with an inner wall, which would shield a force big enough to stop Saladin's advance. There was another reason for speed. Everything had to be carried in – wagons, oxen, food for the troops, grain, tools, all guarded by crossbowmen and other fighters, and all paid for by the king and the Templars with no hope of income from booty. Time was money, and speed saved both.

That demanded improvisation. Designers must have complained that they were being forced to work with one arm tied behind their backs. Normally, there would have been one or two gates. But ox-wagons piled with stones, timber and refuse would create bottlenecks. So the architects had to allow for five gates, though doing so left the place harder to defend. On a base of cobbles, the workforce laid out ashlar blocks as foundations for 20,000 dressed stones for the walls, carried from the stonemasons' workshop by mules (as is suggested by the damage done to the bones unearthed by Ellenblum). The inner walls, 4 metres thick, made a rectangle 150 metres long and 60 metres wide – almost half a kilometre all the way around. Excavated earth was dumped outside the wall, which meant that the second wall, if there was ever time to build it, would stand higher than the first. Mounds of earth stored water, and waterlogged earth put pressure on walls. So the designers had to (a) get as much rock as possible, which took time, wagons, and manpower; and (b) make good drainage, which meant covering the raised earth with a layer of clay, and that too had to be dug and carried in. Every castle designer knew that to hold off sieges you needed towers. No time for those. Or for any buildings inside, except for a single stone vault. And they planned a moat, but that could be built only after the outer wall was finished. Better a bad castle than no castle or an unfinished good one. By the following spring, the castle had walls 10 metres high – what would have become the inner walls, given more time.

The spring campaigning season opened with a skirmish. Saladin received a report that some Franks were on the Golan Heights in pursuit of unguarded flocks. In fact, they were from Jacob's Ford, and were led by Baldwin himself, for his men could do with the food. A force of 1,000 Muslims was nearby, some 30 kilometres from Jacob's Ford and 60 from Damascus. The Muslims, under Saladin's nephew Farrukh-Shah, went looking for the raiders overnight, surprised them at dawn, chased most of them off with volleys of arrows, and took some prisoners, among them the wicked, haughty and arrogant Templar commander Odo de St Amand.

At this unexpected success, a message was sent by pigeon to summon Saladin. As always, pigeon-post was so routine that no one commented on it, but here is evidence that there was a minor industry in Damascus, as in all cities, devoted to pigeon-rearing – cotes of pigeons bred to return to base, and taken out on every patrol so that reports, sent off in duplicate or triplicate in case a bird was lost in flight, could be received within an hour or two.

So Saladin was out there the following day, by which time someone unnamed had provided an eyewitness account of what had happened: King Baldwin fleeing for his life, many deaths, many knights wounded, one of Baldwin's aides so seriously hurt that he died later. And they had Odo himself, who was soon thrown into 'a squalid prison', as William of Tyre put it, where he died a few months later 'mourned by no one'.

A dry winter had become a dry spring. With little new grass for horses, Saladin could not import fresh cavalry from Egypt; could not therefore mount his promised assault on Jerusalem.

All this took place on Muslim territory, just over the Frankish 'border'. This suggested a very odd but original idea to Saladin. Sieges are expensive operations. Did they really have to go through with this one? What if he came to terms with Baldwin? At a stroke, that would make the castle redundant. All that labour and expense would be for no purpose. Why not short-circuit the whole business? So in May 1179, just after Baldwin fled, Saladin made an extraordinary offer. How about making peace and agreeing a deal? He would *buy* Jacob's Ford castle, and save everyone time, money and lives. The Templars in charge took the idea seriously. The border, such as it was, would return to its previous peaceful state, and the Templars would get their money back. It could work, they said, if they were reimbursed the building costs. Saladin offered 60,000 dinars. No, sorry, came the reply, the 20,000 stones cost 4 dinars each. That was 80,000 right there, not taking into account the costs of the garrison, workers, food, etc., etc. So Saladin raised his offer to 100,000 dinars. Still no deal. In a way, it is not surprising, because had it gone through Saladin would have acquired a nice new – though unfinished – castle and a slab of territory. Both sides backed off. When armies prepare for action, minds are made up: it becomes harder to make peace than war.

A sort of trial assault took place a few days later, but Saladin pulled back, seeing he could not take the castle before it received reinforcements from Jerusalem. Then all was quiet for three months, while both sides prepared for something more serious. Saladin arrived again from Damascus on Friday, 23 August, and again he was in a hurry to conclude the siege before Baldwin mustered an army in Tiberias, 23 kilometres to the south, and sent it to drive him off. Collecting his force would take Baldwin four days, the march a couple more. Saladin had a week at most.

In his camp on the east bank of the Jordan, almost within artillery range of the castle, Saladin had the beams with which his engineers could have put together trebuchets; but that would take time, with no guarantee that the giant machines could batter a hole in the walls fast enough. So, with the Franks locked inside the castle and with bowmen all around making them keep their heads down, Saladin set his sappers to work. Undermining had been the normal tactic for decades, so the sappers were expert at their job, digging themselves below ground under the protection of their cross-bowmen, setting wooden pillars and a roof, as in a coal mine. They dug in relays, round the clock, for three days. By the morning of Tuesday, the 27th, they were 10 metres into the hillside, right under the wall.

They stuffed their tunnel with wood, set it on fire, and stood back.

The fire blazed, everyone watched and waited, each side with opposite hopes.

Nothing happened.

The wall held.

Three days to go before the Frankish army arrived, with consequences that would probably be disastrous for Saladin, if the catastrophe of Mont Gisard was anything to go by.

Without a moment to lose, Saladin had to get his sappers to dig further. But the tunnel was full of flaming embers. There was no time to wait for the flames to die and the ashes to cool, so he ordered them to be doused with water, promising an astonishing one dinar for every skinful of water poured on the flames. Imad al-Din witnessed all this: 'I saw the men bringing skins full of water, and when the tunnel was flooded with water, the fire was extinguished and the sappers could renew their efforts.' Meanwhile, in the castle above, the Franks were taking precautions, building a wooden wall to block the hole that would appear if the stone one collapsed.

The following day, Wednesday, the sappers scooped out the water and ashes and mud, and that same night dug deeper, adding a crucial few metres to their work, before once again stuffing the tunnel with wood and setting it alight to burn for the rest of the night.

At sunrise on Thursday morning, 29 August, the flaming roof of the tunnel burned through to the cobble foundations, which tumbled into the hole below. The wall cracked and fell, to wild applause from the Muslims. Moreover, the flames spread to the temporary wooden wall, fanned by a hot, dry wind. It was all over for those inside. Seeing this, the Frankish commander, unnamed in the sources, astounded Muslims gathering at the breach by leaping from a remaining section of wall into the flames. The Christian forces in Tiberias saw the cloud, and knew there was no point in going.

The Franks sent a message asking for surrender terms,

but Saladin – not always as generous as portrayed – refused. The Muslims burst through the gap, killed 800 defenders and took another 700 prisoners. Some of the skeletons were rediscovered by Ronnie Ellenblum's team of archaeologists in their ten years of work, some with skulls and other bones chipped by swords and others with the heads of the arrows that killed them lying alongside. Of the survivors, Saladin interrogated many personally, pulling aside for execution Muslims who had converted to Christianity and crossbowmen who had been the scourge of the Muslim assault force. The 100 captured Muslim stonemasons were brought back on side. Among the booty taken were 1,000 suits of armour and '100,000 weapons' (hard to believe, from a defence force of 1,500; over sixty weapons apiece sounds excessive). The survivors were marched off to Damascus into captivity.

Then the victors completed the job of destruction. Among the victims were three horses, six mules and a donkey, killed by random arrows during the attack, then collected along with human bodies and thrown into a stone vault, which seems to have been deliberately destroyed. All remained buried and untouched by predators, weather or human scavengers until Ellenblum and his team dug them up. There were a lot of other bodies, some of which were tossed into the water-cistern. Not a good idea, because this was late August and within three days the bodies were a health hazard. Saladin ordered his men out. They were back in Damascus by mid-September, just three weeks after their arrival at Jacob's Ford.

Taking the castle was a turning point. It was the first time in many years that the Muslims had captured a Frankish castle. Their success proved a point – that castles were only useful as bases for field armies. True, the Crusaders could retreat into them and be safe for a while. But not for ever. Once they were in, the open mobility of their attackers became the key to victory. If Muslims worked towards a final battle out in the open, they could destroy the Crusaders.

The tide of war was turning.

But it had not quite turned. The whole region was seething. Imagine it as a nightmarish snooker table, with iron balls that are magnets of different strengths and sizes. If you listed them all, there would be dozens. Here are some: Egypt and Syria, Syria's major cities, their rivals for leadership, the Franks in Jerusalem, the other Frankish enclaves, rogue Frankish commanders, Frankish rivals for power, Frankish marriages (Frankish politics being a universe on its own), Bedouin desert-dwellers, Byzantium, the Seljuk Turks of Rum, the caliph in Baghdad, Saladin's own family, and off at the far end of the table a scattering of European rulers and nobles – all these and more governed by the whim or calculation of individuals, all affecting each other by their moves, repelling, attracting, sticking together in perverse alliances, cannoning off each other in a multiplicity of effects, and sometimes vanishing for ever into a side-pocket labelled 'Death' or 'Defeat'. Saladin was not yet the master-player. All he could do for the moment was wait, watch, and hope for an alignment that would favour him.

For three years, from late 1179 to late 1182, very little favoured him. The Nile's annual flood had failed. The people suffered, yet the rich flaunted their wealth. An emir celebrated the circumcision of his sons with 700 slaughtered sheep. In Baghdad, the caliph al-Mustadi died, and so did his vizier, perhaps murdered. There were rumours of a coming invasion from Europe, another Crusade. Turanshah, Saladin's older brother in charge of Damascus, was a problem. He was generous to the point of foolishness and had run up severe debts. Damascus could not be left in his charge. Saladin gave him a new task, to bring back from Syria many Egyptian soldiers recovering from wounds or exhaustion after their crushing defeat at Mont Gisard. It seems the move, or perhaps the shock of demotion, was too much, for in Alexandria Turanshah went on living high, squandering cash on 'buffoons and panders', as a satirical poet said. He developed severe intestinal problems. He would be dead within the year.

Fortunately for Saladin, very little favoured the Christians either. Baldwin's leprosy was getting worse and the Franks started talking about a successor. No help came from Europe, and there would be none from Byzantium either, because Emperor Manuel was dying and his empire was bankrupt from foreign adventures and a terrible defeat at the hands of the Turkish Seljuks. It was then torn by intrigues and mysterious deaths and a massacre (when the Greeks of Constantinople turned on the Latins). The several Christian statelets tried to strengthen themselves through marriages proposed, debated, abandoned or made. Every proposal, negotiation, engagement, marriage, love affair and death added to the chaos.

As an example, follow one of the elements, the princess named Sibylla, daughter of Jerusalem's king Amalric, sister of Baldwin the Leper, and Jerusalem's future queen. Because of her brother's condition, it was vital she produce an heir. So she was married at sixteen and had just fallen pregnant when her husband died of malaria. That left her with a son, but no husband. Envoys sent off all over Europe failed to find a replacement, until at last a French baron,

Hugh of Burgundy, raised a hope that he would sail in to become heir to Jerusalem's throne; which he might have done had not Sibylla fallen for Baldwin – not, of course, the leprous Baldwin her brother, but another one, of Ibelin (a castle in today's Yavne, between Jaffa and Ascalon); but then this Baldwin was captured by Saladin, which put him out of the running, until he was released owing a large ransom, at which point Sibylla refused him anyway because of the debt, a rejection that inspired Baldwin to go to Emperor Manuel in Constantinople to pay it; only to find that on his return Sibylla had fallen in love again, this time with a 'weak and foolish' boy named Guy, to the fury of the Palestinian barons who would have him as their king when Sibylla's brother died if the marriage took place; which it did at Easter 1180.

These were not circumstances in which either side wished to wage war. In May 1180, Baldwin the Leper requested a truce, and Saladin agreed. You might think this was a move that benefited everyone. But there was one man who was extremely put out. The truce turned out to be another of those events with unexpected consequences, which would turn Saladin's war against the Christians into something intensely personal.

8

Reynald's Raid

THE PROTAGONIST OF THIS NEXT PART OF THE STORY IS, OF course, Reynald, at his most excessive, for his idea was to strike at the very heart of Islam, perhaps even the holy cities of Mecca and Medina (on which more later). 'Only one man,' as historian Alex Mallett puts it,[40] 'had the audacity, temerity, and insanity (or possibly genius)' not simply to dream up something so crazy, but then to act on it, resulting in 'one of the most extraordinary episodes in the history of the Crusades'.

No one knows for sure what Reynald's plan was, because

[40] Alex Mallet, 'A trip down the Red Sea with Reynald of Châtillon'; see Bibliography.

he was not there at the end and everyone else was killed. All we have as evidence are reports written by five different sources, all of which mention rumours and surmises about Reynald's intentions and how bad things might have been without the successful intervention of the Egyptian fleet.

So here is what actually happened, as near as it can be gleaned from the letters that describe it.[41]

The truce made by Saladin and Baldwin in May 1180 frustrated Reynald, who was eager to pillage Muslims, especially those who could now in theory cross his territory in peace. He had the idea of mounting a raid into the Red Sea to attack what was then the Hejaz and is now the western coastal strip of Saudi Arabia, a narrow plain backed by rugged, barren mountains. This is the original heart of Islam, containing its holiest city, Mecca (Muhammad's birthplace and where he started to write the Quran), and its second holiest, Medina (where the Prophet is buried). The Red Sea was liquid Islam, virtually sacrosanct, never penetrated by Europeans since the Romans were there 1,000 years previously, long before Islam came into existence. Strategically, the planned raid was a brilliant idea, because if even halfway successful it would both shatter Saladin's claim to be the true defender of Islam and restore sagging Christian morale. And, of course, Reynald had the prime location from which to launch such a raid: Kerak, his newly acquired castle, 200 kilometres north of the Red Sea port of Eilat.

---

[41] The letters are by Imad al-Din, Saladin's secretary, and Qadi al-Fadil, his vizier in Egypt. Another account was left by the great traveller ibn Jubayr. Both ibn al-Athir and Sibt b. al-Jawzi edited the accounts, and added snippets of their own. Additional details are in the biographies of the admiral who ended the raid, Lu'lu'.

It took him the next two years to prepare. It was not immediately obvious how best to mount such a raid. The most direct way was overland. If you made the journey today, it would take you 180 kilometres to the Saudi border, then – if you wished to penetrate to the heart of Islam – another 600 to Medina and 1,000 to Mecca. So to inflict the sort of damage Reynald dreamed of, he would have to take a body of men on a round trip of 1,600 kilometres to Medina and back, or, if he was really ambitious, 2,400 to Mecca. The journey itself, though over desert, was not the main problem; it was, after all, routine for pilgrims and it was not hard to buy the help of local Bedouin as guides. The problem was one of military logistics. He might get through with a small group, not drawing attention to themselves. But what good was a small group when the time came for action? Yet the bigger the group, the bigger the risk and the more support would be needed in terms of camels and food and finance. What he needed was experience and information on which to base a decision. And cash, because whatever his decision it was bound to be expensive.

So he did what other commanders have done in similar circumstances: he mounted a trial raid, which would have the additional advantage of paying for itself and making a fat profit. In 1181, possibly in October to take advantage of the rainy-season grass, he led a raid to the pilgrim staging-post of Tayma, some 200 kilometres outside the borders of his territory, on the way to Medina. The details were not recorded, but he did attack a caravan of pilgrims, perhaps even reaching Tayma itself. Some said that he was really aiming for Medina, and that only a quick response by Farrukh-Shah, Saladin's nephew and boss of Damascus and Baalbek, saved the day by raiding lands around Kerak, drawing Reynald back home. As Saladin himself wrote to the caliph in Baghdad, al-Nasir: 'Thanks to the Almighty for giving us the chance to protect the Prophet's tomb.' True or not, Reynald returned home with rich pickings, and vital information. He now saw that he could not hope to lead a force overland all the way to Medina, let alone Mecca, and spread the sort of mayhem required. It would invite an immediate counter-attack, or highway robbery by the unruly Bedouin, or death by thirst, starvation or sunstroke. To attack pilgrims and get closer to the holy cities, best go by sea.

But his trial raid had unexpected consequences. Saladin complained to Baldwin that Reynald had broken the truce, and demanded compensation, with no effect, because the person who had to pay was Reynald and there was no chance of him doing any such thing. So Saladin arrested 1,500 Christian pilgrims who had arrived by ship in Egypt. He said he would release them only when he received compensation.

Ships were a problem, but not an insuperable one. To stand a chance of landing killer blows on the Muslim heartland, Reynald needed a significant force. Sources mention 300 men and five ships, not much for an army but a good size for an SAS-style raid. If true, the numbers suggest that the ships were so-called dromons, twelfth-century versions of Roman galleys, some 30 metres long, with a single bank of fifty oars, aided by a triangular lateen sail and weighing some 60 tonnes. Each would have carried fifty oarsmen and ten others. For this tricky operation, each ship would have been built in sections in Kerak and then loaded on to camels. A camel carries about 150–200 kilograms, so there must have been some 2,000 of them, hired from local Bedouin.

Not exactly an undercover operation, but it would have been hard for any spy to guess what the purpose was. To launch the attack during the months of pilgrimage, between January and April 1183, the camels, with a military escort, were driven the 200 kilometres (8–10 days) across the desert to Eilat, along with teams of shipwrights. While the task-force isolated the castle of Eilat on its little island, the carpenters put the ships together (easily said, but not so easily done; it must have taken many days).

At this point, Reynald himself vanishes from the story. All we know is that he survived. It would have been out of character for such a bloodthirsty and fearless buccaneer to forgo an adventure without good reason. As it happens, there were several good reasons. Eilat had been taken back from the Franks by Saladin himself in 1170, using precisely the same tactic as Reynald's: dismantling ships and carrying them to the Gulf of Aqaba by camel (though that was a paltry operation by comparison). Reynald would therefore have considered the castle rightfully his. With Saladin's rise and the union of Syria and Egypt, the castle, which took up most of the island on which it stood, was – along with its well on the mainland nearby – in a key position to dominate the road joining the two regions. So he remained behind to seize the fortress. He was in no hurry. He kept two ships, which blockaded the island castle, preventing those inside from leaving to spread word of the assault, and also forbidding them access to the well on the mainland. Given time, the castle would surely fall into his lap.

One thousand kilometres – two to three weeks' travel – later, as all sources agree, the other three ships landed in Aydhab, which no longer exists, but in the twelfth century was a thriving port on the western coast of the Red Sea and a popular point from which pilgrims crossed back and forth between southern Egypt and the two holy cities. Here the raiders gave vent to their hatred and bloodlust. They 'cut the pilgrimage route and began to kill, plunder and take prisoners'. The locals, of course, had no idea that such a thing was possible, because 'the presence of the Franks in that sea had never been known, and such extreme wickedness had never confronted a pilgrim . . . The weak became worried, and the worried became weak.' While some raiders burned sixteen ships and seized a pilgrim vessel that had just arrived from Jeddah, others attacked a caravan coming from Qus, on the Nile 500 kilometres north.

Slowed by booty, prisoners and their own ignorance of currents and winds, the Franks then crossed the Red Sea – 300 kilometres, four or five days' travel – to Rabigh, a little port where some of the pilgrim ferries landed, 150 kilometres north of Jeddah. Perhaps they were aiming for Jeddah itself, a much bigger place, and were blown off course. In any event, they moored their ships, landed and began to work their way inland.

It was now almost a month since the raid on Eilat. The news had travelled at the gallop to Saladin, who was in Harran, just north of today's Turkey–Syria border. Off went orders to Cairo, to the admiral of the recently strengthened fleet, Husam al-Din Lu'lu'. From obscurity, Lu'lu' now leaped to fame, mainly because our sources were eager to flatter the man one of them called 'the gallant favourite, the bold lion, the unyielding charger, the man of unbounded generosity and unlimited hospitality'. He and a hastily gathered force transferred ships to Suez from Cairo (125 kilometres) and

Alexandria – the business of carrying ships on camels was apparently a common tactic, because this is the third time it was recorded, without any description of how it was done. By now, Reynald had a head-start of six weeks. Sailing and rowing to Eilat (550 kilometres) took the best part of another week. There Lu'lu' overpowered the two Frankish ships and headed for Aydhab (two weeks), where they 'witnessed what the people had suffered'.

Locals pointed out the way the Franks had gone – they were, after all, in pursuit of pilgrims. Lu'lu', whose crews were familiar with the sea and its winds, caught up with the raiders at Rabigh, where the pirates' ships were soon taken, the Frankish crew killed or captured, the Muslim captives released, the booty returned.

Ashore, the remaining raiders fled inland, bribing local Bedouin 'as impious as themselves' to guide them to hiding places in the ravines that cut across the semi-desert lowlands behind the town. Over the next five days, Lu'lu's men used the same tactics, carrying bags of money to out-bribe Bedouin horsemen and hunt down the pirates, killing some and capturing others. They returned to the coast with 170 prisoners, who were divided like booty between Mecca, Cairo and Alexandria, where the traveller ibn Jubayr saw them being paraded through the streets, mounted backwards on camels, to the beat of drums and blare of trumpets. None could be allowed to live, since they all now knew how vulnerable the Muslims were in the Red Sea. All were executed. Two of the leaders were sent to Mina, the 'tent-city' near Mecca, where they were sacrificed like animals.

What had the Franks been hoping to achieve? That was what puzzled the Muslim leaders, who read significance into where the Franks had been heading when they were captured – Medina, the city where Muhammad was buried. It was a natural conclusion, because this was the second time, apparently, that Reynald had aimed at Medina, to 'seize, God forbid, the Holy Places. They wished to inflict upon the Arabian Peninsula the worst possible enormity.' Which was what? The Islamic scholars leaped to the most dramatic conclusion possible. To paraphrase a source, Abd al-Latif, who knew all the main participants, they set out to dig up the grave of the Prophet, take his remains with them, display them, and then charge Muslims an access fee.

For Muslims, the reasoning was sound. The Christians, being (in Muslim eyes) dumb and devoted to nothing but evil, would naturally have chosen the ultimate target, the Prophet's tomb, a plot that was then foiled by the brilliance and bravery of their admiral. The story, taken to these extremes, serves an Islamic agenda: to put Islam and its leaders in the best light, the Christians in the worst.

But from the Christian point of view it makes no sense. Reynald was not *that* crazy. In fact, by all accounts he was highly intelligent, admired both for his ruthlessness and his skill in fighting, surviving and fighting again. He would not have backed, let alone taken part in, a mission that was not only suicidal, but which also had no chance of success, especially considering its size. You might take a small, fanatical group on a suicide raid – we have become used to such missions in recent years – but not a force of 300. So it is worth asking again: what was Reynald's purpose?

For an answer, we should take into account his intelligence, his status, the wider context and the consequences. Saladin was in Syria, aiming to gain control of Aleppo, which would have completed the unification of an empire in which the Christian kingdoms would have been isolated and vulnerable. Anything that made his task more difficult would be welcome to all Christians. This was no self-serving, piratical raid. It could well have been a well-thought-out strike that accomplished everything it set out to do, namely slow Saladin's rise to sole rule and give the *impression* that the pilgrims, trade and holy cities were open to attack. After all, the raiders did not first go towards them, but spent a month not doing so. Why? Because the whole idea is ludicrous. Even if they could have reached Medina unchallenged, over landscapes totally unknown to them; even if they could have entered the Prophet's mosque: how could they have dug up his coffin? What would the local inhabitants have been doing? Not standing around watching. And having got the coffin out of the ground, what then? A quick transfer to a waiting camel and a 600-kilometre gallop to the border, unmolested? It was never an option.

But there was good reason to implant the *fear* of such an outcome, and also good reason for our five sources to make the most of it – to present Lu'lu', and through him Saladin, as the saviour of Islam's Holy Places, the defender of pilgrims, the agent of Allah's vengeance on unbelievers.

Perhaps the Franks were hoping to secure a foothold on the coastline of the Arabian peninsula, planting a little Christian colony in the great sea of Islam. What then? Saladin had recently secured Yemen. His brother Tughtukin was still there when Reynald's raiders entered the Red Sea. Their presence would have left him out on a limb, and vulnerable. The pilgrimage routes from the west would have been cut, with a loss of income to Egypt and a loss of Muslim morale.

It would have disrupted the trade with India, which was vital to the Islamic economy. And of course if, as Muslims believed, the raiders had really been intent on digging up the Prophet's coffin and carting it home, the impact on Islam, and on Saladin himself, would have been so catastrophic that no source dared examine the outcome: not charging for access, but using the body as a bargaining chip, which was how the Muslims used the 'True Cross'. It would surely have been the best PR stunt in history, firing the imagination of Europe, attracting reinforcements, perhaps swinging the balance against Islam in the Holy Land for ever.

Or perhaps not. Perhaps there would have been unintended consequences. No act could have been better calculated to unite all Islam against the Christians. Perhaps, if the raiders had achieved their alleged aim, the Christians would have been chased out of the Holy Land a lot quicker.

What of Reynald, of whom we last heard arriving with his camel-caravan of dismantled ships on the bleak shores of Aqaba? His attempt to retake the castle of Eilat had failed, his ships were captured, his task-force all dead. But he had escaped, no one knows how. Perhaps it would not have been hard. Lu'lu' was approaching by sea up the gulf. There were many camels to hand. Reynald could have chosen a few trusty comrades-in-arms and headed north, fast, without meeting any opposition, and arrived back in Kerak in less than a week, living to fight another day.

9

Build-up to the Show-down

REYNALD'S RAID MADE SALADIN ANXIOUS. IN A WAY, HE WAS
responsible, because his absence fighting other Muslims had
given Reynald his chance, leaving him open to the possible
accusation that he cared more about his own interests than
about defending Islam.

At this point, in early April 1183, Saladin received a letter
from the caliph authorizing him to take Amida, today's
Diyarbakir in south-eastern Turkey, the richest and greatest
city of the region known as al-Jazira (or Jazeera, 'the Island',
from which today's TV station takes its name), with a library
said to be the finest in all Islam. With many names over
the centuries of its existence, Amida was always labelled 'the

Black' this or that, after the local dark basalt used in its buildings and its formidable walls. It was famous in Roman times for the great siege of AD 359, when the Persian army spent days attacking the city. The siege was described in detail by the Graeco-Roman historian Ammianus Marcellinus, who took part. One part of his description conjures up an image of the hilltop castle:

> In a remote part of the walls on the southern side, which looks down on the river Tigris, there was a tower rising to a lofty height, beneath which yawned rocks so precipitous that one could not look down without shuddering dizziness. From these rocks subterranean arches had been hollowed out, and skilfully made steps led through the roots of the mountain as far as the plateau on which the city stood, in order that water might be brought secretly from the channel of the river.

A thousand years later, it should still have been impregnable. In fact, it was being run on behalf of an aging emir by an unpopular and incompetent administrator, ibn Nisan, who didn't even adopt the normal practice of paying civilians to join the ranks of his archers and infantry. So there was a good reason to take Amida – namely, in Imad al-Din's words, 'to free the place from Nisanid slavery'. Getting there was no simple matter – it is 500 kilometres from Damascus, a march of two weeks. Saladin arrived and spent three days recovering, then began a bombardment with mangonels, including a giant known as 'the Examiner' (al-Mufattish), with its 10-metre throwing arm and a counterweight of several tonnes of rock. Having cleared the walls of archers, infantry used scaling ladders to capture the outer walls, while the mangonels attacked the main walls from above and sappers attacked from below.

Under this assault, it took three days for the townspeople to see where their interests lay – which was not with the mean-minded ibn Nisan. At the end of April, abandoned by all, he surrendered, partly (as he said in a note to Saladin) because without servants he couldn't even move his possessions to a place of safety. A foolish confession. Saladin sent men to 'help' him, with the result that 90 per cent of ibn Nisan's treasure vanished, unrecorded except for items that survived to be listed in an inventory: 80,000 candles, a towerful of arrowheads, and over a million books (1,040,000 according to an account by ibn Abi Tayy).

The fall of Amida had an unexpected consequence. It seized the attention of the warlord of Mardin, an ancient town built on a steep hill 75 kilometres down the Tigris. Once again, restraint and generosity paid off. In exchange for getting his lands back, the warlord, il-Ghazi, agreed to send troops wherever Saladin wanted. Very soon, that would mean fighting against Mosul's ruler, Izz al-Din, who was now checked at every turn and facing checkmate.

But, if Saladin was to go ahead and take Mosul, he needed authority from the caliph, al-Nasir, in the form of a written instruction known as a 'diploma'. In letter after humble letter, he asked, argued, begged, persuaded. Egypt was his; Egyptian troops had helped take Amida; if he only had the caliph's backing, Mosul would be his, and he was the only one capable of confronting the infidel, the enemies of the truth, because every other leader was busy eating, making money and playing polo; the only blows they exchanged were on the sports ground. The Mosulis were not to be trusted. They wanted the Seljuks to return. They stole money from orphans and places of worship. They were happy to cooperate with Franks and Assassins. They distracted him from the business of holy war. Give him Mosul, and he would retake Jerusalem in no time. Constantinople, Georgia, west Africa and Spain would follow, conquest after conquest 'until the word of God is supreme and the Abbasid Caliphate has wiped the world clean.' Islam united, from Spain to the Caucasus! With such a vision before him, how could the caliph refuse to sanction a small step into Mosul?

But all this had no effect. The caliph would not sanction the move, so Saladin decided to leave Mosul aside and focus on Aleppo. He set up camp there on 21 May. But Aleppo was as tough as Mosul and even trickier politically, because its ruler, Imad al-Din Zangi, was of the same family as the Zangi who had been an ally of Saladin's father, and also nephew and son-in-law of Saladin's mentor, Nur al-Din. Every day, thousands of citizens joined the soldiers in skirmishes outside the walls. Saladin faced the same problem as in Mosul. If there was no surrender, he could not mount a full-scale assault because, as he wrote, 'they are, after all, the soldiers of the Holy War.' There was no point sitting there, exposed, doing nothing, so he moved across Aleppo's river, the Queig (Kuwaig), and started to build what looked like the beginning of a town – a statement that he was not going anywhere, a show of self-confidence designed to put pressure on both Zangi and the Franks.

Often in politics, a show of self-confidence works wonders. 'Speak softly,' as President Roosevelt said, 'and carry a big stick.' Well, Saladin's stick looked very impressive to Zangi, and he decided that it would be better to settle for a quiet, rich life rather than a noisy, violent one. There were negotiations. Zangi would give up Aleppo and promise to supply troops as needed in exchange for four much smaller towns.[42] In mid-June the deal was done, formalized when Saladin and Zangi met in a tent outside the walls. The citizens of Aleppo suddenly saw Saladin's standard flapping from the citadel. By agreement with Saladin, who with typical generosity said he wanted only 'the stones of Aleppo', Zangi left on 17 June with as many possessions as his entourage could carry.

Three days later, Zangi took possession of his new fiefs, and Saladin made a state entry into Aleppo's citadel. Opposition to him evaporated as if by magic and Zangi was reviled 'as a donkey who had sold fresh milk for sour', in the words of a catchphrase.

In June 1183, after eight years of waiting, Saladin was at last in possession of the city he called 'the eye of Syria' and had made himself the most powerful Muslim prince for more than two centuries, controlling Egypt, Damascus, Aleppo and a scattering of fiefs whose leaders awaited his orders. True, Mosul still held out, but Izz al-Din was encircled and impotent. The Byzantines had retreated into their own territory. It was time at last to address the task he had declared to be his destiny: to destroy the Christian intruders whose presence was a lasting shame to Islam.

Both Muslims and Christians knew that a showdown was inevitable. Saladin had an almost-united empire behind him, dedicated to recapturing Jerusalem and driving the Christians

---

[42] Al-Khabur, on the Khabur river, Saladin's old HQ of Nisibin, Sinjar (Zangi's old home) and Saruj.

into the sea. That was an inspiring vision. The Christians had nothing comparable. They were strangers in a strange land, reliant on castles, towers and walls. To oppose and defend and hang on to what you believe is yours is not much of a vision. What would their vision have been, if they had one? A new Christian empire reaching from Europe to Asia, with Jerusalem as its capital? The destruction of all Islam? But for that they would have needed inspirational leadership and the backing of a unified, expansionist Europe. All they had was the occasional burst of energy, grand words, bluster, arguments and a lust for booty. Let alone Europe: even in the Holy Land, a Christian vision and united leadership were absent. There was no central planning for the castles, no Christian commander-in-chief – no strategy, just tactics emerging from circumstances.

Witness what was happening in Jerusalem. The Leper King, Baldwin, was a young man of remarkable qualities. But a twenty-three-year-old could not retain authority when immobilized and almost blind. His disease had eaten away at his arms and legs and eyes, until he 'was scarcely able to hold himself up and was almost totally paralyzed'. He was closely guarded by two women, with an agenda of their own: his mother, Agnes – 'a most grasping woman,' William of Tyre called her, 'utterly detestable to God'[43] – and his sister, Sibylla, both of whom were determined that Sibylla's handsome but dim husband Guy de Lusignan would become the next king. In August, Baldwin caught a fever. Fearing the end was near, his guardians persuaded him to make Guy regent,

---

[43] He was indignant because Agnes was in part responsible for his demotion from the patriarchate.

with responsibility for all the realm outside Jerusalem, to the consternation of his principal barons.

On 30 September 1183 Saladin, with the biggest Muslim army to date, made what might have become his first attempt to seize the Kingdom of Jerusalem. In fact his advance stalled in the face of a strong response by the Christians under Guy de Lusignan. The two forces, both some 17,000 strong, made move and counter-move, each looking for an opening and never finding one. They stared at each other for five days, as Saladin sent out raiding parties to tempt the Christians into an attack and Guy dithered, for he was, in William's words, 'a man totally useless in affairs of this magnitude'. In the end both sides ran short of supplies and withdrew.

So began two years of stalemate as each side waited for an opening that never came. All Saladin could do was focus on the piratical Reynald, immovably fixed in Kerak, and thus a constant menace to Muslim traders and pilgrims travelling to and from Egypt. In October 1183, Saladin set up a joint operation with Egyptian troops under his viceroy and brother, al-Adil, with further help from Taqi al-Din, his half-brother's son. It took time to get under way, because the siege would last a week, perhaps more, depending on if and when Saladin's seven mangonels could batter holes in Kerak's walls. Meanwhile, several thousand soldiers had to be fed. Saladin's army camped for a few days 10 kilometres to the north of the castle, gathering supplies and arranging for the delivery of vast numbers of rocks. This gave Reynald ample time to gather his defence forces.

Defences he would need, not just for the castle, but also to protect some rather special guests, who by chance were there for a grand occasion. Humphrey IV of Toron (today's Tibnin in southern Lebanon), Reynald's wife Stephanie's seventeen-year-old son from her first marriage, was getting married to the eleven-year-old Isabella, the younger (half-)sister of King Baldwin. Humphrey was famed for his beauty, intelligence and gentility, a combination, as an anonymous source put it, that would have suited a girl more than a teenage lad. It was, of course, all about property and politics, the idea being that Toron castle would become Baldwin's property. In some way, the match would also allow Baldwin to repay a debt of honour incurred to Humphrey's grandfather, who had saved Baldwin's life four years previously. So Kerak was crammed with the great and the good, the humble and the bad, depending on the point of view. Another guest, for instance, was Queen Maria Comnena, the bride's mother, former Byzantine princess, who married Amalric when he wanted a closer link with Byzantium. Reynald and she hated each other. This grand occasion was supposed to paper over the cracks. Royalty, aristocrats, friends, relatives, actors, dancers, jugglers and musicians – the castle was so crammed with people that they blocked the soldiers pushing through to their positions.

Kerak, like many castles, was much more than a fortress. Around the stronghold itself – towering walls set on a plateau, with steep slopes and a huge ditch along the front – was a little community of Muslims and Christians, traders, servants, pastoralists raising horses, camels, sheep and goats. At Saladin's approach on 20 November, those who lived at the base of the fortress wanted to flee to safety inside, but Reynald refused them access, partly because the castle was full and partly because he had decided on a first line of defence on the plateau outside. Not a good decision. When Saladin arrived, he took possession of the little township. 'So,' as William of Tyre wrote, 'through the rash tactics of their lord, the wretched citizens suffered the loss of their goods. All their possessions, all their furniture and utensils of every description, were seized by the enemy.' Saladin then ordered his soldiers to storm across the ditches and up the steep slope, where they could shoot at the defenders on the bridge, who ran for safety. Among them was Reynald, who was able to make his escape only because a mysterious foreign knight called Iven wielded his sword like a windmill, holding the bridge until Reynald retreated through the gate. Meanwhile, a few remaining defenders were busy destroying the bridge, which collapsed into the ditch, leaving them to scurry inside the castle before the portcullis slammed down behind them. Saladin set up his mangonels and began a steady, round-the-clock bombardment across the deep ditches.

Schlumberger, Reynald's nineteenth-century biographer, allowed his imagination free rein: 'How to describe this unprecedented sight? The unbelievable noise, the constant movement in the vast mass of warriors, weeping women, terrified children, while every minute the high walls resonated and trembled under the fearful impact of chunks of rock thrown with incredible violence by the Sultan's immense mangonels.'

In reply, those inside the castle tried to build a mangonel of their own – after all, they had enough ammunition in the form of the rocks flying in over the walls. By definition, the mangonel would have to be close to the walls in order to reach its targets. But the bombardment itself made its construction impossible, and the carpenters refused to work in the open.

Yet the town did not fall. The problem was the ditch. It was too deep and too steep-sided for either men or machines to get close to the castle's walls; nor, most crucially, could the sappers. Mangonels alone, operating too far away to reach the inner town, were not enough to do the job.

As often, chivalry trumped every other consideration. Reynald's wife, Stephanie, sent out dishes from the marriage feast to Saladin, who in his message of thanks asked which tower the newly-weds were in. On being told, he ordered his mangonels not to target it.

Sieges never lasted long, because help was always summoned by the besieged. At most, the attackers had ten days; in this case rather less because relief was on its way from Jerusalem, led, unbelievably, by the immobile and nearly blind Baldwin in a litter. There was no time to batter holes in the walls or to fill in the ditches to give access to the walls for sappers. In early December 1183, Saladin gave up the attempt and a week later was back in Damascus, leaving Reynald free to rebuild.

For the next six months, business and the weather ruled. Officials came and went. Mosul, despite many negotiations, remained untaken and unsurrendered. Saladin was eager to gather forces for a new campaign, but the winter of 1183–4 was wet, then snowy, then wet again. Saladin's vizier and secretary al-Fadil said he hoped this was the soap that would wash clean the filth of unbelief, but troops had difficulty moving, and it was summer before Saladin could turn again to jihad.

Except that it was not proper jihad. That summer he was back at Kerak, with nine mangonels this time, smashing the

THE FACELESS LEADER

There are many 'portraits' of Saladin, none of them authentic. His contemporaries recorded only exceptional features, and he had none. He was bearded: that's all we know. His charisma lay not in his looks, but in his self-denial, generosity, politeness, respect for his religion and his dedication to the cause of jihad.

Above: A late twelfth-century miniature portrays Saladin in standard terms: beard, green turban, robe, and sitting cross-legged.

Below: This 1993 statue of Saladin as Arab hero stands in front of the citadel in Damascus.

THE RISE TO POWER

Given a chance by his mentor, Nur al-Din, Saladin made himself a base as ruler of Egypt, and set himself the task of defeating the Crusaders. This could be achieved only if they could be drawn out of their almost impregnable castles and beaten in open combat. It took him twenty years.

Left: An illuminated letter R in the thirteenth-century history by the Christian William of Tyre, Saladin's lord Nur al-Din flees two well-armoured knights.

Below: Cairo's citadel, built by Saladin in 1176–83, was the key defence in the wall with which he surrounded the separate towns of Fustat and Cairo.

Above: *The castle on Pharoah's Island in the Gulf of Aqaba, held by a small Christian force, was taken by Saladin in 1170. Later abandoned, it was restored in the 1980s.*

Below: *Kerak, now in Jordan, was the formidable castle owned by Saladin's despised enemy, Reynald of Châtillon. It remained in use until 1917.*

THE PROBLEM, AND THE SOLUTION

Around 1100, the Crusaders from a Europe rich in castles came with their tactics and designs. Muslims, though preferring open combat, copied them – Aleppo's (*right*) being one of the strongest castles. How to take them? Cross-bows, undermining and towers had their uses. But the best siege weapons were 'counterweight trebuchets', which could toss rocks over 100 metres.

Above left: *A soldier attaches the sling to the throwing arm of a counterweight trebuchet. The weight is in position, ready for release. On the right a tower cracks and topples under the impact of a rock.*

Left: *In an illuminated O, Crusader cross-bowmen assault a Muslim city.*

Right: *Siege towers, or belfries, had long been in use. If there was no moat and the ground was flat, they could roll right up to the wall, providing shelter for troops and a bridge to the battlements.*

Aleppo's castle was extended first by Saladin's mentor Nur al-Din, then by Saladin's son al-Zahir Ghazi, before getting its final present-day form from the Mamluks in the fifteenth century.

VICTORY AT HATTIN, REVENGE AT ACRE

Saladin's victory over the Crusaders on the Horns of Hattin in July 1187 was the prelude to the high point of his career. He destroyed his enemies; seized their prized possession; captured their king; and personally slew his most despised enemy. The way lay open to the re-capture of Jerusalem, and the almost total destruction of the Crusader colonies. Unfortunately for him, the Crusaders still had some fight in them.

Above: *The Horns of Hattin, looking east. On these steep slopes, King Guy made his last stand. Lake Tiberias is out of sight, beyond the gorge in the background.*

Left: *In a fifteenth-century illustration of William of Tyre, Muslim soldiers seize King Guy (in chains) and the 'True Cross' – which was, in fact, a piece of wood in a gold-and-silver setting.*

Right: After Hattin, some 200 Christian soldiers – those who refused to convert or were not sold as slaves – were executed, while Saladin (on the left in this fourteenth-century illumination) looked on 'with a glad face'. This incident contrasts with what happened after Acre capitulated to the English king, Richard I, in 1191, when 2,600 non-combatant Muslims were executed.

Right: In a fifteenth-century French painting by Jean Colombe, Richard watches the execution.

Below: A fifteenth-century version of Saladin beheading Reynald of Châtillon, four years after the battle of Hattin. In the background, King Guy is led away.

RECALLING THE HERO

Though overshadowed by later Muslim dynasties, Saladin re-emerged in the late nineteenth century as a nationalist hero. Under Turkish rule, his tomb in Damascus was restored. In the 1950s, as European colonialism retreated, he became a figure-head for Arab nationalism. Recent events have made him an anti-Western icon.

Above: Saladin's mausoleum in the Umayyad Mosque, Damascus. The marble tomb, a gift from Kaiser Wilhelm II, is a memorial, and empty; the wooden one is said to contain Saladin's remains.

Above right: This wreath, given by Kaiser Wilhelm, is now in the Imperial War Museum, London.

Clockwise from the left: Saladin as icon: on a Syrian banknote in 1991, on a Palestinian poster in 2001 and in an Egyptian film in 1963.

fortifications and towers, and at last filling in the ditch with rubble to build a causeway across to the main gate. In Imad al-Din's words:

On the Sultan's orders, moveable towers were built which were placed to the fore, and then, with beams and bricks made on the spot, long parallel walls were raised, running from the suburbs right up to the ditch. These walls, one covered with roofs, were additionally reinforced with skilfully made stockades. Thus [in early August 1184] were produced three wide, well-protected passageways, in which troops could stroll at ease, and at last undertake the task of filling in the ditch in complete security.

But again, with victory in sight, a Frankish relief forced the Muslims to retreat, leaving Kerak untaken, quickly restored to its former state, and still free to raid caravans travelling back and forth to Egypt.

In Jerusalem, Baldwin died at last, in March 1185, having specified in his will that his six-year-old nephew, Baldwin V, should succeed, under the control of his uncle and Baldwin IV's own one-time regent, Raymond III of Tripoli. Pent-up rivalries simmered.

On one side stood the 'Old Families' headed by Raymond. He was in his mid-forties and cut an impressive figure. William of Tyre described him: slim, swarthy, dark straight hair, imperious in bearing, 'prompt and vigorous in action, gifted with equanimity and foresight, and temperate in his use of both food and drink'. He had been captured by Nur al-Din in 1164, and spent nine years in prison until he and the Hospitallers managed to raise a ransom of 80,000 dinars. He used the time to read as much as he could, and he remained 'indefatigable in asking questions, if there happened to be anyone present who in his opinion was capable of answering'.

On the other side, the 'Party of the Court', as historians have termed them, were new arrivals, the main figures being Reynald of Châtillon, Guy de Lusignan and Count Joscelin, 'of Edessa' as he was known, though Edessa had been lost to the family years before. This freebooting 'count without a county' had been one of Reynald's co-prisoners. Others included Jerusalem's Patriarch, the barely literate but handsome Heraclius, who had once been the lover of Sibylla's mother, Agnes.

The rivalries intensified when the new boy-king died in April 1186, a year after his coronation. The Party of the Court turned to conspiracy, the plot being that Sibylla, the boy-king's mother and the Leper King's sister, would seize the throne and make her husband, Guy, king. The mastermind of this scheme, Joscelin of Edessa, persuaded Raymond of Tripoli to go off to gather other barons, ostensibly to arbitrate on the succession. In the absence of Raymond, Joscelin summoned Reynald from Kerak, proclaimed Sibylla queen and closed the gates of Jerusalem. Raymond, furious at his exclusion, was helpless.

For the coronation, the conspirators needed the royal insignia, which were in a trunk with three locks, the keys to which were held by the Patriarch, Heraclius (no problem there); the Grand Master of the Templars, Gerard of Ridford (ditto); and the Grand Master of the Hospitallers, Roger de Môlins. Roger refused to cooperate, because he said it meant breaking his oath to the newly dead king. Reynald made an unrecorded offer that Roger could not refuse, got the key and the insignia, and took them to the Patriarch, who led Sibylla up the aisle to be crowned. Then she, as queen, crowned her husband, Guy, as king.

Nothing could have more powerfully revealed how divided the Christians were. That suited Saladin, because he was in no state to take advantage, partly because he was determined to secure more territory to the east and north, and partly because in early December 1185 he went down with a fever. The weather that winter was grim. Saladin's secretary, al-Fadil, writing in Damascus, recorded that people could not bear to turn their faces to the wind. Strong men could not walk against it, let alone the weak, among them now Saladin, who had been campaigning, travelling and camping for the past nine months, attempting to juggle a takeover in Mosul with negotiations that would give him part of what is now southern Turkey, all to prepare for more jihad against the Crusaders. It was too much. Saladin developed a 'quartan' fever, one that induced a paroxysm every fourth day. He and his entourage kept the news to themselves, in order not to depress his followers and delight his enemies. He made the occasional public appearance to keep rumour at bay, while his close aides and family hoped for the best.

In mid-January, a brief recovery allowed him to put action against Mosul on hold and turn his attention to winning territory to the north. Driven by dreams of conquest, which was not strategically necessary and almost cost him both his uncertain empire and his life, he rode to Harran, 175 kilometres west of Mosul, just over the present-day Turkish border. Here he relapsed. Doctors came and went. He dictated his will. Hearts were palpitating and tongues filled with rumour, wrote al-Fadil, urging a return to Aleppo and its top-class doctors.

Then to cap it all, Saladin's wife for the last nine years, Ismat, Nur al-Din's widow, died. They were about the same age, approaching fifty, and quite possibly the marriage had never been consummated. It was not important: he already had a dynasty in the making, a dozen sons and unrecorded daughters by several unrecorded wives and slave-girls. Ismat was different, almost an equal. He so valued her advice and support that he had been writing long letters to her almost every day, despite his illness. In his weakened state, the shock of her death might be the end of him. Al-Fadil told Saladin's aide, Imad al-Din, to keep the news from him and censor his incoming mail.

It was a good decision, because, after another seeming recovery and another relapse and more frantic correspondence and doctors muttering that there was no hope, the fever finally left him. It was the end of February. He had been ill for two and a half months. Imad al-Din could at last break to him the news about Ismat without fear of killing him. He was apparently strong enough to accept the blow and mourn in private, because no one recorded his reaction.

There followed a pact with Mosul, which turned Saladin's former rival Izz al-Din into a subject. At last, it seemed, thirty-three months of fighting other Muslims was over – well, for the moment, because he did not rule all Islam, but at least he could turn from civil war to the real issue. As Al-Fadil wrote, everyone in Damascus was looking forward to holy war. This could surely be planned at leisure, since the truce with the Christians still held and they were absorbed in their own disputes.

*

Then everything changed.

In early 1187, Reynald, secure in the knowledge that he was protected by the truce, broke it. This, for Saladin, was a final, unforgivable act of ruthlessness and duplicity, and it led directly to the climax of the war between Muslims and Christians. Of course it might have happened anyway, given Saladin's commitment to jihad. But the cause was now deeply personal, more personal by the month, so it is worth looking more closely at what happened.

This being the month of Muharram (mid-March to mid-April), pilgrims by the hundred were returning from Mecca. Imad al-Din recorded what Reynald – 'the most perfidious, the most evil of the Franks, the greediest, the most zealous to do harm' – did next. Using Bedouin, 'a disgrace to our religion', who were scattered all along the road to Mecca, he 'fell upon an important caravan' – 400 camels, according to one source,[44] travelling in peace – 'transporting a very rich consignment, and seized the lot.' They killed its escort of soldiers, led the survivors to Kerak, stole the horses and equipment, and treated their prisoners cruelly. 'We sent him a message condemning his behaviour and reproaching him for his perfidy and violence, but he only became more obstinate . . . "Beseech your Muhammad to deliver you" was his reply.' Off went messages to Reynald demanding the release of the prisoners, the return of the stolen merchandise and payment with interest for violating the truce. The reply from Reynald was utter disdain: he would repay nothing;

---

[44] The Armenian Vardan Araveltsi, 'the Easterner' (*c*.1198–1272), in his *Historical Compilation*.

king of his territory, he recognized no truce with Muslims.

Whatever the details, Saladin's anger was beyond words, beyond bounds. Again, Imad al-Din has the story: 'The sultan swore that he would take [Reynald's] life with his own hand' – the second time he had sworn this oath, the first having been after Reynald's raid into the Red Sea. It was an oath that would be fulfilled in the most dramatic fashion.

Reynald's ill-considered act was like poking a sleeping tiger with a pointed stick. Leaving contingents behind to protect the northern frontiers and to guard against a Frankish invasion, Saladin arrived in Reynald's territory in mid-April. His move, as usual, set off a chain reaction. A chance meeting near Nazareth[45] of several thousand Muslim troops and a small Christian force of 130 Templar knights ended in disaster for the Templars: the death and beheading of the Grand Master, all Templar knights bar four killed, many others dead, forty captured. The prisoners were paraded beneath the walls of Tiberias, shackled to horses; heads were displayed on Muslim lances.

Aghast, the Franks closed ranks. Old rivalries vanished in the face of this calamity, and the confrontation that everyone knew was coming.

---

[45] Ain Gozeh, known in western sources as the Spring of Cresson.

10

The Horns of Hattin

AT LAST, SALADIN WAS MUSTERING. MESSAGES WENT OUT to all Muslim cities, urging action, vengeance, a war of liberation and annihilation. In June 1187, Saladin's scattered forces re-gathered near Busra, just north of today's Syrian border with Jordan, 75 kilometres east of the Jordan valley. Flat, scrub-covered, with spindly grass, arid (but fertile if watered) – this turned into a parade ground for some 30,000 men, almost half of them cavalry. Saladin formed them into three wings, with Taqi al-Din leading the right; Gökbüri (Keukburi or Kukburi in other spellings), commander of the Aleppan army, the left; and Saladin himself the centre. From Busra, he led his army across the Jordan and in late June camped 10 kilometres west of the Sea of Galilee, where, on rising ground, his army had a fine view of the plateau running up to the hills that would become the scene of the coming battle. Here, near a village called Kafr Sabt (Carfasset), the Muslims had a good supply of water and were within easy reach of Tiberias, 10 kilometres away, where, as it happened, Raymond III's wife, Eschiva, was in residence, with a garrison to defend her.

The Franks, about 20,000 strong and headed by 1,200 knights, gathered at Sepphoris,[46] a village 5 kilometres north-west of Nazareth. This was a little place with a big history, Jewish, then Arabic, then, in recent times, Jewish again. A Roman theatre, mosaic pavements, and a hilltop house built by Crusaders still recall the times. It was a common assembly point because it is halfway between the coast and the Sea of Galilee. The Franks numbered rather fewer than Saladin's army, but with a powerful contingent of armoured cavalry under an impressive aristocratic leadership: masters of the Templars and Hospitallers, the rulers of Tripoli, Kerak and Caesarea. They also had with them their talisman, the True Cross, carried by the Bishop of Acre. With God on their side, what could possibly go wrong?

Saladin knew he had to draw the Christians away from Sepphoris, on to a battleground of his choosing, namely the plain below him. But his array was so daunting that the Christians would have been crazy to be drawn. 'The army, like the ocean, was the most formidable ever to have been seen in the annals of Islam,' wrote Imad al-Din, 'It lapped the Sea of Galilee, the vast plains of which vanished beneath

---

[46] Tzippori, Zippori or Tsipori in Hebrew, Saffuriya in Arabic.

the flow of tents. In vain did the Sultan advance on the Christians and challenge them to combat.'

Saladin had to do something to force the Christians' hand. On 2 July, he attacked Tiberias, hoping that the Christians would come to rescue Raymond's wife. A tower was mined, a breach made, the town seized, plunder taken, and the Franks still did not budge. Raymond's wife locked herself and her four sons safely inside the citadel, protected by a deep moat. While Frankish messengers – with Saladin's implicit blessing – fled the town carrying the news, Saladin's force returned to its base near Kafr Sabt, leaving a few surrounding Eschiva's citadel.

With what response from the Christians? The sources conflict, because the Arab ones were based on hearsay and the Christian ones supported one faction or another. Was Raymond relaxed about his wife's position? Perhaps he pointed out the broken ground which would favour light-weight Saracen horsemen over the heavy Christian ones? Or the summer heat? Or the lack of water? Did he, as told by the chronicler al-Athir, say something like 'Let them take Tiberias! I would be happy if he took the citadel, my wife and our possessions! They won't be able to stay there, because Saladin's men will want to get back home, and we'll retake it'? Did Reynald accuse Raymond of cowardice – 'Enough of making us frightened of the Muslims!' (in al-Athir's words) – even treachery? Or did Raymond beg King Guy to save his wife? Did Guy decide to remain in well-watered Sepphoris? Did the Grand Master creep in to see him later that night and urge him not to follow the advice of a traitor?

Whatever the truth, Guy was under pressure not simply

to confound those who said he could not take decisions, but also because he had received cash from Henry II in England, in a bizarre example of the complex interactions between Crusaders and their homelands. Henry had had his archbishop Thomas à Becket murdered, involuntarily (as the story is usually told), having muttered the words 'Will no one rid me of this turbulent priest?' After four knights had broken into Canterbury Cathedral and cut down the archbishop, Henry had expressed remorse and as part of his self-imposed punishment, which involved having himself lashed by priests and promising to 'take the Cross', had also given cash to support the Crusaders.[47] Now that money was gone, on knights who bore a banner with Henry's arms on it. Guy needed to prove himself worthy of Henry's gift. He opted for action, and set off eastwards. With hindsight, it looks a foolish decision, but possibly justified if he had underestimated Saladin's strength and was planning on using several springs along the way.

Friday, 3 July 1187: from dawn, the sun turned the plains into an anvil, hammering the heavily armoured Franks like forged metal. They set out eastwards towards Tiberias, Raymond in a vanguard of Hospitallers, Guy in the middle with his talisman the True Cross, Balian of Ibelin with the Knights Templar as the rearguard, other contingents to right and left.

---

[47] Henry had promised to defend Jerusalem by providing enough to support 200 knights for a year. He transferred to the Templars and Hospitallers in Jerusalem 30,000 silver marks, about 30 per cent of the national income, which was in a dormant account pending his arrival on a Crusade that was eternally promised and never realized. The money was spent on operations in early 1187: 'They [the Templars and Hospitallers] opened the treasure of the lord king of England and gave stipends to all who could carry a bow or a lance into battle.' Further details are in Mayer, 'Henry II of England'.

From early that morning, everything depended on a single factor: the need for water. Saladin had enough of it, supplied by lines of camels carrying water in skins from Lake Tiberias to his campsite. The lack of it steadily reduced the Christian troops to husks. To their left was a wooded ridge formed by Mount Tur'an, and two low hills known as the Horns of Hattin, sloping down to the village of Hattin beyond. They were only about 25 kilometres from Lake Tiberias, a day's march in the right conditions, but Saladin's army was in the way. By midday, they were at an abandoned village, named Tur'an after its mountain, where there was a small spring, but its flow of water was not enough to sustain an army. The nearest springs of any size were in Hattin, 18 kilometres away. That was where the Christians headed, cavalry shepherding infantry, all guarding their icon, the True Cross, with its acolytes, the bishops of Acre and Lydda. Saladin rejoiced at the sight. 'What we wanted is happening. If we conduct ourselves as we should, it's the end of them.' He sent raiding parties of bowmen to cut the advancing enemies off from their base, and from Tur'an's scanty water supply. Retreat for the Christians was now impossible.

But, with the exhausted troops slowed by thirst and hemmed in by Saladin's forces, Guy decided to camp that night at the base of the slopes leading up to the Horns, with Hattin and its well still 4 kilometres away. Raymond of Tripoli rode in from the front with a shout: 'Ah, Lord God, the war is over; we are dead men; the kingdom is finished.'

The Christians had no rest that short night. The two camps were so close they could hear each other – not much from the demoralized Christians, but the sound of drums, prayers and singing from the confident Muslims – and the pickets guarding their outer limits could exchange words. Muslim cavalry circled the Christian camp, firing arrows at the horses, for a Christian knight without his horse was nothing. A few daredevil Christian soldiers sneaked out of their camp in the hope of stealing water from some lone Muslim, but 'not even a cat' could leave the camp unseen, and all were killed. To the west, across the gentle hills and in among the trees, Muslim infantrymen collected brushwood which would be used to smoke out the Christians the next morning, if they decided to stay where they were.[48]

The Muslims could return to their camps, to refresh themselves with water brought from the lake by a steady stream of camels and poured into temporary ponds dug in the ground. All was made ready for the battle to come. Saladin ordered 400 camel-loads of arrows, with more to follow – 66 camels carrying arrows would be on hand all the next day, for arrows were used by the hundred thousand.[49] The bowmen were given particular targets: the Christian horses. Few wore horse-armour, because their owners couldn't afford it. If a horse went down, its heavily armoured rider was as helpless as a beetle on its back.

Saturday, 4 July, dawn. The Muslim army was well rested, well watered, well armed and ready for slaughter. For a short

---

[48] 'The whole mountain is thickly covered with dry grass,' wrote the traveller and orientalist Johann Ludwig Burckhardt in 1812, 'which readily takes fire, and the slightest breath of air instantly spreads the conflagration.' (Quoted in Kedar, 'The Battle of Hattin Revisited'.)

[49] We know how many arrows a master-bowman could fire, because the experiment has been done by the man who single-handedly resurrected horseback archery, the Hungarian Lajos Kassai. After years of training, he can fire ten arrows in twenty seconds; and in one marathon session lasting most of a day he fired over 1,000 arrows. In a battle, 1,000 bowmen could use over half a million arrows.

while, Saladin made no move, waiting for the heat to rise, and to see what the Christians would do: retreat, or prepare for a last stand, or go for the lake, or for Hattin's well. Saladin, as good generals do, rode up and down the ranks, praising and exhorting his troops. 'They were full of confidence,' recorded Imad al-Din. 'This one sharpened his lance, others tightened harnesses, adjusted arrows, or thanked Heaven for Allah's help. Here, during the wait for the morrow, one could hear the cry of *Allahu Akhbar* [God is Great]; there, a desire to be among the happy ones chosen to survive; elsewhere, the hope for martyrdom.'

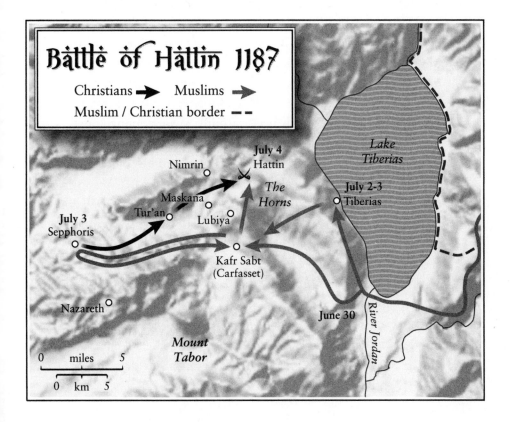

One of the young mamluks of the Sultan's entourage by the name of Mangouras made a superb charge into the Frankish ranks, challenging any of them to single combat: 'But a great number of Franks attacked him and his horse, in a moment of stubbornness while carrying him back to his own ranks, threw him. The Franks threw themselves on him and killed him. Thinking for a moment that they had massacred one of the Sultan's sons, they raised his severed head on the tip of a lance.'

The Christians, now tormented by thirst, had only one aim: Hattin's well. They set off along the floor of the valley, aiming for Hattin, in three squares, the infantry framing the cavalry. Ahead, as before, was Raymond of Tripoli, in the centre King Guy, shepherding the True Cross, and in the rear Balian of Ibelin's rearguard. Behind them, Saladin's men roamed through the tree-covered slopes starting scrub fires, which sent clouds of smoke drifting on a westerly breeze. Flames licked at Frankish heels, clouds of smoke enveloped them, the sun smote down from a clear sky.

Saladin sent one wing galloping forward to block the valley ahead. Muslim skirmishers rode in close, testing the flanks of the Christian squares like picadors goading a bull. The archers then unleashed a fusillade of arrows, filling the sky 'like a swarm of locusts'.

All Christian leaders saw they were dead men unless they could break clear. Only cavalry had a chance. Raymond of Tripoli, out in front, was edging away from King Guy's force, with Muslim outriders increasing the gap minute by minute. Raymond did the only thing possible: he led a charge at the Muslim force ahead, Taqi al-Din's cavalry, which parted, showering arrows on the galloping Christians, then closed ranks, making return impossible. Later, Raymond was accused by both sides of treachery and cowardice for abandoning the main force. True, his departure weakened the Christians, but his presence would not have saved them; and perhaps if Guy had followed his lead, the whole force might have broken through to the lake. As it was, Raymond chose possible life over certain death. He and his men headed for Saphet, then Tyre, and home.

Back in the smoke-filled valley, the Christian army was dying. There was a gap left in Muslim ranks by those closing in after Raymond's exit. It led up the slope towards the ridge made by the two low peaks, the Horns of Hattin. This was a last, desperate gamble. There were a few shallow pools up there, at an abandoned hamlet called Maskana; and on top of the Horns there were the remains of a prehistoric redoubt, the ruined walls of which stood a metre or two high and offered a little protection. At least in that position there would be no attack from above, where the slopes were steep.

Infantrymen dragged slow and thirsty feet up the northern hill, refusing orders to rejoin the battle, leaving Guy and the cavalry in a melee around the True Cross and its retinue of two bishops and their acolytes. Now the cavalry too retreated uphill, and found no relief. The pools were either dry or too scanty for an army, and the walls too low[50] for a defence. Guy had his red tent pitched to provide a focal point. Cavalry surrounded him, but to no great effect. Muslim cavalry advanced up the only gentle slope, engaged, and all became confusion. Some must have cut their way through to the True Cross, held aloft by the Bishop of Acre until he was

---

[50] They are still visible today in low light.

killed, when it was seized briefly by the Bishop of Sidon, until it was snatched from his grasp. 'The seizure of it was one of their greatest misfortunes,' wrote al-Athir, 'after which they were sure they were doomed to death and destruction.'

It was not yet over. Saladin's oldest son, seventeen-year-old Al-Afdal, taking part in his first battle, was with his father, watching on horseback, probably from the gentle slopes between the two hills. He described what happened to al-Athir. The surviving Christian horsemen rallied and charged downhill, forcing the Muslims back to where father and son stood. He glanced at his father, and saw that Saladin had turned pale at the possibility of defeat. He tugged at his beard nervously, then shouted, 'Satan must not win!' or 'Away with the Devil's lies!' (Translations vary.) Inspired, the Muslims returned to the assault up the hill. Al-Afdal's account continued:

> When I saw them retreating with the Muslims in pursuit, I cried out in joy: 'We have beaten them.' But the Franks charged again as they had done before, and drove the Muslims up to my father. He did what he had done before, and the Muslims turned back against them and forced them up the hill. I cried again, 'We have beaten them.' My father rounded on me and said: 'Be quiet! We have not beaten them until that tent falls.' As he was speaking to me, the tent fell [its ropes cut].

Saladin moved forward as the fighting died. The surviving Christian knights dismounted and collapsed on the ground, awaiting whatever fate was coming. King Guy, too, was on the ground beside his fallen tent, utterly exhausted, with hardly the strength to hand over his sword. The sultan dismounted and prostrated himself in a prayer of thanks, weeping for joy.

He then remounted and made his way back to his own tent, while his officers gathered prisoners from among the body-strewn battleground, so many of both, said al-Afdal, that 'to see the dead, you would not think there could have been any prisoners; and to see the prisoners, you would not think there could have been any dead.' Imad al-Din said he saw thirty or forty prisoners bound by the same rope and led by a single horseman. Elsewhere, 100 or 200 were overseen by a few guards.

Prayer tents were set up, prayers said, messengers sent out to spread the good news. Then Saladin, seated on a blanket-covered divan in his huge, cool pavilion, ordered the top Christian leaders to be brought to him, a dozen or more, including King Guy and Reynald of Châtillon. Imad al-Din recorded the drama that followed, as did several other chroniclers. Details vary; this account is a composite.

Saladin is seated, surrounded by aides, with a few empty chairs. First to enter is King Guy, hardly able to stand with exhaustion, his head lolling as if he were drunk. Saladin indicates the chair beside him, and the king collapses on to it. Reynald comes in, and is seated next to Guy. By tradition, a prisoner who is offered refreshment is spared, but nothing is offered yet. Perhaps Saladin wishes to test his captives to see if they could be more useful alive than dead. It is on his arch-enemy, Reynald, that Saladin focuses first, addressing him through an interpreter.

'How many times have you sworn an oath and then violated it?' he says. 'How many times have you signed an agreement that you have never respected?'

Saladin the victor can afford to be magnanimous, even to a man he has sworn to kill. Perhaps even now he is prepared

to show the generosity that he knows would win over enemies. But Reynald, who in other circumstances has shown
an ability to act the penitent, does not know that Saladin has
sworn to kill him. Perhaps even now the right form of words
might save his life. But he is too foolish, or headstrong, or
arrogant to resist a smart answer.

'Kings have always acted thus. I did nothing more.'

To equate his own actions with Saladin's is no way to win
sympathy. Besides, Reynald is not a king. That is enough to
tilt the balance against him. But Saladin is restrained. He
turns to Guy, murmurs 'reassuring words', orders an aide to
bring some iced water –

(Yes, iced water. There was a regular supply of snow from
high in the Lebanon and Anti-Lebanon mountains, where
peaks are snow-covered for most of, and sometimes all, the
year round. It was packed into containers, which camels
carried as far as Cairo, a month-long journey of 600 kilometres. That July, a mere two or three days from the point
of origin, merchants would have been well aware of the
potential market among the officers on both sides, whoever
emerged victorious.)

– and offers it to Guy, a gesture of further reassurance.

Guy drinks; but then, perhaps ignorant of Arabic tradition,
or made stupid by exhaustion, he hands the cup to Reynald.
Saladin does not move to prevent him. Reynald takes the cup
and drains it, which must take a few seconds, time enough
for Saladin to see a pretext for what he is about to do. He
says to the interpreter, 'Tell the king: it is you who have
given him to drink,' meaning that since he himself has not
handed the water to Reynald, he no longer has an obligation
to preserve his life.

There is a pause. The two Christians are led out, surely appalled by the sultan's ominous words. Saladin himself leaves the tent, remounts and rides out briefly to see how the army is recovering in the wake of the battle. Standards and flags are brought to his tent. When he returns, he doesn't hesitate. He orders Reynald to be brought in and tells him about his twice-made vow to kill him. According to one source, he offers Reynald the chance to convert to Islam, and upon his refusal,

> he advanced towards him, sword in hand, and struck him between the neck and shoulder-blade. When Arnat [as the Muslims called him] fell, he [Saladin, or more likely his aides] cut off his head and dragged the body by its feet past the king, who began to tremble. Seeing him thus upset, the Sultan said to him in a reassuring tone: 'This man was killed only because of his maleficence and his perfidy.'

According to another source, he also tells Guy he can stop trembling: 'Kings do not kill kings, but he had overstepped the limit.'[51]

His bloody deed was apparently a source of pride, because Reynald's head was sent on tour, being shown off in all the main cities controlled by Saladin. But this has bothered Islamic commentators. It is not good form to slay helpless captives. There are two defences. Firstly, Islamic law authorizes the

---

[51] There are several versions of what happened, all with the same outcome. One copy of Ernoul's *Continuation* has Saladin asking Reynald: 'If you had me in your prison, what would you do with me?' 'With God's help,' the prisoner replies, 'I would cut your head off.' Saladin: 'Well, you are in my prison, and yet you reply with arrogance.' He then runs him through, and his aides cut off Reynald's head.

beheading of a prisoner who refuses to convert, because he remains a threat to the Muslim community. Secondly, Saladin had an oath to fulfil. As he himself wrote to the caliph, 'the servant [i.e. he himself] had sworn to shed the blood of the tyrant of Kerak.' The business with the water was nothing but a pretext. Any excuse would have done.

Reynald was not the only one. Many Templars and Hospitallers had been taken prisoner, along with 'Turcopoles', Turkish or mixed-race mercenaries recruited locally by the Franks as mounted archers and considered traitors by the Muslims. According to one historian,[52] there were some 200 of them. Saladin gave their captors 50 dinars a head, and offered them all a chance to convert to Islam. Some did, becoming perfectly good Muslims, according to Imad al-Din. The rest would have been kept alive if they were worth anything in ransom money; but they weren't, so they were offered for execution to volunteers who did the job as Saladin looked on 'with a glad face'. A grim business, as recorded by Imad al-Din: 'There were some whose strength gave out, so they backed out and were excused; there were others who did not hit strongly enough and were laughed at by the crowds and had to be replaced by others', suggesting images of half-severed heads and gruesome sounds, 'but there were some who revealed their noble descent in administering their blows.' One who escaped execution was Gerard of Ridefort, Grand Master of the Templars. He would fetch a good ransom, so he was spared.

There were other prisoners, ordinary soldiers by the hundred, who in normal circumstances would be sold off as slaves.

---

[52] The polymath historian, poet and scientist ibn Wasil (1208–98).

But the circumstances were not normal. There were so many captives that the price of slaves collapsed to 3 dinars a head, and in one case a Christian slave fetched a pair of sandals.

And what of the True Cross, the taking of which was for Christians 'a graver matter than the taking of the king', as Imad al-Din put it? It was tied upside down on a spear and two days later paraded through the streets of Damascus, as proof of its uselessness as a talisman and as an insulting rejection of the tale – not of Jesus himself, revered in Islam as a great man, but of his resurrection.

How many died that summer's day? Saladin claimed 40,000, others 30,000, while the numbers of those who escaped ranged from 200 to 3,000, most of them fleeing to Tyre. Of the 1,200 knights, about 1,000 died. Of the common soldiers, no one knew the numbers then, no one knows them now. Saladin had a monument built on the summit of Hattin's Horns,[53] but no one buried, or even counted, the decaying corpses that lay scattered across the site for months, or the bones that remained for years. Whatever the numbers, the truth was that the Frankish army was destroyed, and with it the possibility of defending Jerusalem.

Days later (perhaps a couple of weeks, if the stench was anything to go by), Imad al-Din wandered over the battleground, recorded a litany of horrors, and rejoiced. Bodies were scattered across the hillsides and over the valley:

Everywhere around Hattin stank of corpses . . . I saw heads tossed far from lifeless corpses; eyes dug from sockets;

[53] 'The Dome of Victory' was short-lived. Thirty years later, it was an untended ruin.

bodies sullied with dust, disfigured by birds of prey; limbs mutilated during battle and scattered, bare, torn to shreds, lying unattached, skulls split open, feet cut off, mutilated noses, extremities detached from bodies, empty eyes, opened stomachs, contorted mouths, open foreheads with liquid pupils, necks wrung, inanimate and shattered bits and pieces, as still and stiff as the rocks around them.

But what sweet smell of victory arose from this charnel-house! What vengeful flames swirled around those bodies! How this hideous sight made hearts rejoice! . . . How many arrogant lords were hunted down, how many leaders were leashed, how many kings enchained!

Later, he and many other poets turned the victory into verses, spreading the news across all Islam. Here is Imad's contribution (in my English translation of Schlumberger's French. Imad was a good poet; the nineteenth-century French is not bad; by the time it reaches modern English in my translation, it's a disaster as poetry but still captures Imad's sentiments):

O day of Hattin! The bravest faces were darkened and the
    sun was veiled by clouds of dust:
You saw the leader of the Infidels humiliated, his brow
    sullied with mud and his pride cast down.
Noble and pure sword, which cut off the prince's head and
    struck faithlessness in its vilest form.
In falling, this head bathed itself in its own blood, like a
    frog plunging into a pond.
Driven by treachery, he raged like a wild beast; but to the
    onslaughts of a traitor death was the only answer.

The Sultan ordered swords drawn from scabbards, and
    the impious blood they spilled clothed their blades with
    purple robes.
He it was whose blade plunged in the blood of a people
    who had always immersed themselves in faithlessness.
Struck by death and captivity, they fell, and their impious
    rule was cleansed of all its blemishes.

11

Retaking the Holy City

HAVING CAMPED AT THE BATTLE SITE THAT NIGHT, SALADIN led his force to Tiberias, where Raymond's wife saw that resistance was useless. She surrendered, allowing Saladin to act the chivalrous victor and let her keep all her possessions and followers. He could afford a little tactical chivalry, because he now had strategy to consider. Sometime, a new army would arrive from the west. Should he go for Jerusalem, his main objective? Or take the ten cities that guarded 550 kilometres of coast, and forestall any Christian reinforcements? He chose to seal the coast. With those ports gone, the inland castles could be surrounded one by one and starved into surrender.

Speed was vital. Acre, 40 kilometres from Hattin, was the kingdom of Jerusalem's second richest and most densely populated city. Standing on a peninsula overlooking a well-sheltered sandy bay, it was protected in the north and east by great walls that met at a fort known as the Cursed Tower. It was the hub of trade between Egypt, Palestine, Syria and Italy – for Genoa, Venice and Pisa controlled several sections – with a mass of houses, churches, warehouses and shops. Food, cloth, hemp, copper, iron, spices, incense, medicines, perfumes, silk, sugar – all flowed in from the region, from Arabia, from the east. 'Its roads and streets are choked by the press of men,' wrote the traveller ibn Jubayr. Muslims and Christians shared both markets and shrines.

Acre was a walkover – a display in battle order produced instant surrender, followed by a typical display of imprudent generosity, imprudent because so much was pillaged and wasted. The town was handed to Saladin's son al-Afdal, who distributed much of it and its contents to his followers: the Templars' property to Diya, the sugar refinery to Taqi (who pillaged it), and a house to his secretary, Imad al-Din. It was not just the top people who benefited. Some 4,000 Muslim prisoners were freed to return to their homes.

Other inland towns, villages, castles and roads fell in days, because there was no one to defend them or no defence mounted: Nazareth, Sepphoris, Tabor, Sebaste, Nablus. Then on the coast south of Acre, Haifa and Arsuf surrendered, Caesarea put up only a brief resistance. Al-Adil, Saladin's brother, approached from Egypt, mopping up southern cities. Jaffa was taken by force. Its Christian inhabitants were sent to the slave markets and harems of Aleppo, where al-Athir brought a girl carrying a one-year-old baby, weeping because, as she said, 'I had six brothers, all of whom were killed, as well as a husband and two sisters, and I do not know what happened to them.'

Tyre, with a hard core of survivors from Hattin, would be a challenge, the more so because it had just acquired a new leader, Conrad of Montferrat (in northern Italy), cousin of kings, rich, handsome, intellectual, experienced in Europe's wars and civil wars, and about to play a major role in what followed. Now in his mid-thirties, he was at the height of his considerable powers and beauty: 'Comely in life's springtime, exceptional and peerless in manly courage and intelligence, and in the flower of his body's strength', according to one chronicler. Another made him a paragon: vigorous, astute, amiable, virtuous, wise, multilingual, politically smart. He had been intending to join his crusading father, William, in Jerusalem, but William was one of those captured at the battle of Hattin. Conrad could not have heard the news as his ship approached Acre, but noticed something was wrong – no bell to announce the ship's arrival, no Franks coming out to meet him, the reason being that the city had just been handed over to Saladin's son al-Afdal and was in the process of being looted. A Muslim port official arrived to find out more about the new arrival. Conrad welcomed him, pretending to be nothing but a merchant, and learned what was happening. So did the official. Each bid the other a courteous farewell, the official returning to raise the alarm, Conrad putting back out to sea and finding a safe haven in Tyre, which, as it happened, was desperate for strong leadership. He was greeted as a hero come by happy chance to rescue the city in its hour of need, and to provide perhaps a foothold for some future Crusade.

Tyre could be taken only after much else had been secured. So Saladin ignored it, turning instead on Tyre's forward bastion, Toron – which he took after a seven-day siege – and Sidon, 40 kilometres to the north, where he arrived on 29 July 1187 to receive immediate surrender. Next day he was another 40 kilometres further on, at Beirut, which capitulated a week later. The only difficulty was administrative: Imad al-Din fell ill, and no scribe could draw up the surrender terms. Eventually Imad al-Din dictated them from his sick-bed – 'the minds of the healthy men were sick,' he wrote, 'but mine was not' – before retiring to Damascus for two months to recuperate. Jebail,[54] 30 kilometres north of Beirut, fell into Saladin's lap because its master, Hugh Embriaco, had been captured at Hattin and ransomed himself by handing over his city. The town, close to the Kingdom of Jerusalem's northern border, marked Saladin's high-tide mark in the north.

Jebail fell on 4 August. Less than three weeks later, on the 23rd, Saladin was back in Ascalon, 300 kilometres south, which is about as fast as an army can move – some 15 kilometres a day. He brought along his two chief captives, the Grand Master of the Templars, Gerard, and King Guy, who was given the task of negotiating the city's surrender, with himself as the main bargaining chip:

So he went and called the burgesses of the city, for there were no knights there, and said to them, 'Sirs, Saladin has said that if I will surrender the city to him he will let me go. It would

[54] Jbail, Jubail or Jubayl: also known from ancient times by its Greek name Byblos.

not be right for such a fine city to be surrendered for just one man, so if you think you can hold Ascalon for the benefit of the Christians and for Christendom do not surrender it. But if you do not think you can hold it, I beg you to surrender it and deliver me from captivity.'

At first, the city's leaders opted for resistance. Guy was clearly making his request under duress, and they had no faith in the deal. So Saladin attacked, undermining the outer-works and hauling mangonels to bombard the walls. Guy was once again allowed to summon the leaders from inside the city, and this time managed to talk sense into them. After ten days of siege, they surrendered and left with their families – but, since the town had not surrendered freely, Guy was not given his liberty.

Ascalon fell just in time to allow Saladin in before he welcomed a delegation from Jerusalem, summoned to discuss terms for their surrender as well. Saladin offered reasonable terms: no assault, a peaceful surrender, the inhabitants allowed an exit with their possessions. Respect for Christian Holy Places, future pilgrims welcomed. This was on 4 September, about midday, as people remembered, because by coincidence the sun dimmed and vanished, bathing the proceedings in the shadow of a total eclipse. Perhaps the Christians saw in this some good omen, for they refused the terms point-blank. Surrender the place where their Lord died? Never. They returned to prepare its defences.

Gaza's Templar garrison surrendered in obedience to their master, who was then granted his freedom. Other strongholds followed: Darum, Ramla, Yubna, Latrun, Ibelin, Hebron, Bethlehem. Now all the Christians had left were Tyre, a few scattered castles and Jerusalem itself. Tyre or Jerusalem? Well, Saladin had been ill, might fall ill again, and if he did and had not captured Jerusalem, what of his reputation? As Saladin's brother al-Adil put it, 'If you die tonight, Jerusalem will stay in the hands of the Franks. Strive therefore to take it.' And Tyre was a tough nut, especially with Conrad in command. An assault would delay things, allowing the possibility of reinforcements arriving from Europe.

Jerusalem it would be.

There now occurred one of those incidents that revealed the paradoxical, almost schizoid nature of the struggle between these two enemies, both claiming to observe chivalric ideals. Balian of Ibelin, head of one of the most eminent of Crusader families, had escaped from Hattin with Raymond and was now holed up in Tyre. His wife, Maria Comnena, was stuck in Jerusalem. (Ibelin, 30 kilometres east of Ascalon and almost the same distance from Jerusalem, is today's Beit Guvrin.) Balian sent a message to Saladin, asking to be allowed to get her. Can you imagine any general in any recent war making a similar request to his main opponent? Since the seventeenth century, war has become ever more 'total'; in Saladin's day it was partial, with soldiers doubling as farmers, generals as leaders of towns and castles, enemies who became allies overnight. Why, of *course* Balian could retrieve his wife, if he agreed to spend only one night in Jerusalem and to travel unarmed. He agreed; but when he arrived he found the city leaderless and so keen to keep him that he had to stay, with profuse apologies to Saladin for breaking his promise. Saladin, ever polite, accepted the apology, and Balian duly set about finishing Jerusalem's defences.

*

On Sunday, 20 September, Saladin arrived outside Jerusalem. It seemed formidable. The fortifications had been strengthened, the ditch around the walls deepened and mangonels set up, all defended by fighting men drawn from a population of 60,000, according to Saladin's advisers. The west end, where he camped, was particularly forbidding: deep wadis, towers, a massive wall. Why focus the assault there? Possibly because the Citadel, also known as the Tower of David, looked like the key to the city. For the next five days, mangonels, crossbowmen and bowmen filled the air with missiles. Though holed in places, the walls held, and Saladin's troops huddled beneath shields with their rock-damaged machines. Jerusalem seemed impregnable.

In fact, it was a city in crisis. Swollen by refugees, deprived of fighting men by the battle of Hattin, it had one man to every fifty women and children, and only fourteen knights. So Balian, the city's new master, knighted every lad of noble birth aged sixteen or over, as well as thirty non-noblemen. He seized all the treasure he could find – the remainder of King Henry II's cash, even silver from the roof of the Holy Sepulchre. He had a greater problem: the crisis was in part one of loyalty. There were Greek, Syrian and Armenian Christians who had been poorly treated by the westerners and would welcome Saladin as a liberator. The mass of common people saw disaster looming: William of Tyre says they begged the city's leaders to surrender.

After five long days – days he could ill afford – Saladin de-camped, raising hopes in the city that he was about to leave, but he was only shifting to the Mount of Olives, ready for an assault from the north and north-east, the place chosen by the Crusaders when they took the city almost a century before. In their new positions, as archers kept the walls clear of Christians, forty mangonels began a bombardment, with sappers working at the base of the walls to burn away the foundations. It took three days to breach them.

In the city, a proclamation called for fifty volunteers to guard the gap, promising a lavish reward of 5,000 gold coins. No one came forward.

Obviously the city was doomed. Officials came to talk terms. But now Saladin had the whip-hand, and chivalry played no further part in his strategy. Jerusalem, he claimed, could be cleansed only by Christian blood. He reverted to the terms he had set himself, to take the city by the sword. 'I want to take Jerusalem, the way the Christians took it from the Muslims 91 years ago,' he said, according to Imad al-Din. 'They inundated it in blood . . . The men I will slaughter, and the women I will make slaves.'

Balian, the city's leader, came to plead with Saladin, without effect. But he still had a strong card to play: the razed-earth tactic, which would leave Saladin with nothing worth having. His words – or rather his approximate words and his passion – were captured in two different versions. Here he is as quoted by Imad al-Din, promising an existential confrontation:

> If we despair of having our lives spared, if unable to count on your kindness, we have everything to fear from your might, if we remain convinced that there is neither salvation nor happiness nor peace nor settlement remaining for us, no longer truces or security, no longer benevolence or generosity, we shall set out to meet our deaths; it will be a bloody struggle of despair; we shall exchange life for the void; we shall throw

ourselves into the flames rather than accept destitution and shame.

And here are al-Athir's more specific words:

O Sultan, be aware that this city holds a mass of people so great that God alone knows their number. They now hesitate to continue the fight, because they hope you will spare their lives as you have spared so many others . . . But if we see death is inevitable, then, by God, we will kill our own women and children and burn all that we possess. We will not leave you a single dinar of booty, not a single dirham, not a single man or woman to lead into captivity. Then we shall destroy the sacred rock, the al-Aqsa mosque, and many other sites; and we will kill the 5,000 Muslim prisoners we now hold, and will exterminate the mounts and all the beasts . . . not one of us will die without having killed several of you.

Was he serious? Who knows? But he had to be believed, because otherwise Saladin would have risked losing the prize he had been fighting for all this time. Only by coming to terms could he be sure of getting what he wanted. So it was as much for tactical reasons as personal ones that he abandoned vengeance for mercy. When executing a U-turn, a leader who values the opinions of his advisers may be greeted with opposition. Not so in this case. When he asked to be released from his earlier promise to take Jerusalem by force, they agreed, insisting only that the Christians be made to pay for their freedom.

Terms followed on 2 October. The Christians would ransom themselves, 10 dinars per man, 5 per woman, one per child, to be paid within forty days, and slavery for those who couldn't. Horses and military gear were to be surrendered, all other possessions to be kept. Balian agreed in principle, then haggled for the 7,000 he said could not pay – the old, the widowed, the children. How about 30,000 dinars for them all? He, Balian, would pay. So it was agreed.

Imad al-Din returned from his convalescence in Damascus the following day and saw total chaos. The gates were shut, so that in theory no one could leave without payment and a receipt from a clerk, which was to be shown to the guards. But there was no way to check up on the clerks, the receipts or the guards. In practice, the clerks took whatever money was offered, handed over receipts, gave a cut to the guards, who let the prisoners go and 'mislaid' the receipts. Those without enough to ransom themselves – 20 or 30 dinars for a family was income for a year or more – climbed over the walls or were lowered in baskets or fled disguised as Muslims. Much of the ransom money went into the pockets of Saladin's generals. 'Complete negligence,' Imad al-Din wrote. 'General disorder. Anyone who made a gift under the table was released.' Saladin himself, again giving way to his innate generosity, allowed the widows of top leaders to leave without payment. Those without ready cash or wagon-space put household goods up for sale. Traders had a field day, picking up furniture for a tenth of its true value. Patriarch Heraclius snatched 200,000 dinars worth of treasure from the Church of the Holy Sepulchre – gold, carpets, ornaments – loaded the lot into several chariots and drove out with them. Balian himself escaped to Tyre. A Christian chronicler said he saw church treasures being sold off in the marketplace and churches turned into animal sheds and brothels. Even the ransom money that was collected vanished. Saladin himself gave away one day's collection of 70,000 dinars, using ransom money a second time to ransom Christians of his own choosing, and simply granting others their freedom. His officials despaired at the waste. The great man himself was intensely relaxed. Christians everywhere 'will speak of the blessings we have showered upon them'.

These were showered particularly on Christian women. Saladin fulfilled his promise to Balian, allowing his wife, Maria, to leave with her children, a nephew and all her possessions, even entertaining her and her children in his tent, in an incident told in sentimental terms by an anonymous Christian author:[55]

> When the children came before Saladin, he received them honourably as the children of free men, and had them taken off and given robes and jewels and ordered them to be given something to eat. After he had had them clothed and they had eaten, he took them and sat them on his knees, the one on the right and the other on his left, and began to sob. Some of his emirs who were there asked why he was weeping. He said that no one should wonder at it because the things of this world are merely on loan and are then recalled. 'And I shall tell you the reason. For just as I am now disinheriting other men's children, my own will find that after my death they will be disinherited.'

This author recorded other acts of charity as well, because he had an agenda: to explain Saladin's success as God's way

[55] The Old French *Continuation of William of Tyre*.

to punish the Christians for their sins. 'For the stench of adultery, of disgusting extravagance and of sin against nature would not let their prayers rise to God. God was so very angered at that people that he cleansed the city of them.'

Now I shall tell you of a great act of courtesy that Saladin did for the ladies of Jerusalem. The women and daughters of the knights who had been killed [at the battle of Hattin] had fled to Jerusalem. After they had been ransomed and had left the city, they came before Saladin and craved mercy. When he saw them he enquired who they were and what it was they were asking. They told him they were the wives and daughters of the knights who had been killed or taken in the battle. He asked what they wanted . . . They called on him for the sake of God to have mercy on them and give them counsel and aid. When Saladin saw them weeping, he had great pity on them and said they would be informed as to which of their husbands were alive and he would have them all freed . . . Then he ordered that the ladies and maidens whose fathers and lords had been killed in the battle should be provided for generously from his goods . . . He gave them so much that they praised God and man for the kindness and honour Saladin had showed them.

Queen Sibylla left to join her husband, King Guy, a prisoner in Nablus. Finally there was Stephanie, the widow of Reynald, the embodiment of Christian malevolence. She was freed, with a deal: that her son, Humphrey, captured at Hattin, would be released if she surrendered the two castles – Kerak and Montreal – she had inherited from her dead husband. It was agreed. Humphrey joined his mother in

Kerak. But it didn't work out that easily, because the garrisons refused to surrender. Stephanie, displaying an integrity that owed nothing to her husband, actually sent her son back into captivity. The gesture so appealed to Saladin that he released Humphrey anyway.

Well, negligence, disorder, wastage and 'kindness' were better outcomes than many other possible ones. Jihad on the one hand (for many jihadists resented Saladin's generosity) and Christian fervour on the other might have led to extreme violence and appalling bloodshed: torture, rape, looting, destruction, thousands dead.

Saladin was never happier. As he proudly wrote to the caliph – or rather dictated to Imad al-Din in one of seventy letters taken down by his long-suffering secretary – he had fulfilled his main aim: to unify Islam.[56] True, it had meant fighting other Muslims, but only for the greater good of unity. Tongues had wagged in criticism and the 'cauldrons of men's thoughts' had boiled against him, but patient endurance had quenched the fire. Muslims had had their revenge for the loss of Jerusalem, and it had all been achieved without the bloodshed and destruction unleashed when the Christians had seized it. Islam was victorious twice over, militarily and morally.

The first Friday for prayers in the al-Aqsa mosque after the taking of the city was 9 October 1187, and it was the first *khutba* (sermon) in eighty-eight years. Who would have the honour of pronouncing it? Imad al-Din described many

---

[56] Well, the Sunni heartland: north Africa, Arabia and Persia remained beyond his reach.

imams standing by in hope, 'preparing themselves, observing, insinuating', as well they might, because Imad al-Din was ready to hand the chosen one a long black robe given him by the caliph, al-Nasir, himself. At the last minute, Saladin made his choice: the chief *qadi* (judge) of Aleppo, Muhyi al-Din ibn al-Zaki. Having put on Imad's cloak, his voice trembling slightly, the *qadi* pronounced to a tight-packed and silent congregation the names of the rulers, the caliph and Saladin together; quoted the Quran ('So the people that committed wrong were eliminated. Praise be to Allah, Lord of the Universe', 6:45); and spelled out the significance of the place and the occasion – the Muslims supreme, the Franks evicted, filth purified, the land of Abraham and the site of the Prophet's ascent into Heaven all saved. And now on with jihad! Reconquer the remaining territories held by the infidel! Do not be like the woman who unravels her firmly spun web! 'And may salvation be upon you, Salah al-Din Yussuf, son of Ayyub, you who have restored the spurned dignity of this nation!'

That was the formal part. Then the *qadi* was followed in the pulpit by someone with a more common touch, ibn Naja, a long-time friend of Saladin's from Cairo. The themes were the same, but ibn Naja was an orator who knew how to pull at heartstrings. The congregation dissolved. 'Some noisily wept; others shouted . . . Hearts softened; sadness was alleviated; howls rose up; tears flowed; sinners repented; the afflicted returned to God; the penitent moaned; the repentant lamented.'

As the city's Franks scattered to Christian enclaves in Tyre, Tripoli or Alexandria, Jerusalem changed fast. Some 16,000 of the poor – those not covered by Balian's contribution

– were enslaved: there was a limit to Saladin's generosity, but enslavement was better than mass murder. Churches and monasteries became places of Muslim worship, with new decorations and Quran reciters. In the Dome of the Rock, paintings and statues vanished, as did the gilded cross above the dome itself and a Christian cemetery nearby. There was some debate about what to do with the Holy Sepulchre, the fourth-century complex that marked Golgotha, the place of Christ's crucifixion and resurrection. To leave it would attract Christian pilgrims; to destroy it was unthinkable. Well, it had been left untouched when the city was first taken by Muslims in the seventh century. Guided by considerations of tradition and commerce, Saladin decided to leave it untouched once more and charge pilgrims to enter. It was put in the care of the Melkites, a fifth-century term for a sect that traces its rituals back to the Apostles. What should be done with another important institution, the House of the Hospitallers, the warrior-monks originally charged with the care of pilgrims, which was now a place for medical treatment? Many patients were still there. Saladin decreed that ten knights could remain for a year to care for them. Christian churches became Muslim charities and schools. The Tower of David, a Frankish fortress, acquired an imam.

All of this was a stark contrast to the mayhem and murder let loose on the city by the Christians in 1098. Everyone knew it, because those terrible things had happened only three generations before, and the children of 1187 had heard the story from their grandparents. Saladin performed countless acts of mercy and generosity to individuals throughout his life, but nothing formed his reputation more effectively than the retaking of Jerusalem. Strategy played a part in his decision – the need to preserve the Holy Places intact – but there were many of his advisers who wanted a violent conclusion; it was he alone who had the sense and humility to change his mind.

Of course, Muslims have admired him for it ever since. So have many Christians, down the centuries. Gibbon put it as well as anyone. In his day (he said), it had become a cliché to compare the humanity of Saladin with the massacre of the First Crusade. It is worth remembering that the Muslims in 1098 had put up a long struggle, whereas the Christians in 1187 surrendered by treaty. But still, 'Justice is indeed due to the fidelity with which the Turkish conqueror fulfilled the conditions of the treaty; and he may be deservedly praised for the glance of pity which he cast on the misery of the vanquished . . . In these acts of mercy, the virtue of Saladin deserves our admiration and our love.'

A month after the fall of Jerusalem, duty called. Several fortresses held out, among them Kerak. Tyre was the outstanding problem. But Tyre, set on a peninsula linked to the mainland by a causeway, was hard to besiege. Its causeway was cut across by a ditch and ship-based bowmen could stitch it with arrows. The city needed a blockade of Muslim ships, but there were only ten of them. The balance of forces had changed. The city was well led (by Conrad), well defended, and well manned by refugees from Jerusalem, while Saladin's forces were scattered between conquered cities. Victory demanded inspiration, a new fleet and death-defying assaults. Instead, morale washed away with December's rain. Saladin's money was running out. The troops just wanted to go home.

To cap it all, from the caliph in Baghdad came a depressing

reaction to the retaking of Jerusalem. Saladin's successes had made the caliph nervous. An empire based on Syria was all very well. But if that empire spread south and east, across Iraq, why, pretty soon the caliph himself would be in Saladin's pocket. The caliph's advisers wondered out loud if Saladin had ambitions to overturn the Abbasid dynasty. It happened that Imad al-Din's brother, Taj, was in the caliph's service, so he was sent off to find out Saladin's intentions, bearing a letter in which the caliph responded to Saladin's triumphs with petty carping about sectarian disputes, overly generous welcomes to men who had fled Iraq, and the usurpation of the caliph's title (al-Nasir, 'the Victor', the full title being al-Nasir li-Din Allah, 'the Victor for the Religion of God'). He finished by blaming Saladin for consorting with unreliable elements, like Turkmens and Kurds, on the caliph's borders, 'causing their feet to slip and blunting their resolution', which was as good as implying he was a rebel himself. To save Islam for the caliph, recapture Jerusalem, be praised by all – then this. It hurt. Usurping his title? 'By God!' he told Taj, 'I did neither choose it nor usurp it. It was given to me by Caliph al-Mustadi after I had destroyed his Ismaili enemies!' Some advised an angry reply. But Saladin kept a cool head. The caliph, he said, was too great to allow for harsh words.

The blockade of Tyre, inadequate since it started in July, became ever more so. At the end of December 1187, five of Saladin's ten ships were captured in a dawn raid by a dozen of Conrad's ships, along with their crews and commanders. Saladin ordered the other five to safety in Beirut, but Christian ships pursued them, and the Muslims simply jumped overboard and swam ashore or beached their ships and ran away. That was the end of his attempt to take Tyre.

Impotence capped by humiliation: this was the end of Saladin's run of victories. Failure spotlit the problems of his leadership. The caliph's antipathy was mirrored by the reluctance of north African leaders to rally behind him. There were those who worried that his generosity smacked of weakness. In brief: he had more nobility than common sense. Al-Athir – from Mosul, always reluctant to follow Saladin – complained that 'he never evinced real firmness. He would lay siege to a city, but if the defenders resisted for some time, he would give up and abandon the siege. Now, a monarch must never act in this way.' Look at the results of his generosity. Enemy soldiers had been allowed to leave Acre, Ascalon and Jerusalem to seek refuge in Tyre, and as a result, well, 'ought we not to say that in a sense it was Salah al-Din himself who organized the defence of Tyre against his own army?'

He had a point. Tyre remained a Christian outpost, awaiting help from Europe, and Europe was preparing its response.

12

The Third Crusade: The Gathering Storm

ALMOST INSTANTLY, RELATIVELY SPEAKING, ALL EUROPE KNEW about the disaster of Hattin, and rallied.

In September 1187, with Jerusalem under attack, its Patriarch, Heraclius, had written to Pope Urban III, lamenting and begging: 'Alas, alas, O Reverend Father, that the Holy Land, the inheritance of the Crucified, should be given into the hands of pagans . . . Unless your Fatherhood shall have stirred all the princes of the west to bring aid speedily to the Holy Land, we despair.'

Soon after Jerusalem's fall, Joscius, archbishop of Tyre, set off in a black-sailed ship, bearing appeals for aid, including propaganda drawings of the horses of Saladin's army stabled and urinating in the Church of the Holy Sepulchre. His first stop was Sicily, where King William II dressed himself in penitential sackcloth at the news and promised a fleet, which by chance was on duty near Cyprus. The next stop for Joscius was Rome, where his tale shocked Pope Urban, already a sick man, to death. His successor, Gregory VIII, wrote to all Europe's leaders urging everyone to repent, take up the Cross, fast, abstain and hand over all their worldly goods to Rome for protection. He died two months later (of a fever, after just fifty-seven days on the papal throne). Joscius went to France, where Richard, Count of Poitou, eldest son of Henry II of England, had already vowed to go on Crusade. In January 1188 Joscius met with Henry himself and Henry's long-time enemy Philip II of France, among others. So powerfully did he speak that the old enemies made peace and promised to back the Crusade, thus setting one of four stages – Anglo-French, German, Sicilian (William's fleet) and Muslim – all of which acted and interacted at once.

Help was coming, wrote Henry to Amaury, the aging, scholarly Patriarch of Antioch (the one who had been vilely treated by Reynald of Châtillon). Well, yes and no. In England, Henry promulgated the 'Saladin Tithe' to pay for the Crusade, a 'tithe' being 10 per cent on revenues and movable properties. Anyone who joined the Crusade was exempt from the tithe altogether, and many did, for objections led to imprisonment and/or excommunication. The tax was the largest ever collected in England and in English territories in France. Collecting it was not easy, because England and its French possessions were torn apart, like Henry's family, by strife between Henry and his son, Richard, who was in alliance with the French king, Philip. The fighting drove Henry into an early grave in summer 1189. Richard, now king, took over the task of collection. He sold estates, offices (by firing officials and then auctioning their posts), virtually anything he could lay his hands on to add cash to the Saladin Tithe. After more delays, he met Philip in France in July 1190 to set out on their joint adventure.

But the delays meant that Richard and Philip were not the first of the land forces to move. A contingent was already under way from the Holy Roman Empire, the 600 or so un-Roman and not very holy entities – from duchies and princedoms to pocket- handkerchief estates – that would one day evolve into Germany and several of its neighbours. Emperor Frederick I, known as Barbarossa (Red Beard), had pretensions to make himself a new caesar. Indeed it was he who added the 'Holy' to what had been the Roman Empire in the West (as opposed to Constantine's one in the East). With imperial restoration in mind, he had himself crowned emperor in Rome and spent much of his life trying, and failing, to seize Italy. So in the end he won a reputation not as conqueror but as the unifier of Germany, working with, rather than against, the German princes. In his old age, he became a passionate Crusader. In response to Gregory's letter urging a new Crusade, Frederick convened a congress, the Diet of Mainz, at Easter 1188. To wild excitement caused by a reading of Gregory's letter, Frederick, a grizzled sixty-eight-year-old, 'took the Cross', along with his son, another Frederick.

The response was astonishing: many other noblemen and thousands of ordinary men, perhaps 50,000, were keen to go, for glory, for loot, for the forgiveness of sins. This gave the commanders a problem. The easiest route was by sea, via northern Italy. But there were not ships enough to carry such a crowd such a distance. So most of the troops – not all, because a few nobles did take the sea route – went overland, through Hungary (picking up 2,000 Hungarian fighting men) and south-eastern Europe, to Constantinople, and onwards across present-day Turkey. That route presented another problem: the Byzantine emperor, Isaac II Angelus, although a Christian, detested his western co-religionists so much that he had allied himself to Saladin. The Crusaders would (perhaps) have to fight their way through Christians in order to fight Muslims.

The German force was more migration than advance, including an archbishop, eight bishops, three margraves, twenty-nine counts, and tens of thousands of troops – more than enough, as it turned out, to cow the Byzantine emperor, who, under threat of attack, let the Germans rendezvous with Italian ships to carry them across the Bosporus and set them on their way southwards, skirting the territory of the Seljuks (Anatolia, today's eastern Turkey).

The Seljuks, being Turkish Muslims, were *real* enemies, harassing Frederick's army for 400 kilometres in bitter conditions, this being the new year of 1190. As al-Athir says, the Turks would 'kill anyone who became isolated and steal what they could. It was wintertime and the cold in those lands can be intense and the snow deep.' A rare victory at Iconium (today's Konya) scattered the Seljuks and reinvigorated the Christians.

Then fate took a hand. Having negotiated a truce with the Turks, the Germans were on the very edge of Christian territory, on the road which for almost two millennia led along the Göksu river (known as the Calycadnus in the ancient world), which cuts through limestone gorges down from highlands to the town of Silifke (then Seleucia). Now it was summer, brutally hot, and the old emperor had been on the road for months. According to conflicting stories, he came to the river where the road crossed from the east bank to the west[57] and decided either to refresh himself or to walk his horse across instead of using the crowded bridge. Either way, his horse slipped, Frederick fell, his armour weighed him down, and he was swept to his death. Some officers retrieved his body and put it in a barrel of vinegar to preserve it for the rest of the Crusade.

It is on the leader and his vision that a noble cause depends. With the emperor's death, the German army lost its head, and its inspiration. His son, young Frederick, Duke of Swabia, was no match for his father. Some of his princes headed home, others went south to the coast and hired ships to take them to the Holy Land. The troops were hungry, sick, demoralized – 'as if they had been exhumed from their graves', as al-Athir put it – and far too happy to reach Christian Antioch. Here Prince Bohemond fed them for two months. By the end of August, one of Europe's greatest arrays had been reduced in number and spirit to a pampered rabble unwilling to face more hardship, and without even the symbol of a leader, for vinegar is not a good preservative. Frederick's rotting flesh was boiled from his bones and given a hasty burial, while the disarticulated skeleton was kept for burial in Jerusalem, thus ensuring that part of him would reside for ever in the Holy City. That at least was the hope of his heir, young

---

[57] Perhaps where the road crosses the 100-metre-wide river today, about 15 kilometres north of Silifke.

Frederick of Swabia, as he proceeded by sea from Antioch to Tyre.

In Palestine, meanwhile, Saladin had had to face the problem of the principal surviving Christian enclaves, Tyre first and foremost. All attempts to take it – a blockade by ships, assaults with mangonels – had failed. Saladin turned to politics in an attempt to ensure that the Christians remained at each other's throats.

King Guy, his prisoner in Nablus since Hattin, was his main asset and, as king, he was more the leader than Conrad in Tyre. So in July 1188, Saladin set him free, along with ten high-ranking followers, in exchange for a promise that he would never, ever take up arms against Muslims again. Guy rejoined his queen, Sibylla, in Tripoli – but promptly forswore his oath, or rather got a priest to release him from it on the grounds that an oath should not be kept if it endangered religion.

He then marched to Tyre and demanded to be received as king. Conrad refused to admit him. 'The very fact that I have preserved and am preserving Tyre,' he wrote to the Archbishop of Canterbury, 'is grievous and insupportable to Guy of Lusignan', whom he disdained as *'the former king'*. He said he would hold the place pending the arrival of the Crusaders from Europe. Guy returned unhappily to Tripoli. The two main Christian enclaves (and several smaller ones) remained separate but intact. They were down, but not yet out.

Help came to the Christians in early 1189, in the form of ships from both Pisa and Sicily, and more would surely follow. On this slight foundation, Guy, who had risked all and lost at Hattin, took another high-risk decision. He left Tripoli to besiege Muslim-held Acre. Well repaired, well provisioned and well garrisoned, it was no easy target. Guy settled in for the long haul – for a two-year siege, as things turned out, which would become the central event of the Third Crusade. In fact, it would quickly evolve into a double siege – the Muslim population inside Acre; the Christians outside the walls, supplied by sea; and hemming them in Saladin's land army, with his ships occasionally breaking through the Christian fleet to keep the city alive.

13

Acre

MORE AID BEGAN TO TRICKLE IN TO THE CHRISTIANS. WITH
counts, margraves and bishops by the dozen, ships by the score
and sailors by the hundred, Acre was solidly blockaded.

All this took Saladin by surprise. He broke off attacks on
lesser fortresses to set up camp near Guy, and on 3 October
prepared for battle. Placing himself in the centre of the
line, he had his two sons al-Afdal and al-Zafir on his right,
then the Mosulis, those from Diyarbakir (under their lord,
Qutb al-Din Suqman, who was only fifteen), his nephew
Husam al-Din, a contingent from Damascus and, as his
anchor, Taqi al-Din; on the left were contingents from
Kurdistan, Sinjar, Gökbüri's men and mamluks. After brief

advances and retreats as both sides probed for weaknesses, the Franks saw that Saladin had sent troops from his centre to support Taqi al-Din – failing to understand that Taqi was making a planned retreat to draw the Franks on. Saladin's order exposed the inexperienced Diyarbakiris. A Frankish charge broke them, drove many into headlong flight and inspired servants to loot their masters' tents, convincing many Muslims that the Christians were victorious. That was what many Christians believed, too. It was very nearly true. A bunch of them started to pillage Muslim tents, and were close to Saladin's – almost close enough to cut it down and create panic among the Muslims – when they saw they were in trouble. Having charged through the centre, they risked being cut off from left and right, and paused.

Something changed. Those who analyse battles know about this moment, when, for some apparently inexplicable reason, one side senses victory or the other defeat. Perhaps it was leadership. Saladin, galloping back and forth in a very un-general-like fashion, yelled at five of his knights, who re-formed the centre and, magically, as a flock or herd will respond to an unseen signal, the tide of battle turned. Perhaps it was the sight of a riderless horse pursued by a few Christians in apparent flight, as recorded by some eye-witnesses. Perhaps it was down to Saladin's boldness, or the Christian knight Adrienne of Brienne, who galloped back and forth, yelling exhortations, only to be cut down, a symbol of defeat instead of victory.

Whatever seized them, the Franks became sheep in confused retreat, and easy victims. Some 6,000 were killed, according to Baha al-Din, though estimates like this should be taken with pinches of salt. But there is no reason to doubt his next statement, that the Muslims threw bodies into the little river[58] on which the Christians depended. 'The river flowed with blood, dead bodies and grease for more than eight days,' wrote the anonymous author of the *Continuation*, 'so that the people of the host could not drink the water.'

A great victory, but not one on which Saladin could build. His own troops had been robbed and others had fled. Some goods were recovered, piled up in front of Saladin's tent, and returned to their owners, but that took time. Help for the Christians was flowing into Acre from the ships offshore, with more apparently to come from Frederick Barbarossa – reports spoke of 200,000 troops or more, enough to make all Muslims quail, for they were weary, the horses saddle-sore and Saladin himself drained of energy, borderline sick. There could be no follow-up attack on the city. In mid-October, Saladin pulled his army back to reconsider his options.

That winter of 1189–90 there were few options on either side except more of the same: more reinforcements – including a fleet of fifty Christian ships, which caused Saladin to remark, 'By God, it seems to me that the Franks have gone mad and built their towers on the sea'; occasional breakthroughs, now by Christian ships, now by Muslim ones; skirmishes here, duels there; much sickness in both camps, Guy's wife, Queen Sibylla, and their two daughters being among the victims. For weeks, famine stalked the Franks; troops ate grass, bare bones and their own horses. Both sides – Muslims in Acre surrounded by Franks, who were surrounded by Saladin's Muslims – settled into a dismal stalemate, enlivened, believe it

---

[58] Then known to Christians as the Belus or Belos, now the (Hebrew) Na'aman.

or not, by parties thrown by knights and emirs for each other, and Saladin's everlasting generosity to Christian prisoners. The Crusaders were as much their own enemies as Saladin's, being torn by a dispute over the kingship: King Guy, already weak, was king only because his now-dead wife had made him so; Conrad would be better, but would have to marry Sibylla's already-married sister, Isabella, to have a claim. So Conrad had her marriage annulled on the grounds that she had been underage when she was married (eleven, actually). Her 'cowardly and effeminate' husband, Humphrey of Toron, failed to object, and Conrad would marry her in November 1190, with no great effect, because Guy refused to abdicate.

Come the spring of 1190, both sides mounted further attacks, with no breakthroughs. The Franks, who had no expertise with mining, somehow managed to hire a team of renegade miners from Aleppo, to no effect, because they could not get close enough to Acre's walls to mount a successful operation. The Franks used wood brought in by sea to build siege-towers, which the Muslims sent up in flames, thanks to a coppersmith from Damascus who devised a way of tossing Greek fire (*naphtha*) with a mangonel. One battle in July 1190 led to an astonishing discovery. After one failed Christian assault, which left bodies littered across the battlefield, Saladin's aides, Baha al-Din and Imad al-Din, rode out together to examine the dead. To their astonishment, as Baha al-Din recorded, 'I noticed the bodies of two women. Someone told me that he had seen four women engaged in the fight, of whom two were made prisoners.'

Accounts of the Crusades give the impression that they were wholly masculine enterprises. Not so: many women were involved, as passing references in both Muslim and

Christian sources testify. Aristocratic women accompanied their Christian husbands. Christian sources speak of washer-women and women who helped fill in a ditch around Acre so that mangonels could be brought up close. Then there were the prostitutes. They were not mentioned in any Christian sources, which were almost all written by clerics not eager to publicize the lusty habits of their own side. But Imad al-Din is happy to record Christian immorality – their abominable treatment of women being proof of their barbarity – because it contrasts nicely with the civilized morality of the Muslims:

> There arrived by ship three hundred lovely Frankish women, full of youth and beauty, assembled from beyond the sea and offering themselves for sin. They were expatriates come to help expatriates, ready to cheer the fallen and sustained in turn to give support and assistance, and they glowed with ardour for carnal intercourse. They were all licentious harlots, proud and scornful, who took and gave, foul-fleshed and sinful, singers and coquettes, appearing proudly in public, ardent and inflamed, tinted and painted . . . selling themselves for gold, bold and ardent, loving and passionate, ink-faced and unblushing.

How, I wonder, did he know? But even if it's half true, what a story. Back in England, according to many accounts, women sent their men off with the sort of enthusiasm that marked the start of the First World War: *Oh! We don't want to lose you, but we think you ought to go.* There was an eager female supply back in England, and a lusty male market in the Holy Land. The link between the two is a blank. Who did the supplying? How were these beauties recruited? Were they willing volunteers, or compelled, or bribed, or persuaded with honeyed words about how they would contribute to the zeal of the Crusaders? Who paid for their transport? What happened to them? And their inevitable children?

Other women, as the two secretaries recorded, actually took up arms.[59] There were many female knights, wrote Baha al-Din, who could not be told apart from the men until they were killed and their armour removed. Later, he recorded another instance, in July 1191, when the siege of Acre was still rolling on:

> One very intelligent old man . . . was amongst those who forced their way into the enemy's trenches that day. 'Behind their rampart,' he told me, 'was a woman wrapped in a green *melluta* [a kind of green mantle] who kept on shooting arrows from a wooden bow, with which she wounded several of our men. She was at last overpowered by numbers; we killed her, and brought the bow she had been using to the Sultan, who was greatly astonished.'

Messages went back and forth between Acre's Muslim inhabitants and their would-be rescuers, carried by pigeons or strapped to swimmers (a dangerous occupation, which led to several deaths). News of the German approach and the Anglo-French preparations exhilarated Christians and appalled Muslims. Saladin sent frantic messages to local

---

[59] Many of these details are from Helen Nicholson, 'Women on the Third Crusade'; see Bibliography. She points out that both sides had an agenda in their attitudes to women as fighters: Muslim historians emphasized them as examples of Christian barbarism; Christian historians avoided mentioning them 'to defend the Crusaders against charges of immorality.'

emirs and the reluctant caliph urging support, and an apprehensive army gathered in northern Syria. When news came of
Frederick Barbarossa's death, it was the Christians who were
appalled, the Muslims exhilarated.

Still the double siege continued, the inhabitants of Acre
always starving – with 200 a day dying – but always saved
by some last-minute arrival. Once Saladin arranged for a ship
in Beirut to be filled with food, in an incident described by
Baha al-Din. A group of Muslims boarded the ship dressed
like Franks. They shaved their beards, sewed crosses to the
mast and positioned pigs – taboo to Muslims, of course, but
favoured by Europeans – prominently on the deck. Then they
approached Acre, cutting through the Frankish blockade. A
Frankish ship accosted them. Officers ordered them to furl
their sails and shouted at them, asking why they were heading
for Acre.

> Our soldiers, feigning astonishment, asked, 'Haven't you
> taken the city?' The Franks, who thought they were dealing
> with their own countrymen, replied, 'No, we haven't yet
> taken it.' 'Well then,' our soldiers replied, 'we will moor near
> the camp, but there is another ship behind us. You had better
> alert them so they do not sail into the city.' The Beirutis had
> indeed noticed that there was a Frankish ship behind them.
> The enemy sailors headed towards it immediately, while our
> sailors unfurled all sails for a rush to the port of Acre, where
> they were greeted with cries of joy, for hunger was stalking
> the city.

Now it was the spring of 1191. Enter Saladin's European
counterpart, the most awe-inspiring Crusader of them all,

Richard 'the Lionheart', the recently crowned king of England, thirty-three years old, tall, strong, good-looking, with golden-red hair, seemingly the archetypal hero. But this often charming and courageous young man was also the product of a dysfunctional family, which was in an almost constant state of rivalry, rebellion, war and civil war. Henry II and Eleanor of Aquitaine, however, had been highly competent rulers, right up until Henry's death two years previously,[60] while Richard was prone to hot temper and impetuous action. He was both idealistic and mean, chivalrous and treacherous, a wonderful ally and a fearsome enemy, mercurial in turning from one to the other, a man equally in love with music and slaughter. With a will of iron and adoring followers, he was free to use his vast wealth – as king of England and ruler of Aquitaine, which was half of France – to indulge an urge for foreign adventures. In this case, he had personal reasons to do so: he was a relative of Jerusalem's queen and King Guy's dead wife, Sibylla. Retaking Jerusalem would be the perfect way to serve his religion, his kingdom and his family.

Richard, well financed by the Saladin Tithe, had some 6,000–8,000 men, whose transport he master-minded: 14,000 pig carcasses, for example, gathered from most of southern England, 60,000 horseshoes, arrows by the million, 150 ships, a complicated land–sea operation which had Richard crossing France (because he suffered from seasickness) and meeting his ships in Marseilles. Further complications followed, for Richard's brilliant and imperious mother, Eleanor of Aquitaine, was determined he should marry a Spanish princess in order to protect Aquitaine's southern

[60] Eleanor lived on until 1204.

border. Queen Eleanor and the princess, Berengaria by name, pursued Richard all across Europe and caught up with him in Sicily. En route to the Holy Land, there was a storm. Berengaria was cast ashore on Cyprus. Richard rescued her, and captured the island. The two were married there, making Berengaria queen of England, not a happy position for her, given that Richard's crusading zeal and his consequent absences (which we will get to shortly) would mean that her marriage was likely never consummated and she probably never set foot in the country of which she was queen.

Richard joined his ally, the French King Philip, in Acre in early June, to the kindling of bonfires and the sounding of trumpets. Already Philip had built new mangonels, one named the Evil Neighbour, and another God's Own Sling, which had been hammering at the walls. What was needed was energetic leadership, and Richard was the man for the job: he was not only a powerful figurehead but also an expert in the 'arbelast', or crossbow. His first move was an attempt to meet Saladin, to see if politics could replace warfare. Saladin refused, saying, 'Kings meet together only after the conclusion of an accord.' He agreed that his brother al-Adil could meet the English king, but sickness of some sort fore-stalled the summit.

Both sides continued to build their forces, the Crusaders digging in behind earthworks, the Muslims receiving reinforcements from Egypt – fifty ships under the command of Lu'lu', the hero who had ended Reynald's raid in the Red Sea – and Mosul, the inhabitants of Acre continually re-shoring their much battered and undermined walls, the occasional Muslim ship breaking through the ring of Crusader vessels. Pigeons kept up a flow of information, but for the system to work someone had to retrieve the birds once they had flown to their bases, and that sort of contact was rare. During the summer of 1191, the main messengers were commandos who swam back and forth, at great risk.

Baha al-Din told the story of one of them, a Muslim swimmer named Isa, who used to dive under the Frankish ships at night and swim to the shore beneath Acre's walls. He usually carried money and messages for the garrison, these being attached to his belt. The besieged soldiers would confirm his arrival by releasing a pigeon. One night, when he had dived down carrying three bags containing 1,000 dinars and several letters, he was seen and killed. Saladin's officers guessed what had happened, because no pigeon arrived:

> A few days later, some inhabitants of Acre happened to be walking along the water's edge and saw a body washed up on the shore. As they approached it, they recognized Isa the swimmer; the gold and wax with which the letters were sealed were still attached to his belt. Who has ever heard of a man fulfilling his mission in death as faithfully as though he were alive?[61]

Inside Acre, hope was dying, as Saladin heard from a message carried out by a swimmer on 7 July. There was nothing he could do. Five days later, the city capitulated, buying freedom by agreeing – in Saladin's name, but as yet without his involvement – to hand over its population, contents, ships, military stores, 100,000 dinars (with another 10,000 for Conrad personally) and 1,600 anonymous

---

[61] Adapted from Amin Maalouf, *The Crusades Through Arab Eyes*.

Christian prisoners held by Saladin, 100 of them 'men of rank' who were listed by name. Saladin would also have to return the True Cross. Conrad would release his Muslim prisoners *if Saladin kept the pledge.* Another swimmer bearing another message brought the news to Saladin. Horrified, he was in the process of writing a reply forbidding this unilateral surrender, when he saw Frankish flags waving over the walls.

It was over. Distraught 'as a mother who has just lost her child', he had no choice but to accept the deal.

How could this reverse have come about? True, his forces were spread too thinly, fending off rivals to the east and north. But the main reason was that the caliph had sent no help, to Saladin's distress. 'Jihad is the personal duty of all Muslims,' he wrote. 'Yet your servant is left to bear that oppressive burden all alone.'

The inhabitants trailed out, some 3,000 ordinary soldiers being taken prisoner, and the Franks moved in, along with a small contingent of Germans. There were four leaders – King Richard, King Philip, Conrad (who still claimed the kingship of Jerusalem over Guy) and Leopold of Austria (commander of the Germans following the death of Barbarossa's heir, Frederick of Swabia). They squabbled over who would stay where. Richard seized the prize, the Royal Palace. But then Leopold claimed equality by raising his standard beside Richard's, until English guards tossed it over the walls. Remember this, as Leopold did with bitterness, because there would be consequences for Richard when the Crusade was over.

Acre was quickly re-Christianized, the churches reconsecrated, and the business of the kingship settled. Guy would keep the crown until his death, when it would pass to Conrad and Isabella and their line. That done, Philip, who was sickly and nervous that Richard was more rival than ally, sailed for home, leaving Richard in charge of dealing with Saladin.

Saladin played for time. He needed two months, he said, to gather the cash and release his Christian prisoners. Richard's officials demanded half the amount after a month, plus the True Cross and the prisoners. Yes, the True Cross was safe and sound in Saladin's hands, as Baha al-Din witnessed: 'It was shown to them, and when they saw it they displayed the most profound reverence, prostrating themselves on the ground till their faces were covered with dust, and humiliating themselves in adoration.' Saladin agreed to the new terms, provided that Richard release his own Muslim prisoners; moreover, he would leave hostages as a guarantee that the high-rank Christians would be released. Richard's men said they would release only the prisoners of their choice.

With too many new conditions, trust was broken. The deal was off.

Richard was keen to set off for Jerusalem, but could not leave while burdened by the 3,000 prisoners. His patience ran out, and he took a terrible decision. In his own words:[62]

On Saladin's behalf it had been agreed that the Holy Cross and 1,500 living prisoners would be handed over to us, and he fixed a day for us when all this was to be done. But the time limit expired, and as the pact which we had agreed was

[62] In a letter to the Abbot of Clairvaux dated 1 October 1191, quoted in Peter Edbury, *The Conquest of Jerusalem and the Third Crusade*.

entirely made void, we quite properly had the Saracens that we had in custody – about 2,600 of them – put to death.

They were roped together, led out to the open space before Acre, in full view of Saladin's advance guards, and executed by Christian swordsmen, along with 300 of their wives and children, sparing only 'prisoners of note and such as were strong enough to labour'. The watching Muslim troops rushed to stop the slaughter, but were repulsed. Bodies were left for relatives to recognize, bury and mourn.

Two thousand six hundred: not many, perhaps, by the standards of a modern genocide, but a show of brutality far beyond anything done by Saladin. It is not a question of numbers. This was a political act, revealing the difference between personalities and between cultures. Richard might have released them; he might have made them slaves; but – according to Baha al-Din's Christian sources later – he had intended to kill them anyway, proof to the Muslims that he was not to be trusted. What a difference between the generosity Saladin, as a Muslim, usually (not always) showed to his enemies and the ruthlessness that Richard, as a Christian, showed to his.

'Jihad' now has a dire reputation as a justification for indiscriminate violence against non-Muslims and Muslims, soldiers and civilians, men, women and children. But the original concept is more subtle than the superficial ideology of a suicide bomber. Jihad, as portrayed in the Quran, was a hard and unpleasant duty, which involved killing – when necessary and within limits. 'Fight in the Way of Allah those who fight you, but transgress not the limits. Truly, Allah likes not the transgressors' (2:190). Islam, spread by the sword, contains enough to justify tolerance; Christianity, spread by persuasion, contains enough to justify atrocity. There is much room for interpretation. What makes killing necessary? What are the limits? Choice is available. Saladin frequently chose tolerance; Richard chose atrocity.

14

The End of the Third Crusade

TWO DAYS AFTER THE MASSACRE, ON 22 AUGUST 1191, Richard led his army out of Acre, shadowed by Saladin, looking for a chance to strike, but not seeing one. It was not a happy army, for the troops had indulged in a month of R&R, with good food and female company. On the march Richard's will ruled. The only women allowed were elderly washerwomen – no ardent beauties. Since Saladin held the roads to the east, Richard headed south along the coast, with his ships tracking his progress a little out to sea, ready with food and water. His aim: to reach Jaffa, 130 kilometres away, then head inland another 65 kilometres to Jerusalem. It was brutally hot. Richard, well aware of the dangers of dehydration, ordered a slow pace – no more than 6 kilometres a day, resting in the afternoon. Even so, his troops, dressed in thick felt and chain-mail to ward off Muslim arrows, began to suffer.

Saladin was with him, marching in parallel, a few kilo-metres inland, looking for a place to attack, his light horsemen occasionally swooping in to seize some heat-stricken trooper. After questioning, all were killed – sometimes, as Baha al-Din says, 'in the most cruel manner, for the Sultan was terribly angry at the massacre of the prisoners from Acre'.

An anonymous Christian[63] described Muslim tactics:

> The Turks were not loaded with armour like our men, and with their ease of movement distressed us so much the more severely; for the most part they were lightly armed, carrying only a bow or a mace bristling with sharp teeth, a scimitar, a light spear with an iron head, and a dagger suspended lightly. When put to flight by a greater force, they fled away on horse-back with the utmost rapidity, and they have not their equals for agility throughout the world. If they see their pursuers stop it is their custom to turn back – like the fly, which, if you drive it away, will go, but when you cease, it will return.

Chivalry and generosity did not stand much of a chance now. At one point, a Frankish knight was captured, 'evidently a person of consequence', in Baha al-Din's words; 'Indeed, I never saw a man so well made, with such elegant hands and feet, and such a distinguished bearing.' Through an interpreter, he was questioned about the price of provisions, which was rising daily as merchants exploited the shortage;

[63] In the *Itinerarium Peregrinorum*.

and about the loss of horses since the Christians had left Acre. Answer: about 400 horses. At this point, Saladin ordered the man's head to be cut off. The prisoner asked what the sultan had said, and on being told:

> he changed colour and said, 'But I will give you one of the captives in Acre.'
> The Sultan replied: 'God's mercy, it must be an emir.'
> 'I cannot get an emir set at liberty,' answered the Frank.
> The interest shown in him by all present, and his fine figure, all spoke in his favour . . . The Sultan therefore postponed the execution of his commands, had him put in chains, and reproached him with the treachery of his fellow-countrymen and the massacre of the prisoners. He acknowledged that it was an abominable act, but said it was the King alone who had decreed and commanded it to be done. After the afternoon prayer, the Sultan rode out according to his custom, and on his return ordered that the prisoner should be put to death. Two other prisoners were then brought in before him, whom he likewise ordered to be put to death.

After two weeks of progress the armies approached Arsuf, and one of Palestine's rare forests. Saladin, ahead of Richard's slow-and-steady advance, saw a good place for battle, open ground between the woods and the sea. On 7 September he attacked. But the Christians were well prepared, the experienced Templars out in front, other contingents – Angevins, Bretons, English, Normans – shepherding King Guy, with Richard in the centre and the other knightly order, the Hospitallers, bringing up the rear. 'They kept so closely together that an apple, if thrown, would not have fallen to the ground without touching a man or a horse.'

In mid-morning, with a bloodcurdling clash of cymbals and gongs and war-cries, the Muslims charged from the woods, infantry first discharging arrows and javelins, followed by the cavalry, the aim being to break the Christian line, scatter them and get in among them for hand-to-hand slaughter. But the arrows could not pierce the Christians' thick armour, and the line held. A later assault on the Hospitallers forced them back, but they simply retreated facing the Muslims, re-loading their crossbows as they went. Richard was magnificent, riding back and forth, rallying, taking risk after risk. 'No one escaped when his sword made contact with them; wherever he went his brandished sword cleared a wide path on all sides. Continuing his advance with untiring sword strokes, he cut down that unspeakable race as if he were reaping the harvest with a sickle, so that the corpses of Turks he had killed covered the ground everywhere for the space of half a mile.' There would be a counter-attack, but not yet; not until the Muslim troops and horses began to tire. Richard ordered restraint until the signal, a sixfold trumpet blast. In the event, two Hospitaller knights could not bear the delay, broke through their own forward ranks to join battle, and inspired the men behind them into a charge. Richard saw that they might fail unless supported, and ordered the whole army to charge. Within minutes, he had regained command. The Muslims fell back and opened to let the Christians through. 'Then might be seen numbers prostrated on the ground, horses without their riders in crowds, the wounded lamenting with groans their hard fate, others drawing their last breath weltering in gore, and many lay headless whilst their lifeless forms were trodden underfoot by both friend and foe.'[64] But Richard, afraid that the Muslims would close ranks, called them back. Despite the thick dust, in which men struck about them indiscriminately, hitting friend and foe alike, they regrouped, charged again, and again, until the Muslim rout became a general collapse, with several hundred dead. 'The king, mounted on a bay Cyprian steed which had not its match, bounded forward, and scattered those he met on all sides; for the enemy fled from his sword and gave way, while helmets tottered beneath it and sparks flew forth from its strokes.' Richard himself wrote of his victory: 'So great was the slaughter among Saladin's more noble Saracens, that he lost more that day . . . than on any day in the previous 40 years.'

The battle of Arsuf almost did for Richard what Hattin had done for Saladin. The Muslim army was not wrecked, but the Christians were jubilant, Saladin humiliated, and his troops so demoralized there would be no further assault. All he could do was pull back and guard the road eastwards. With no further opposition, Richard moved on that evening to enter Jaffa, his base for his planned advance inland to Jerusalem.

Now there came another pause. Richard had to be sure of securing Jaffa, because through Jaffa's port would come all his supplies. Besides, his troops were once again living in comfort, with good food and women brought in from Acre. He would be there for weeks, rebuilding the place, but also 'enjoying ease and pleasure'.

During this time, the Christians very nearly lost their king, in an incident recorded in the *Itinerarium Peregrinorum*.

[64] *Itinerarium Peregrinorum.*

Richard was out hawking with a few companions. At some point he dismounted to rest and fell asleep. Suddenly a small force of Saladin's men appeared and attacked. Four knights died in the fight. The Muslims had no idea that they had stumbled upon the king, who, remounting his 'Cyprian steed', led a counter-attack. One of his companions yelled in Arabic something like, 'To me. I am the king!' and held the Muslims' attention long enough to be captured and allow Richard to escape.[65] Advisers rebuked him for taking such a risk, but he was unrepentant: 'in all expeditions, he was the first to advance, the last to retreat.'

Saladin was not sure what Richard would do next: either go for Jerusalem, or build himself another base in Ascalon, 50 kilometres further south. This would have an important strategic advantage by giving him control of the road to Egypt, thus preventing the arrival of help for Saladin. To forestall such a possibility, Saladin took the decision to use scorched-earth tactics. 'Knowing that it would be impossible for the Muslims to hold the city, with the remembrance of Acre and the fate of its garrison fresh in their minds, and being convinced, moreover, that his soldiers would be afraid to shut themselves up in the city, he . . . decreed that Ascalon should be destroyed.'

The following day, accompanied by Baha al-Din, he reached Ascalon, a famously lovely city, 'pleasant to look upon and delightful to the senses; its walls were strong, its buildings beautiful, and it occupied a most charming situation.' The decision was a hard and painful one:

---

[65] His name was William of Pratelles. He was ransomed by Richard on his departure for home.

His tent had been pitched at some distance from the city, and he spent the night there, though he slept very little, for the thought of being obliged to destroy the city filled his mind. I had left him after midnight, but at daybreak he summoned me again, and began to discuss his plans with me. He then sent for his son, el-Melek el-Afdal, to consult with him on the subject, and they talked together for a long while. He said to me, whilst I was on duty in his tent: 'I take God to witness I would rather lose all my children than cast down a single stone from the walls, but God wills it; it is necessary for the Muslim cause, therefore I am obliged to carry it through.'

With the city's governor, workmen were hired, and the ramparts, the market and other areas allotted to emirs and soldiers, all of whom well understood Saladin's decision. The inhabitants, overwhelmed by the news that they would have to give up their homes, 'uttered loud lamentations, and began at once to sell everything they could not carry away with them . . . even selling ten hens for one dirhem.' Some of them set out for Egypt, some for Syria, many on foot, having no money for a horse or donkey. As the buildings were stripped, the stone towers and ramparts were undermined and the spaces filled with wood, the purpose of which could hardly be kept a secret from the Franks for long. The work was like that of a siege, but from within. 'One of the stone-masons,' wrote Baha al-Din, 'informed the Sultan in my hearing that the wall of one of the towers which he was undermining was as thick as a lance is long.' Saladin urged the workmen on, sending his own servants and animal-handlers to help, apprehensive that if the Franks heard what was happening, they would attack. Meanwhile, even

as outriders between Ascalon and Jaffa fought small engage-
ments, messages passed back and forth between the two sides
discussed possible peace terms, negotiations that were deliberately drawn out on Saladin's orders to ensure Ascalon's
destruction. Finally, after two days of frantic preparation,
the moment came, the signal was given. Every building was
set on fire, burning up whatever property had been left by
the fleeing inhabitants. Towers fuelled with wood above and
below collapsed, ramparts tumbled.

With Richard's army, mainly the French, settled in Jaffa
and Saladin camping near Jerusalem, peace talks started in
earnest, in two separate strands, Richard talking to Saladin's
brother al-Adil, and Saladin with Conrad. Proposals ranged
from realistic to bizarre. Richard demanded Jerusalem,
the whole country west of the Jordan, and the True Cross.
Saladin, who vetted all proposals, rejected all three out of
hand: Jerusalem was as much Muslim as it was Christian, the
land was Muslim, and the True Cross was his main negotiating asset. Richard countered by proposing marriage between
al-Adil and the king's sister, Joanna of Sicily; the release of
prisoners; guaranteed Christian access to Jerusalem. That
suggestion was scotched by Joanna herself, who was appalled
at the idea of marrying a Muslim. In that case, Richard said,
how about his niece, Eleanor of Brittany?

Time passed, and still there was no conclusion. In the winter
of 1191–2, Saladin kept guard on Jerusalem, waiting for
reinforcements from Mosul, from al-Jazira, from anywhere.
Richard took over ruined Ascalon and set about repairing
it, a task that took four hard months. But this would not
solve his problems. Amongst the Christians, old rivalries re-
emerged: Guy's supporters versus Conrad's, men from Pisa

versus their ancient enemies the Genoans. Richard, having tried and failed to patch everyone together, was more ready than ever for peace, mainly so that he could go home to end his brother John's ambitions to seize the English throne.

Before he could go, there were vital matters to be sorted out: peace was the first; but that depended on the second – the simmering dispute between Guy and Conrad over the kingship of Jerusalem. In early April 1192, Richard, as commander-in-chief, called a council of all the top Christians to resolve the dispute. To his surprise, he discovered that Guy was universally despised, Conrad by far the favourite. He agreed to replace Guy with Conrad, and sent off a messenger to Tyre to tell him so, the messenger being a young man called Henry of Troyes, Count of Champagne. Upon hearing the news, Conrad fell to his knees in joy, and prayed that if he were unworthy of the kingship it should not be given to him. It wasn't, as the result of a piece of high drama that almost at once became the subject of rumour and distortion.

This is one account of what happened.

A few days later, on the evening of 28 April, a Tuesday, Conrad was expecting to have dinner with his pregnant wife Isabella, to whom marriage had made him the future king. She was in her bath. He waited, and waited, until finally, in a fit of impatience, he decided to go and dine with his kinsman and friend, Philip, Bishop of Beauvais, who lived nearby. A quick walk with his bodyguards took him to the bishop's house. But the bishop had already eaten, so Conrad set off home, plus guards, hoping no doubt that Isabella would be ready to join him. Suddenly, rounding a sharp corner and temporarily separated from his guards, he was accosted by two monks, their faces covered by their cowls, one of whom handed him a letter. For a second or two, he was distracted. The other monk stabbed him twice in the side and back. His guards killed one of his attackers, captured the other, and carried Conrad home, dead or dying.

Who was responsible? The captive confessed. The two were not just assassins, but Assassins, with a capital A, employed by their boss, Sinan, the same man who had tried to assassinate Saladin seventeen years before. Ever since then, the Assassins had kept a low profile, strengthening their castles and amassing wealth without bothering anyone. But Conrad had apparently offended Sinan by seizing a ship carrying a cargo that Sinan had bought.

Was the confession true? Was this really just revenge? The timing was strangely coincidental – just after the announcement of Conrad's coming coronation. Rumour quickly spun other explanations. Yes, perhaps Sinan was responsible, not seeking revenge, but in order to forestall a strong Christian state that would limit his freedom of action. Or perhaps Saladin had paid Sinan to kill both Richard and Conrad (unlikely, given the animosity between Saladin and Sinan). Or Richard had paid them (but this made no sense, because he needed to leave Palestine in Conrad's hands). The mystery endures.

What now? At a stroke, or a stab, Jerusalem, which a few days previously had a choice of two kings, now had none. Almost at once, a solution emerged, in the form of the young man who had rushed the news of Conrad's elevation to him and then returned to Acre. The twenty-six-year-old Henry of Troyes was well qualified for kingship. He was a grandson of Eleanor of Aquitaine by her marriage to Louis VII of France, so his mother was half-sister to the kings of both England and

France. They were, if you like, his half-uncles. On his arrival in Acre two years before, he had been given command of the siege. As soon as he heard of Conrad's murder, he returned to Tyre and found that Isabella would see only someone representing either the king of England or the king of France. Young Henry stood for both, and was also wildly popular. Henry himself had his doubts, but Richard had none. Both Isabella and Henry bowed to the pressure. Only a week later the pregnant widow of twenty, already twice married, was married a third time to Henry, who thereby became the new king, and by happy chance the famously good-looking couple fell deeply in love with each other.[66]

For Richard, there remained the problem of the ex-king, Guy. For this too he found a solution. Cyprus, his new possession acquired on his approach to the Holy Land, needed a governor. Guy, with no obvious role to play in Palestine, bought the right to govern it, and there he went in May 1192.

With that problem solved, Richard was keen for a peace settlement with Saladin, for which he could do with a little more leverage. Further down the coast, just over 30 kilometres from Ascalon, was Saladin's most southerly coastal castle, Darum (or Daron, today's Deir al-Balah in the Gaza Strip). It was his last stop before Egypt, in effect a frontier post, and very handy for protecting the coast road. It was not heavily guarded, but it had four towers and good, thick walls

[66] Isabella went on to be very fecund (seven children) and unlucky in her husbands. Henry died in 1197 when he stepped backwards through an open first-floor window. Her fourth husband, Amalric of Jerusalem, died of food poisoning caused by bad fish. She herself died four days later, aged only thirty-four.

which would need undermining. The Crusaders had not yet acquired any expertise in this vital skill, so Richard again hired the renegade miners who had been employed in Acre. The garrison didn't stand a chance. They surrendered after five days, on 28 May. Richard should have been going home, but with all the coast between Darum and Tyre in his hands, suddenly Jerusalem called once again. He moved eastwards, and set up camp halfway between Ascalon and Jerusalem, some 30 kilometres away.

Saladin had been preparing: the walls were strengthened, battle-stations allotted, outlying wells poisoned, spies briefed to report Richard's movements. Reinforcements had arrived, and more were expected from Egypt in the form of a large caravan – 3,000 camels and horses – and a military escort of over 500. But Richard also had his spies, a group of three Bedouin, who kept an eye on the caravan's progress. On 21 June, Richard left camp in force, with 700 cavalry, 1,000 foot-soldiers and 1,000 of the 'Turcopoles', the locally recruited mercenary archers. Saladin feared for the Egyptian caravan, and sent off a detachment to warn them. The commander seems to have bypassed Richard's force, but camped on a hill near the caravan a few kilometres inland between Ascalon and Gaza. The following morning, at dawn on 23 June, just as the caravan had been loaded, Richard struck, scattering camels, horses and troops. It was a walkover. The Christians seized almost everything and almost everyone. Only a few escaped, one being a groom who reported to Saladin later that day. The sultan was appalled – 'no news ever came that grieved his heart more,' wrote Baha al-Din – for now Richard had all the baggage animals and cash to move easily against Egypt. If he did that, Saladin would have to follow, and expose Jerusalem.

But Richard didn't. Jerusalem remained too strong an attraction. Yet, having got himself into position at Bayt Nuba,[67] just 18 kilometres from Jerusalem, he hesitated. The weather was miserable, cold and wet. There was no water to sustain a siege, he was far from supply ships on the coast and Saladin was on home ground, with help close at hand. Watched at a safe distance by Saladin, Richard pulled back.

From the safety of Jaffa, he returned to diplomacy. Saladin was willing to listen. He would allow Latin priests in Jerusalem's Holy Places. He would recognize Henry of Champagne as king of Jerusalem, with his little coastal strip as his kingdom, provided only that Ascalon, newly rebuilt, be dismantled again. At this point negotiations broke down, opening another round of tit-for-tat moves: Richard went to Acre intent on seizing Beirut, from which he would depart; Saladin to Jaffa for a three-day attack which left Christians barricaded in the citadel; Richard back to the rescue in an advance guard of fifty galleys carrying eighty knights, 400 bowmen, 2,000 Italian sailors, and just three horses, with his main force approaching by land. On deck, Richard saw Jaffa apparently in Muslim hands and thought it lost, as the author of the *Itinerarium Peregrinorum* relates:

> and at that moment [Richard] saw a priest plunge into the water and swim towards the royal galley. When he was received on board, he addressed the king with palpitating heart and spirits almost failing him: 'Most noble king, the remnants of our people, waiting your arrival, are exposed like

---

[67] The village which Saladin had himself used in his approach to Jerusalem in 1189. It is now the Israeli settlement of Mevo Horon.

sheep to be slain, unless the divine grace shall bring you to their rescue.'

'Are any of them still alive, then?' asked the king, 'and if so, where are they?'

'There are some of them still alive,' said the priest, 'hemmed in and at the last extremity in front of yonder tower.'

'Please God, then,' replied the king, 'by Whose guidance we have come, we will die with our brave brothers-in-arms, and a cursed light on him who hesitates.'

The word was forthwith given and the galleys were pushed to land. The king, dashing forward into the waves with his thighs unprotected by armour and up to his middle in the water, soon gained footing on the dry strand.

Saladin was talking about surrender terms to Jaffa's leaders when Richard waded ashore at the head of part of his army. His sheer audacity and the ferocity of his attack swung the tide of battle. An aide whispered to Saladin what was happening, but Saladin kept his visitors talking until a mass of fleeing Muslims revealed the truth. The city was reclaimed by the Christians, but Saladin was able to stay where he was, in his camp, undefeated.

Now it was Saladin who was wrong-footed. He sent a message to Richard again proposing peace. Again, they argued over terms; again, Ascalon proved a sticking point; and now Richard's main force had arrived. Saladin attacked with his cavalry, Richard fended them off with spears and volleys of arrows, then headed a counter-charge, all of this going on in full view of Saladin, who was aghast with admiration at Richard's élan. When the king's horse fell wounded, Saladin sent an aide leading two horses as replacements. The battle of Jaffa, the last of the Third Crusade, ended in a draw. Saladin retreated to Jerusalem, leaving Richard to collapse into an exhausted fever.

In the end, it was not further victory or defeat that ended the Crusade, but sheer fatigue. Saladin offered the same terms: give up Ascalon, or there would be no deal – an offer he backed up with a gift of peaches and pears and an ice-cold drink from his store of snow from Mount Hermon. Richard could not go on. He was sick, his troops were tired and his brother John looked likely to seize the English throne. He agreed. Pilgrims could come and go, the Christians would keep their little rump-state – 100 kilometres of coast – well clear of Jerusalem, and Ascalon would remain out of reach, disarmed.

On 2 September, he signed the Treaty of Jaffa, ending the Third Crusade, and so the next day did Saladin. It really was over at last.

A small party of Crusaders made a final visit to Jerusalem, where Saladin gave them an audience, chatting affably with Hubert Walter, bishop of Salisbury, about Richard's virtues and vices (brave, certainly, but lacking wisdom and moderation, in Saladin's opinion). And what, asked Saladin, do they say in England about me and my people? The bishop was the soul of diplomacy: 'My lord, in my humble opinion, if anyone were to bring your virtues into comparison with those of King Richard, and were to take both of you together, there would not be two other men in the world who could compete with you.' After such flattery, Saladin was magnanimous. At the bishop's request, he allowed for four prelates to serve the needs of Christian pilgrims in Jerusalem, Bethlehem and Nazareth. This was not generosity, but pure politics. When the Orthodox asked for an extension of their responsibilities to full control of the Orthodox Church, Saladin refused. Peace depended on every religion and every sect having its fair share, and no more.

The True Cross? He still had it. Queen Tamar of Georgia offered to buy it for 200,000 dinars. He turned her down. He would keep it as a bargaining chip, a 'trump', as he put it, in case of future need.

Richard left on 9 October 1192, to start an adventure that became one of the best-known in English history, in both its factual and legendary versions. It is also a story that spotlights the power of coincidence and the significance of the inter-relationships of Europe's royal families.

A storm forced him into Corfu, which was owned by the Byzantine emperor, Isaac Angelus. After being the victim of extreme violence by crusading Europeans, the Orthodox hated the westerners almost as much as they hated Muslims (more, perhaps, since they had a treaty with Saladin). Fearing arrest, Richard disguised himself as a Templar knight and fled with four aides in a pirate boat that was wrecked on the other side of the Adriatic. On they went, aiming for Saxony and its ruler Henry the Lion, who was his brother-in-law, being married to his sister Matilda. To get there, he had to cross Austria, ruled, as bad luck would have it, by the same Leopold whose flag he had cast down when taking over Acre. Stories about Richard's spiteful act had spread, and so had the rumours connecting him to the murder of Conrad, who, by another unfortunate coincidence, had been Leopold's cousin. So Richard was infamous in Austria. And now it was somehow known that he was on the run.

At an inn near Vienna he was recognized, arrested and delivered to Leopold, who accused him of the murder of Conrad, imprisoned him in Dürnstein castle for three months, then handed him on to the emperor, Henry VI, whose father, Frederick Barbarossa, had been a long-time opponent of Richard's brother-in-law Henry the Lion. The emperor promised to release him in exchange for an oath of vassaldom and an immense ransom – 65,000 silver pounds, as much as the whole Saladin Tithe and over twice the English Crown's annual income. Richard's mother, Eleanor of Aquitaine, the government and the Church taxed, begged, borrowed and seized cash and treasure, while his brother John actually offered half the amount of the ransom to the emperor to keep his prisoner captive. The emperor declined, the ransom was raised and Richard released. He then spent five years fighting in France, never learned English and spent only six months of his life in the country he supposedly ruled. Eventually, he forgave John his treachery and named him heir. He died in 1199, aged forty-two, of gangrene after being hit by a crossbow bolt fired from a rebel French castle. In his magisterial *History of the Crusades,* Steven Runciman sums up Richard's life: 'He was a bad son, a bad husband and a bad king, but a gallant and splendid soldier.'

Much later, a legend arose telling the story of Richard's minstrel, Jean, nicknamed 'Blondel' for his long, blond hair, who supposedly went from castle to castle singing a special song outside each of them as a way of finding his master, until eventually Richard revealed his presence by joining in the song. Details vary, but in any event it's probably nothing but legend: the tale – not mentioned in the *Itinerarium Peregrinorum* (though Richard's capture and imprisonment are) – emerged only seventy years later, and scholars are not sure whether 'Blondel' was Jean I, the father, or his son, Jean II. From the eighteenth century onwards, the story became part of the romance surrounding Richard as portrayed in songs, novels, films and a musical.

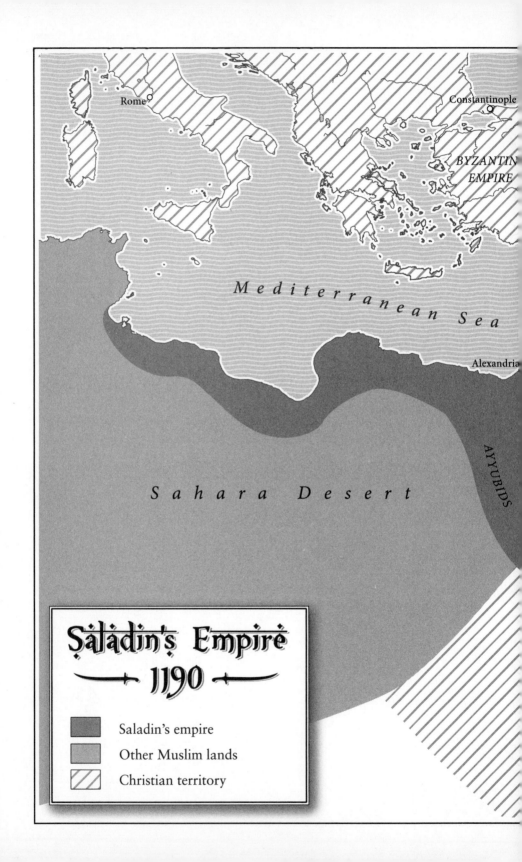

Rome

Constantinople

BYZANTIN
EMPIRE

M e d i t e r r a n e a n   S e a

Alexandria

AYYUBIDS

S a h a r a   D e s e r t

Saladin's Empire
1190

Saladin's empire

Other Muslim lands

Christian territory

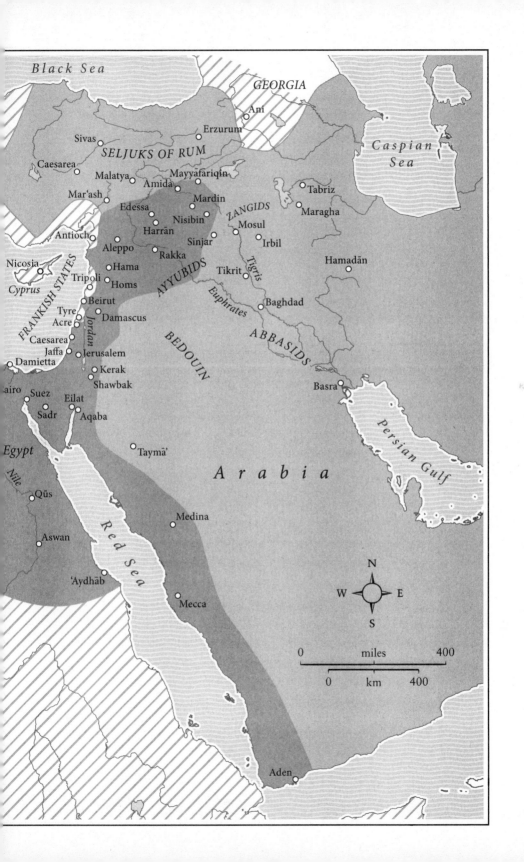

Black Sea

GEORGIA

Ani

Erzurum

Sivas

SELJUKS OF RUM

Caspian
Sea

Caesarea

Malatya

Mayyafariqin

Tabriz

Mar'ash

Amida

Mardin

Edessa

Nisibin

ZANGIDS

Maragha

Harrān

Mosul

Antioch

Rakka

Sinjar

Irbil

Aleppo

Hamadān

Hama

AYYUBIDS

Tikrit

Nicosia

Tripoli

Homs

Cyprus

Beirut

Euphrates

Baghdad

FRANKISH STATES

Tyre

Damascus

ABBASIDS

Acre

Jordan

Caesarea

BEDOUIN

Jaffa

Jerusalem

Damietta

Kerak

Shawbak

Basra

Cairo

Suez

Eilat

Sadr

Aqaba

Persian Gulf

Egypt

Taymā'

Arabia

Nile

Qūs

Medina

Aswan

Red Sea

'Aydhāb

Mecca

N

W   E

S

0   miles   400

0   km   400

Aden

15

Death, and Enduring Life

SALADIN HAD FREED JERUSALEM; BUT THE CHRISTIANS WERE still there, not tossed into the sea. He could do no more. He was fifty-four, old for the times, and tired and ill. All this while, he had hoped to make the pilgrimage to Mecca, and still kept hoping, but duty called him home to Damascus, where he arrived on 4 November 1192.

Next day, he held an audience, 'to which everyone was allowed to come and satisfy their thirst to see him'. The words are those of Baha al-Din, who recorded his master's decline in vivid and painful detail. Saladin's status was that of national hero and saint, a sort of medieval version of Nelson Mandela. 'People of all classes were admitted, and poets recited poems in his praise: "that he spread the wings of Justice over all, and rained down boons on his people from the clouds of his munificence and kindness".' Death was far from Saladin's mind – he worked during the day, and occasionally went hunting gazelles. The mood was more of recuperation than decline.

Actually, this part of Baha al-Din's report was second-hand, because he came to Damascus from Jerusalem only in mid-February 1193, through torrential rain that turned the roads to mud. When Baha arrived, Saladin summoned him through a crowd of officials: 'Never before had his face expressed such satisfaction at the sight of me; his eyes filled with tears, and he folded me in his arms.'

But by now Saladin was a shadow of his former self. There were no more receptions, and he had trouble moving. Once when he was surrounded by some of his younger children, the sight of ambassadors with shaven faces and close-cropped hair made one of the boys cry, so, according to Baha, Saladin dismissed the visitors without hearing what they had to say. '"It's a busy day," he said, in his usual kindly way. Then he added: "Bring me whatever you have ready." They brought him rice cooked in milk and other light refreshments, and he ate them, but without much appetite as it seemed to me.'

Saladin asked about the pilgrimage to Mecca. When Baha said the pilgrims would arrive through the mud the next day, Saladin said he would go and meet them, despite the fact that 'he no longer had the good spirits I knew so well.'

As they rode out together – with people crowding round to get a glimpse of the great man – Baha noticed that Saladin had forgotten his usual cloak. When Baha pointed this out, 'he seemed like a man waking from a dream', and asked for it, but the wardrobe master was not to hand. The incident upset Baha. He thought, 'The Sultan is asking for something he never used to be without, and he cannot get it! . . . I was heavy of heart, for I feared very much for his health.'

That evening and the next day, lassitude and a low-grade fever set the sultan on a downward path. On the fourth day of his illness, his physicians 'thought it necessary to bleed him and from that moment he grew seriously worse.' On the sixth day, he drank some water – too hot, he complained, and then, when he tried the next cup, too cold: '"Oh, God," he said, but not in an angry way, "perhaps there is no one who can make the water at the right temperature." Al-Fadil [Saladin's secretary] and I left him with tears streaming from our eyes, and he said to me, "What a great soul the Muslims will lose! By God, any other man in his place would have thrown the cup at the head of the man who brought it."'

Three days later, Saladin's mind began to wander and he became unconscious. Everyone – his staff, his family, the whole city – knew the end was near. 'It is impossible to give any idea of the sorrow and trouble with which one and all were oppressed . . . When we came out, we used to find the people waiting to gather from the expression of our faces what was the Sultan's state.' A brief moment of conscious-ness, a sip of barley-water, a little perspiration on the legs – tiny signs of life brought temporary hope.

Saladin's son and heir, al-Afdal, caused consternation by demanding that the Syrian emirs take an oath of loyalty to Saladin, each one pledging 'from this moment forth, with single aim and unflinching purpose . . . consecrating to his service my life and wealth, my sword and my men, as long as he lives, and afterwards I will keep the same faith with his son', swearing to God, failure being punished by enforced divorce, sale of slaves and a barefoot pilgrimage to Mecca. Some agreed, some refused outright, some agreed if they were assured of their estates. It left a bad feeling: oaths are not demanded by the strong.

On the evening of Tuesday, 3 March (27 Safer in the Muslim calendar), the twelfth night of his undefined illness, 'he remained sometimes with us, sometimes wandering'. A sheikh stayed with him all night, reading from the Quran. Saladin died around dawn the following morning, the 4th. 'I was reciting the Divine Word to him,' reported the sheikh to Baha al-Din, 'and had just reached the great verse 59:22, *He is God; there is no god but He. He is the knower of the Unseen and the Visible; He is the All-merciful, the All-compassionate*, and I heard him say – God have mercy on him – "It is true!" And this at the time of his passing away, and it was a sign of God's favour to him.'

Could it have been so perfect? Well, the truth in these circumstances is more about what is fitting than about facts. The same sheikh gave a slightly different version, equally perfect, to others – that he was reading 9:129, *Allah is sufficient for me, there is no god but He; in Him I have put my trust*, when Saladin smiled, his face grew radiant and he went in peace.

Either way, it inspired Baha al-Din. Never since the time of the first khalifs had Islam suffered such a blow, he wrote. God alone could fathom the intensity of the grief. 'I had often heard people say they would lay down their lives for that of someone very dear to them, but I thought it was only a manner of speaking . . . but I swear before God that had we been asked that day "Who will redeem the Sultan's life?" there were several of us who would have replied by offering his own.'

The body was washed and put in its shroud. 'All the products used for this purpose had to be borrowed, for the Sultan possessed nothing of his own.' Baha al-Din was asked to watch, but could not bring himself to do so. The coffin was carried in, draped with a piece of striped cloth, and carried out through the wailing crowd to the palace where the sultan had spent his last days. Since he had not had either the time or the will to arrange the building of a mausoleum for himself, he was buried in the *soffa* (summerhouse).

A few months later, al-Afdal sent an embassy to al-Nasir, the caliph in Baghdad, to obtain recognition that he, al-Afdal, was Saladin's true heir. He sent along Saladin's sword, coat of mail and other war equipment, and a letter in praise of his father, which ran in part:

> It was he who subjugated the infidel princes and placed a chain around their necks; he who captured the fiends of idolatry and bound them with heavy bonds; who subdued the worshippers of the Cross and broke their backs; who unified the Believers, preserved them, and put their affairs in order; who closed our borders, directing our affairs with a sure hand; humiliated every enemy outside your august house.

Next door to the Umayyad mosque, al-Afdal had a domed building built with a window so that the people could look out over a small, square, domed mausoleum into which his father's coffin was moved two years after his death. The historian ibn Khallikan recorded that the coffin was inscribed with the date of Saladin's death, and these words: 'Almighty God! Let his soul be acceptable to thee and open the gates of Paradise; that being the last conquest for which he hoped.'

And what of the True Cross, the symbol of what the Christians had been fighting for, the loss of which had deprived them of hope at Hattin? After Saladin's death, his son al-Afdal sent it to the ungrateful caliph in Baghdad. In 1221, it was supposed to be returned to the Christians as part of the peace that ended the Fifth Crusade, but, in Runciman's words, 'when the time came for its surrender, it could not be found.' No one has heard of it since.

16

A Brief History of Leadership

HERO AND 'UNIFIER' OF ISLAM, THE LEADER WHO CRUSHED the Crusaders and reclaimed Jerusalem, admired by followers and enemies alike, admired then, admired now: what was Saladin's secret?

The answers involve more than biography and the history of the period. It is possible to draw on other examples and other ideas of great leadership, and on modern psychology and leadership theory.

One key to his success was that he combined two styles of leadership, exercising what modern theorists call hard and soft power. Several times in history leadership has been equated with the ruthless exercise of power. One exponent was Lord Shang, writing in China in about 400 BC. He advised that for those who rule might is right, power everything. Human beings are idle, greedy, cowardly, treacherous, foolish and shifty. The only way to deal with them is to entice, terrify, reward and punish. He was writing when China was divided between seven warring states. Two thousand years later, Machiavelli was confronted by similar circumstances, Renaissance Italy's warring mini-states, and argued that without the ruthless – indeed cynical, even deceptive – exercise of power there is no state, no guarantee of peace, no possibility of progress.

Saladin might have taken the same hard-power approach across the board, imposing his will on Shia and Sunni alike, then turning with unremitting ruthlessness on the Crusaders. But he didn't. He mixed force with persuasion. Such subtlety makes him seem an exemplar of modern leadership. It's not quite that simple, because he was also capable of brutal acts. It was the combination that made him so effective.

But where did that come from?

It has become a cliché of leadership theory that the quality we should be looking for in a great leader is 'charisma'. Originally, a charisma (or 'charism', as the *OED* puts it, without the 'a') was any 'gift or favour specially vouchsafed by God; a grace, a talent', such as the power of healing or prophecy. It has the same root as 'charity', the divine gift of generosity. It was the German political philosopher Max Weber (1864–1920) who popularized the word as the quality 'by virtue of which [a person] is set apart (originally by prophets, healers, law-givers, hunting-leaders or war-heroes) and seen as possessing supernatural, superhuman, or at least in some way exceptional powers or qualities not available to anyone else. These powers are regarded as of divine origin or as exemplary, and on this basis he is treated as "leader".'[68]

There is a problem here: if charisma is magical, or the result of divine inspiration, it explains nothing. It's tautological, like saying 'he's a leader because he's a leader'. What we are after is understanding: *how* did he become charismatic?

One key almost certainly lay in Saladin's childhood, about which we know nothing. In an article in the *Harvard Business Review* devoted to leadership, the psychoanalyst Manfred Kets de Vries comments on business leaders: 'They can't be too crazy or they generally don't make it to senior positions, but they are nonetheless extremely driven people. And when I analyse them, I usually find that their drives spring from childhood patterns and experiences that have carried over into adulthood.'[69] The successful leader carries enough insecurity to inspire a desire to change the world, and enough of a sense of security to confront this challenge without lapsing into paranoia, criminality or any number of behaviour patterns that undermine his aims.

I once interviewed a number of survivors for TV and radio, about twenty-five of them. They were all people who had endured terrible experiences, yet come through well psychologically, as opposed to others who were left with debilitating emotional scars. It seemed to me that what they shared was

---

[68] *Wirtschaft und Gesellschaft*, 1922; translated as *Theory of Social and Economic Organization*. Chapter 3 on 'The Nature of Charismatic Authority and its Routinization' translated by A. R. Anderson and Talcot Parsons, 1947.

[69] Diane L. Coutu, 'Putting Leaders on the Couch: A Conversation with Manfred F. R. Kets de Vries'; see Bibliography.

a belief that the universe is fundamentally a supportive place, that it rewards action, and that any setback is a challenge to be overcome. Insecurity in early childhood can act like acid, eating away at this foundation, destroying the very basis of survival, simply because a setback becomes a symbol of a malevolent universe that will get you in the end, undermining your will to fight. Security – whether provided by parents, or a wider family, or a group, or a class system, or education – gives a foundation for independence, self-confidence, and possibly leadership.

Young Saladin seems to have had that crucial balance between security and insecurity – the immediate security of family and religion, the wider insecurity of religious strife, Sunni versus Shia, Islam versus Christianity, local leaders versus each other. His father Ayyub is described as kind, upright and generous. Saladin would have grown up 'resilient', in a term favoured by modern psychologists. Meaning what exactly? Here are some of the traits identified in a range of studies that tend to 'promote resilience':[70]

- problem-solving skills
- social competence
- a sense of purpose
- an ability to stay removed from family discord
- an ability to look after oneself
- high self-esteem
- an ability to form close personal relationships

[70] Summarized in Russell Hurd, 'A teenager revisits her father's death during childhood'; see Bibliography.

- a positive outlook
- focused nurturing – i.e. a supportive home life
- a well-structured household
- high but achievable expectations from parents

In *Outliers*, his book analysing what it takes to make highly successful people, Malcolm Gladwell points out that one key element is a mentor, a guiding light, someone who provides both an example and a helping hand. If his father provided an example of good behaviour, Saladin's two mentors were his hard-fighting uncle Shirkuh and Nur al-Din, ruler of Aleppo and Mosul, anti-Crusader, would-be unifier of Islam, Saladin's master and employer, the man who gave him the chance to seize power in Egypt. Without these two – the one a campaigner, the other a ruler – Saladin might have remained insignificant.

So he was programmed for leadership. What now? The first and most vital element for a leader is the agenda, the vision, about which today's leaders and leadership theorists talk a good deal. An inspiring vision is a rare combination of the right circumstances, the right vision and the right person, who must dream it up, communicate it and get followers to believe in it. You can only get so far by brute force. Even China's First Emperor, though unremittingly ruthless, had a vision: national unity the better to fight off the 'northern barbarians'. Far better than mere brutality is to have a Noble Cause, something bigger than the leader himself.

In Saladin's case, the vision was an Islamic world free from the non-Islamic, anti-Islamic outsiders. As Daniel Goleman comments, leaders with vision 'exude resonance: They have genuine passion for their mission, and that passion is contagious.'[71] In his vision, Saladin had two great advantages. Firstly, the cause had been in the air for a generation, since the arrival of the Franks on the First Crusade in 1098. He did not have to invent it, but apply it. Secondly, when rallying support among wary rivals, it is always useful to be able to direct attention on to foreigners. Xenophobia works, especially in conjunction with a higher purpose.

Another prime element of his leadership was his readiness to share adversity. The nature of revolutionary leadership demands it. In the words of James MacGregor Burns, 'The leaders must be absolutely dedicated to the cause and able to demonstrate that commitment by giving time and effort to it, risking their lives, undergoing imprisonment, exile, persecution and continual hardship.' Saladin campaigned, fought, risked his life and almost died from disease. Shared suffering does not guarantee success, and many a brave, misguided leader has died in vain, forgotten; but a refusal to share suffering is an almost certain guarantee of failure. Saladin is in good company. Successful revolutionary leaders who suffered for their cause and followers include Alexander, Jesus, Muhammad, Genghis Khan, Mao, Lenin, Castro and Mandela.

Many leaders have known how to inspire by combining present suffering with a noble cause. Witness Churchill on 13 May 1940, after just three days as prime minister, and three days after the German invasion of Belgium and Holland. France would soon fall. Britain would stand alone. He told his Cabinet: 'I have nothing to offer but blood, toil, tears and sweat.' He repeated that phrase later in the day when he asked the House of Commons for a vote of confidence in his

---

[71] *The New Leaders* (UK), *Primal Leadership* (US). See Bibliography.

new all-party government, and added grim, inspiring words – inspiring because of their grimness. Saladin might have made similar speeches to rouse his troops:

> We have before us an ordeal of the most grievous kind. We have before us many, many long months of struggle and of suffering. You ask, what is our policy? I can say: It is to wage war, by sea, land and air, with all our might and with all the strength that God can give us; to wage war against a monstrous tyranny, never surpassed in the dark, lamentable catalogue of human crime. That is our policy. You ask, what is our aim? I can answer in one word: It is victory, victory at all costs, victory in spite of all terror, victory, however long and hard the road may be.

One other benefit of sharing hardship is that it is impossible for both leader and followers to deny harsh facts. For military commanders and corporate leaders alike, seeing, telling and absorbing the unpleasant truth is an important part of retaining morale, for there is nothing so destructive as optimism that is constantly confounded by events. Poor leaders hide limitations and lay claim to genius, often with ludicrous results. Mussolini was 'always right', Idi Amin proclaimed himself Conqueror of the British Empire. Great leaders acknowledge inadequacies and seek to make them good. In his analysis of what makes good companies great, leadership expert Jim Collins concludes: 'There is a sense of exhilaration that comes in facing head-on the hard truths and saying, "We will never give up. We will never capitulate. It may take a long time, but we *will* find a way to prevail".'

Related to Saladin's readiness to share adversity were two

other qualities. First, his austerity. This is rare in leaders. Few can resist the urge to collect riches. Part of Genghis Khan's appeal was his refusal to do so, adopting the guise of a simple Daoist sage: 'In the clothes I wear or the meats I eat, I have the same rags and the same food as the cowherd or the groom.' Saladin too considered his followers before himself, so much so that in death he had nothing to his name. Baha al-Din says his treasury held just 47 dirhems and one gold piece. 'He left neither goods, nor house, nor real estate, neither garden, nor village, nor cultivated land, nor any other species of property.'

To this must be added his integrity. He kept his word. Lord Shang and Machiavelli were all for duplicity, if it served the leader's purpose. That was not Saladin's way. Keeping promises is a fundamental attribute of good leadership, for without it the trust of allies and those further down the chain of command vanishes, morale plummets, concerted action becomes impossible, creating what Daniel Goleman refers to as a 'toxic organization', in which 'resonance' gives way to 'dissonance'.

All these qualities combine to strengthen morale. Someone who gave the matter of morale much thought was General Sir William Slim, who in 1943 was faced with restoring the morale of Britain's 14th Army after the Japanese drove it out of Burma into India. As he recounts in his book *Defeat Into Victory*, 'morale is a state of mind', which must be created on three levels: spiritual, intellectual and material. By 'spiritual' he was referring not to religious fervour, but to belief in a 'great and noble cause', that must be tackled at once with aggression, by every man, each of whom must feel his actions have a direct bearing on the outcome. Intellectually, they must feel that the object is attainable, that their group is efficient, and that their leaders are to be trusted. Finally, they must feel they are provided for materially, with the tools for the job, in both weapons and conditions. This is virtually a blueprint for almost every force facing apparently overwhelming odds (not, however, for those few unusual cases in which men see a greater virtue in self-sacrifice than in victory: Japan's kamikaze pilots, today's Islamic suicide bombers).

Thanks to Shirkuh and Nur al-Din, Saladin's career took off in Egypt. He was there supposedly to establish Nur al-Din's authority. Egypt's wealth would provide a basis for unifying Islam and confronting the Crusaders. But no one foresaw the consequences – that Saladin would gain the experience he needed to take power for himself and emerge as Nur al-Din's rival. To do this he exercised the most basic of his leadership skills: ruthlessness. He fought the Franks, collaborated in the murder of the vizier Shawar, built up a formidable army, bullied the young caliph into naming him vizier with power to command both the government and armed forces (including its fleet, the only Muslim one in the region).

His new position presented problems. Sunni Syrians and Shi'ite Egyptians were old rivals. Each despised the other. Saladin could not rule by charm, or by claiming legitimacy, but by force and duplicity. He engineered plots, arrested and tortured the plotters, dismissed troublesome rank-and-file members of the Egyptian army and palace guards – black troops and black eunuchs who formed a non-Egyptian minority. At a stroke he rid himself of a danger, without antagonizing the majority. That came later, when he imposed Sunni practices – but by then he had donned the mantle of

Islam's protector against the Frankish threat. On this basis, he put an end to the Fatimid caliphate, scattered the caliph's library, divided Cairo's palaces among his family, crushed revolts – even crucified two ringleaders in central Cairo – and spread his control to Yemen, all to ensure that he was master of Egypt. These are the acts of a leader more devoted to force than subtlety.

But now what? Egypt's wealth was the key to conquest, but the door was Syria. Only from Syria could the Franks be confronted. It was obvious that he was a rival to his master, Nur al-Din. There could have been civil war – except that the two shared the same vision, and both held back for three years. Then Nur al-Din's death gave Saladin a chance to claim his former master's realm. This would not be easy, because major cities – Damascus, Aleppo, Mosul, Homs, Hama, Baalbek – were held by Nur al-Din's heirs or allies. It was now that Saladin's skill in exercising soft power came to the fore. Considering himself well qualified to take over by his record of conquest, anti-Crusader campaigning, wealth and power, he had to usurp, while pretending deference to Nur al-Din's lineage. There was no point forcing himself on those cities and regions whose support he needed, if by doing so he turned them from rivals into enemies on a par with his real enemies, the Crusaders. If he besieged a city, he had to do so with a hand tied behind his back. If he won a battle, he took care not to pursue, slaughter and pillage. He often wrote to the caliph in Baghdad, asking for his backing, pointing out what he had achieved – ending Ismaili rule in Egypt, struggling against Shi'ism. Why, no one was better qualified to rule and take on the Franks – all, of course, as the humble instrument of Allah.

It took ten years of steps forward, steps back, negotiations, appeals, shows of force followed by displays of magnanimity, but in the end it worked. The caliph granted him a 'diploma of investiture', exhorting him to respect justice, surround himself with honest men, govern without violence – but also to pursue jihad and reconquer lost territories. There were limits – the caliph did not want Saladin approaching Baghdad, and there would be no money. But Saladin was free to turn his unified army against the Crusaders. He had the legitimacy he sought.

Success went only briefly to his head, for his ambitions were even more imperial. He dreamed of wider conquests – Iraq, Turkey, north Africa – even on occasion of spreading Islam to Europe. But this dream was a mistake. The first steps took him away from his main target, the Crusader states and Jerusalem. Fate stopped him, in the form of the fever that almost killed him. More by luck than judgement, he survived, to return to jihad.

Perhaps the most remarkable aspect of his soft leadership was that he applied it in his dealings with his enemies. He probed, retreated, consulted, negotiated, agreed, kept promises, exchanged and released prisoners, changed his mind, dealt courteously with Christian women. He acted like this partly because that was his character, partly because it worked. Negotiation often saves fruitless fighting and unnecessary losses. If xenophobia works in conquest, clemency works in victory. If you do not humiliate an enemy, you will not drive him into permanent hostility. Integrity paid off. 'If we refuse what we have promised and are not generous with the benefits,' he said once, 'no one will ever trust us again.'

Saladin was not always great and good; he was not always successful; many of his successes were reversed; but it is remarkable that he clung to the virtues of good leadership, resisted the evils of poor leadership, and achieved as much as he did. That is why he is an object of admiration today.

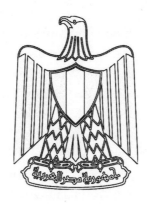

17

Legacy: A Glowing Image,
a Grim Reality

LONDON'S IMPERIAL WAR MUSEUM HAS MANY OBJECTS FROM
many wars. But there are some things that just don't fit with
weapons and battle-scenes. On the third floor, a certain
corridor displays a small collection of such curiosities. One
is a bronze wreath of laurel leaves which sports a number
of Arabic inscriptions, many little eagles and a monogram
made up of the initials IRWII. The story behind this strange
object makes an unlikely link between four people: Saladin, a
Turkish sultan, Kaiser Wilhelm of Germany and Lawrence of
Arabia. It also reveals a good deal about Saladin's reputation
in both the West and the world of Islam.

Though hero-worshipped by Muslims at his death, Saladin was shortly afterwards forgotten, ignored, and disparaged for reasons we will get to later. Only in the late nineteenth century, with the rise of nationalism and Islamic internationalism, did Saladin once again become a Muslim hero. First off the mark was Abdul Hamid II, sultan of Turkey from 1876. As part of his despotic attempt to re-knit the decaying fabric of the Ottoman Empire, of which Syria was still a part, he claimed Saladin as his model. For Abdul Hamid, the European powers were latter-day Crusaders, busy tearing at the flanks of Islam and his empire. To symbolize his self-proclaimed role as saviour of his empire and Islam's new unifier, he 'restored' the mausoleum and saved Saladin's decaying wooden coffin by encasing it in marble.

Next to take an interest in the tomb was Germany's Kaiser, Wilhelm II, in 1898. This had nothing to do with Saladin, and everything to do with European politics. Wilhelm's Germany was on the rise. It faced enemies to east and west – Russia and France – and needed allies. The Turks had long feared that Russia wanted to dominate the Bosporus, because that was her gateway for her navy to get from the Black Sea through the Mediterranean to the Atlantic. Culturally, Germany and Turkey had nothing much in common. Politically and militarily, they had lots. So during a whirlwind trip around the empire, the Kaiser took in Damascus and the mausoleum, where, according to his aide Ernst Freiherr von Mirbach, there were two wooden coffins, one being Saladin's, the other that of an unnamed vizier.

At a banquet that evening Wilhelm as good as inferred that Abdul Hamid, pan-Islamist that he had become, was Saladin reborn. The Kaiser offered his thanks, he said, 'moved by the thought of standing on the place where there tarried one of the most chivalrous rulers of all time, the great sultan Saladin, a fearless, blameless knight who often had to instruct his followers in the correct ways of knighthood.'[72] He finished: 'May the Sultan and may the three hundred million Muslims – who, living scattered over the earth, honour him as their caliph – be assured of this: that the German Kaiser will be their friend for ever.'

Next day, he laid flowers on the tomb and promised to pay for a new one. His odd contribution to the mauso-leum is still there – a very un-Islamic sarcophagus of white marble, which, as a plaque says, is empty. Saladin's remains supposedly lie alongside, in the tomb restored by Abdul Hamid, which is covered in green cloth embroidered with Quranic verses. What happened to the 'vizier' is a mystery. Today's visitors crowding into the little mausoleum, only a few metres square, admire the purity of its coloured marble walls and high white dome, but many must surely wonder why Islam's hero needs two coffins. It may also occur to some that there is no certainty that Saladin is actually there, in the fabric-draped sarcophagus. Only by opening it will we know. Frankly, that's not about to happen.

Wilhelm also left another reminder of his presence: the bronze wreath that now resides in the Imperial War Museum. The scattering of little eagles are German imperial eagles, the monogram IRWII is made from the initials of Imperator Rex (Emperor-King) Wilhelm II.

Now for the final link. The wreath lay on Saladin's tomb

---

[72] The phrase 'fearless, blameless knight' was a reference to the pan-European medieval ideal of knightly perfection: *der Ritter ohne Furcht und Tadel, le Chevalier sans Peur et sans Reproche.*

for twenty years, surviving the turmoil that replaced Abdul Hamid with a new revolutionary government in 1908. In 1918, Lawrence of Arabia, leading light in the British-backed Arab insurgency against the Ottoman Empire, arrived in Damascus a few hours after it fell to British imperial troops (in fact Australians). Here he helped establish a provisional Arab government under his friend and co-insurgent Emir Feisal, soon to become king of Iraq. According to one story, Feisal presented Lawrence with the Kaiser's wreath to symbolize the supposedly imminent end of European imperialism in Arabia. On his return to England, Lawrence presented it to the museum. Lawrence, who liked to dramatize things, had a slightly different version of what happened. The museum records that in his 'deposit note', he claimed to have removed the wreath himself from the sarcophagus 'as Saladin no longer required it'.

This tale raises questions. Why did Muslims forget about Saladin for 500 years? Why did they resurrect him? And why did Christian Europeans, who were otherwise eager to dismiss Islam, never falter in their admiration?

Let's first take the fall and rise of his reputation in the Muslim world.

One reason for his demotion was that, in the cold light of history, he did not succeed in his aims. He wanted to free the Middle East of the Crusaders (and even dreamed of spreading Islam to Europe, a sort of reverse Crusade). But in this he failed. Jerusalem was taken and the Franks were down, but not out. They retained Acre and much of the Syrian coast, enough to stage a comeback and retake Jerusalem fifteen years later. The Crusaders were not finally thrown out until 1291, almost a century after Saladin's death, by the Mamluk rulers of Egypt – who, incidentally, also threw out the Mongols, a far greater threat than the Crusaders had ever been.

Secondly, successor dynasties in both Egypt and Syria had agendas of their own, and lasted much longer. Saladin's dynasty, the Ayyubids, ruled for seventy-six years in Egypt and eighty-six in Syria, whereas the Mamluks of Egypt were in power for two and a half centuries and the Turks, after their seizure of Constantinople in 1254, created the Ottoman Empire that would last into the twentieth century. It is virtually a law of history that new dynasties disparage those they displace. In addition, they liked to celebrate heroes and epic struggles of their own, against both the Franks and the Mongols.

Thirdly, Saladin was not quite the unifier he seems at first glance. There was no doubting his piety, of course. He eliminated taxes that did not conform to Islamic law, rebuilt mosques, founded *madrasas* – nine in Cairo, a dozen in Damascus – defended the caliphate, fought heresy, did much for the poor, and encouraged pilgrims. But all this was done in the name of his own brand of Islam, Sunnism, and at the expense of its great rival, Shi'ism, the predominant creed in Egypt. There was some justification for this: from Egyptian Shi'ism had sprung the Assassins and their murderous agenda, which threatened the life of any less extreme ruler. But Saladin imposed his own beliefs in other ways. For example, he restored the Shi'ite sanctuary in Cairo that sheltered the head of al-Husain, the son of Muhammad's son-in-law, Ali. The head had been rescued from Ascalon in the mid-twelfth century to save it from the Franks. Saladin created 'a mausoleum so superb as to be beyond description', in the words of ibn Jubayr, decorating it with brocades, and silver and gilt candlesticks, its upper part 'encircled by golden spheres like apples, skilfully executed to resemble a garden and holding our eyes in spell by its beauty.' This in effect hijacked the shrine for Sunnism. In Islamic eyes, Saladin was less a unifier than a dictator imposing his will, and Shi'ites – some 15 per cent of Muslims – have never forgiven him.

There is no such long-term ambivalence in the European – that is, the Christian – view.

Yes, to start with he was the enemy who was committed to driving the Christians from the land they considered holy, theirs by right as the homeland of the fount and origin of their faith. To them, it was self-evident that the Muslims were wrong, that Saladin was illegitimate, treacherous, cruel, low-born, tyrannical and utterly evil; that they were right and that God was behind them at every step: taxes, military preparations, campaigns, the lot, all the way to total Christian control of Jerusalem and the rest of the Holy Land. For two Crusades, faith ruled supreme, breeding arrogance and brutality.

Then, suddenly, within a century of Saladin's death, everything flipped. Saladin's successes revealed that God was not on the Christian side after all. How to explain this reversal? Christians had the answer, embedded in the concept of sin. They had fallen short in some way. They were guilty, they deserved to be punished. What better punishment than defeat by their enemy? Saladin was God's instrument, sent to scourge Christians back into the ways of righteousness, as if he were the penance imposed on a sinful people – the '*flagellum*

Christianorum', the Scourge of Christians, as the thirteenth-century chronicler and cardinal Oliver of Paderborn called him.

This, by the way, was not the only time those who claimed to be civilized explained away victorious 'barbarians'. Attila, the most successful of the many barbarian chiefs tearing at the flanks of the Roman Empire in the fifth century, was also called God's Scourge. And when Genghis Khan fell upon the Islamic world in 1219, not long after Saladin's day, the thirteenth-century Muslim historian Ata-Malik Juvaini says that Genghis told Bukhara's wealthiest and most eminent citizens, 'If you had not committed great sins, God would not have sent a punishment like me upon you.' Juvaini was writing with hindsight, for his masters the Mongols, justifying their brutality and success by blaming the victims.

But wait: Saladin was not a Christian. How could he possibly be the instrument of a Christian God? Again, an answer was to hand, a twofold one. Firstly, he displayed obvious virtues, like courage, courtesy, generosity – *Milte*, generosity of spirit, as the medieval German poet Walther von der Vogelweide put it – austerity and forgiveness. These were more in line with the ideals of Christian chivalry than the base qualities of a pagan barbarian. So it stood to reason that he was not a true Muslim, but a closet Christian, knighted (according to one of several accounts) by Humphrey of Toron. Several stories actually proposed that he had French ancestors. Others say that he baptized himself; that he travelled incognito through Europe, undergoing many adventures;[73] that various monks, even Francis of Assisi himself, came

---

[73] Christians have a similar legend about Jesus: 'And did those feet in ancient time/Walk upon England's mountains green ?' No, they didn't. But that doesn't diminish the appeal of the myth.

to the Holy Land to convert him. All this was the stuff of
good drama, making Saladin a near-equal to England's hero,
Richard the Lionheart.

Adventures apart, Saladin struck a chord in Europe because
his generosity offered a way to resolve a problem much
pondered by those who were not totally in thrall to
Christianity: the three major religions – Islam, Christianity
and Judaism – overlapped in their histories, ideals and ways
of life. How could one choose between them?

One story, which existed in many versions, had Saladin
wondering on his deathbed which of the three main religions
was the best, and summoning the wisest priests of all three
so that he could question them. In the words of a thirteenth-
century Latin version:[74]

'Mine,' says the Jew, 'but if I abandoned it I would adopt
Christianity, which is its heir.'

'Mine,' says the Saracen, 'but if I abandoned it, I would
adopt Christianity, which is its heir.'

'Mine,' says the Christian, 'and I would not abandon it at
any price.'

Then says Saladin: 'Those two, if they abandoned their
faith, agree they would adopt this one's; but he would never
have any other but his own; so I judge this to be the best, and
choose it.'

Here is another very different approach to the question of
the truth of the three religions. It is by a thirteenth-century
Viennese chronicler and poet called Jans der Enikel, Jans 'the

---

[74] Quoted in Gaston Paris, *La Légende de Saladin*, 1893.

Grandson'. His main work was a world history in 30,000 lines of verse, much copied in its day, now virtually unknown. It starts with Satan being cast from Heaven, runs through the Bible and merges into a mish-mash of pseudo-history, folk-lore and Chaucer-like stories. Graeme Dunphy, Professor of Translation at the University of Applied Sciences of Würzburg-Schweinfurt, has recently produced an edited version and a translation. One 125-line segment tells the story of Saladin's table, a symbol of whatever underlies the three religions that dominated the thoughts of many Europeans during and after the Crusades. Where lies the truth, and what should be done about it? Jans's response is rather unexpected, given that his listeners were Christians. Saladin – generous, austere, curious – struggles to find an answer, but fails:[75]

> I really cannot keep this from you: I want to tell you about a King, whose name was Saladin. Truly he could not have been more generous. He gave stallions, and robes, the best that could be found on sale. Silver, gold and gemstones, all of these he gave. His generosity was not feigned for the sake of honour, for he kept only one table for himself. It was made of a gigantic sapphire, the likes of which no one had ever seen, more valuable than a ruby. No treasure could be better than this same table was. I have seen its length written: it was three cubits long. It was set in a frame of gold, as if God himself had perfected it.

---

[75] The original is in verse, with very short lines. It begins:
Ich kann iu wærlich niht verdagen   I really cannot keep this from you:
Von einem künig wil ich iu sagen   I want to tell you about a King,
Der was geheizen Salatin   whose name was Saladin.
I have run it as prose to make it read more easily in modern English.

The gentleman was generous, so they say, so generous that he had nothing left. He distributed his whole treasure. As generous as this gentleman was, he fell sick and did not recover. When he became aware of his illness, he sent for the best doctors and had them check a urine sample. They all declared that he certainly could not recover, and would definitely die. Then he was sorely lamented, the whole population in chorus lamented for him so utterly that I cannot put it into words.

When the pious heathen saw that he would have to leave his honour and his wealth, his heart was sad, for he was dissatisfied with his life. He said: 'If I must now depart, I must ask what will happen to my soul? Who will take care of it when it departs from my body? If I entrust it to Mohammed, the Christians will mock; they say that their Lord God is stronger than Mohammed. And I know full well that the Jews are quick to say that their God is stronger. This is a sorry state of affairs. If only I knew for sure which of them is the best, to that God would I give my table without a moment's hesitation. Since I cannot know which is right and I mistrust all of them, I shall divide that whole gemstone between them – I mean that table of mine.'

He had the table brought before him. And I can tell you the truth of the matter: an axe was prepared. No more time was wasted, he had the table neatly split into three parts. At once he gave one part to his God Mohammed, the second part – honestly! – he gave to the Christians' God: the third part in truth he gave to the God of the Jews. He said: 'Whichever of them is strongest, let him take away my worries, for I cannot know better than that.'

Thus spoke the righteous man. With that, his soul departed.

Saladin as knight became a popular motif. He appears in a minor French poem of the early fourteenth century, *Le Pas Saladin*, which tells of a battle between Christians and Saracens for a narrow pass. The Christians are victorious and Saladin retreats, not however because he is overwhelmed but because, being a knight imbued with the ideals of chivalry, he does not want to cause the death of other knights. He generously frees his impoverished captive, King Guy, without a ransom being paid. It was a popular tale, in several versions, one being a play still liked well enough decades later to be performed for the eighteen-year-old queen Isabel of Bavaria – wife of the French king Charles VI – when she made a lavish state entry into Paris in 1389. The historian Jean Froissart was there to record the scene (in this sixteenth-century translation by the soldier and statesman John Bourchier):

> On the stage was ordained the pass of king Saladin, and all their deeds in personages, the Christen-men on the one part and the Saracens on the other part, armed with such armour as they then used . . . The personage on the stage of King Richard . . . went to the French king and demanded licence to go and assail the Saracens; and the King gave him leave. Then King Richard returned to his twelve companions; then they all went and assailed the king Saladin and the Saracens . . . There in sport there seemed a great battle, and it endured a good space. This pageant was well regarded.

But it was Saladin's virtues – his generosity, his magnanimity – that captured the European imagination more than his fighting skills. In Italy, the legend of Saladin's virtue took root, partly based on the account of his death, according to which he died with hardly a penny to his name and left nothing but his burial shroud. In many versions, one of his subjects parades the shroud through his realm suspended on a lance, proclaiming this to be the only object to accompany his master in death.

Dante, writing in the early fourteenth century, twice mentions Saladin and his austerity. His *Convivio* (*The Banquet*) is a sort of philosophical compendium in verse and prose. One section discusses the dangers of wealth and the rewards of generosity, considered a prime virtue among poets and philosophers, perhaps because they stood to benefit. This is what he writes, in a condensed version:

> I say then, 'It is evident that riches are imperfect, and base as well, for however great they are, they bring no peace, but rather grief.' How fair an exchange does he make who gives of these most imperfect things in order to have and acquire things that are perfect, such as are the hearts of worthy men! Who does not still keep a place in his heart for Alexander because of his royal acts of benevolence? Who does not keep a place for Saladin?

A few years later, in his *Divine Comedy*, Dante grants Saladin a place among the virtuous non-Christians in the First Circle of Hell, along with a host of great pre-Christian figures, among them Dante's guide, Virgil. Why are they here? Virgil explains: they have not sinned, but were not baptized and did not know Christ, and therefore did not worship in the right way.

For this defect, and for no other guilt,
We here are lost. In this alone we suffer;
Cut off from hope, we live on in desire.

And there, among the great and good, 'I noticed Saladin', *solo in parte*, by himself alone. Why alone? Perhaps because, of all those named, he is the only one who in life was a near contemporary, and close enough to Christians to have been baptized – but was not, and so remains in limbo.

Meanwhile, the matter of how to identify the one true faith had seeded, propagated and flowered. A story had arisen long before in Persia of a prince who, when entreated by his three beautiful daughters to say which he loved the most, gave them each a wonderful ring in secret, so that each believed herself the best-beloved. The story spread, and changed. The rich man becomes the caliph, the ring becomes a pearl, which evolves into a symbol of True Religion, and at last it migrates to Europe, where daughters become sons and the pearl becomes a ring again, and the story absorbs that of Saladin's table, turning into a fable about religious toleration.

This is the version in the 100 stories told by Boccaccio in his *Decameron* around 1350. Saladin runs out of money. Melchizedek, a Jew, has money enough to cover the shortfall, but Saladin believes he will not lend it fairly. Saladin tries to trick Melchizedek into giving offence (and justifying the seizure of his wealth) by asking him which is the true word of God: Judaism, Christianity or Islam? Melchizedek evades the trap by telling the story of a merchant who had a precious ring and three virtuous sons. Having promised the ring (and, with it, his estate) to all three, the king had two equally precious copies made and gave one ring to each son. Thus it could not be determined who was heir to the estate. Likewise, it cannot be determined which faith is the truth. Saladin gets his loan and repays it, and Melchizedek gains Saladin's respect. In this form, the story entered the European imagination, where it inspired numerous versions for the next three centuries.

This humanist view found expression in another cycle of stories, which suggested that the major religions were not truly separate, that Saladin was actually a mix of Muslim and Christian. A thirteenth-century novel suggests that its heroine, the anonymous Lady of Ponthieu, was Saladin's grandmother, a myth repeated in many versions for the next 500 years. The Catholic church had its fanatics; but Europe also had a more subtle tradition that drew inspiration from Islam's greatest leader.

In the eighteenth century, scientific advances produced a new age of scepticism and a renewed appreciation of the need for tolerance. Saladin was recruited to serve the Enlightenment. 'It is said that he ordered in his will that the same alms were to be distributed to poor Muslims, Jews and Christians.' This was the philosopher Voltaire writing in his *Essai sur les Mœurs* (*Essay on Customs*) in 1756.[76] 'He wanted to show through his command that all men are brothers.'

In the German-speaking regions, the Enlightenment included the playwright and theatrical all-rounder Gottfried Lessing, who was a great friend of the Jewish philosopher

[76] That was the first edition. He went on adding to it for the rest of his life.

Moses Mendelssohn, grandfather of the composer. Lessing was famous as a free-thinker, warning against taking the Bible as literally true. His views brought him up against established powers of church and state, and he was forbidden to publish them. To smuggle them into the public domain, he turned to the stage, principally in his most famous play, *Nathan der Weise* (*Nathan the Wise*), in which the main characters are the Jew Nathan; a Christian friar, Conrad; and Saladin (generous to a fault, to the despair of his treasurer). When asked by Saladin which religion is true, Nathan – partly based on Lessing's friend Mendelssohn – replies by picking up the allegory of the three rings, which ever since Boccaccio four centuries before had been symbols of the three main religions. Since they cannot be told apart, there is no alternative but tolerance. 'Marvellous! Marvellous!' says Saladin when Nathan concludes his tale. 'You have set my mind at rest.'

Lessing makes tolerance work in practice. All the characters – Christian, Muslim and Jewish – turn out to be interrelated by blood or adoption, and all will live in harmony ever after.

In Britain, a few decades later, with revolution in the air across the Channel, the historian Edward Gibbon emphasized virtues that turned Saladin into a rough-and-ready hero of the underdog. He was, after all, a Kurd, 'a people hardy, strong, savage and impatient with the yoke . . . the garment of Saladin was a coarse woollen; water was his only drink.'

In nineteenth-century fiction, the chivalric qualities return, though the tone becomes ever more patronizing as British power increases. In 1825, Sir Walter Scott in the introduction to *The Talisman* says he was drawn by the old paradox in which 'the Christian and English monarch showed all the cruelty and violence of an Eastern Sultan; and Saladin, on the other hand, displayed the deep policy and prudence of a European sovereign'. Why, he would sound like a European statesman, except for one little disadvantage: 'true-hearted and loyal, so far as a blinded infidel may be called so'. Certainly he has the manners for the part. Richard challenges Saladin, who declines, being the epitome of prudence and politeness, saying that if he fell to Richard's sword he 'could not pass to Paradise by a more glorious death'. At the turn of the century, with the British Empire at its adventurous zenith, in George Henty's *Winning Spurs: A Tale of the Crusades* and Rider Haggard's *The Brethren*, Saladin is a virtual public-school boy, a model for those aspiring to make their mark in the great game of life, the rules of which were by happy chance written in English.

In the real world, Islam and Europe were largely apart still. Arabs ignored Saladin and Europeans admired him, without much interaction. That was changing, even as Henty and Haggard were writing. European powers sought to increase control over the decaying Ottoman Empire, particularly Germany, with Kaiser Wilhelm II's state visit in 1898, during which he flattered the Turkish sultan Abdul Hamid by implying that he was Saladin resurrected (and placed the funereal wreath with which this chapter began).

During the First World War European powers fought across Muslim lands, and then imposed themselves in a final outburst of imperialism – no crusade, but comparable in the exercise of power and influence. From Lawrence of Arabia's dream of Arab independence sprang kingdoms that were new colonies, under the thumbs of Britain and France and Britain's protégé, Palestine. Islam remained divided, theologically by its sects, strategically by its new borders. No wonder that Arabs hoped for a new resurrection, a new Saladin who would unite all Arabs, perhaps even all Muslims.

For a while, it seemed to many in the 1950s that they had one. The creation of Israel in 1948 focused Arab discontent. While Israel developed fast, new Arab nations did not. Oil revenues flowed into the pockets of ruling elites. Ordinary people remained poor. The Suez Canal stayed in British hands. To many, the whole region was ripe for revolution. So when a young nationalist named Gamal Abdul Nasser came to power in Egypt in 1954, he seemed like Saladin reborn. He certainly acted the part, seizing the Suez Canal, drawing Britain, France and Israel into a disastrous invasion to seize it back, speaking up for the poor and dispossessed, promising Arab unity, and then, like Saladin, linking up with Syria to make the United Arab Republic.

Yes, the new Saladin, despite supposedly being above religious disputes (his wife was a Shi'ite, but he avoided commitment). Nasser ignored Saladin as a religious leader and explicitly co-opted him as an Egyptian nationalist – which is arguable, since Saladin was a Kurd first, then Syrian, and Egyptian only as a conqueror. There is on the walls of Cairo's citadel, rebuilt by Saladin from 1176 onwards, a stone bas-relief of an eagle, now headless. Known as the 'Eagle of Saladin', it was taken by Nasser as the nation's emblem and it remains on the flag today. (It was also adopted as a symbol of Arab nationalism by Palestine, Yemen and Libya, and appears in some of their past flag designs.) In 1963, Nasser promoted a film that made the same point – *Al*

Nasser Salah Ad-Din (*The Eagle Saladin*) – because 'Nasser' was not only his father's name, but also means 'eagle'.[77]

In the end, it all amounted to not very much. Egyptians resented being shoe-horned into union with other Arabs (indeed Egyptians don't necessarily always identify themselves as Arabs). The United Arab Republic collapsed after three years, though Egypt still called itself the UAR for another twelve years. After Egypt was humiliated in the 1967 war against Israel, pan-Arabism foundered, honoured at best as wishful thinking.

What of Syria, the rump-state of Nasser's dream, the home of Saladin, which fell to the Assads? The current Assad's father, Hafez al-Assad, identified with Saladin as much as Nasser did, which is also a bit of a stretch, considering that he was an Alawite, a branch of Shia Islam, the minority denomination suppressed by the Sunni Saladin. He, like Nasser, called himself 'the new Saladin' and summoned his hero's shade whenever he needed support. Behind his presidential desk he hung a picture of Saladin, victorious after the battle of Hattin. As the conqueror of Jerusalem, Saladin was an obvious symbol for a president who said his main purpose was to destroy Israel, that latter-day Crusader state. But Saladin, the anti-Crusader, had a wider religious and political agenda, which made him extremely useful to Assad as a symbol: a pan-Arabist when it suited, or – since he was not an Arab at all, but a Kurd – a pan-Islamist. As Christopher Phillips says, 'His achievements were so wide that the regime could interpret them as they wished'[78] – though not

---

[77] Its English title is *Saladin the Victorious*.
[78] *Everyday Arab Identity: The Daily Reproduction of the Arab World,* p. 54.

so wide that they are of much use to the current Assad, fighting for survival in a kaleidoscope of sects and interests.

It continues, this belief in Saladin's virtues, increasingly shared between the two worlds, Islam and the collection of peoples that used to be just Europe and is now what is vaguely known as 'the West'.

In the 2005 film *Kingdom of Heaven*, Saladin comes over as tough, smart, magnanimous and gracious. The film is a Hollywood blockbuster, which has to create its own internally consistent universe, part of which involves a claim to be historical. It's not. The claim that it is 'true' is part of the fiction. Like many films, it uses history when it suits and distorts it or discards it at will. Websites are dedicated to pointing out the distortions, but they miss the main point. The prime question for a Hollywood blockbuster is: does it work? Or in other words, will it put enough bums on seats to repay the investment? The director, Ridley Scott, knows his business, and the answer is yes. Cost: $130 million. Revenue so far: over $200 million, and rising.

And yet the history *does* matter, because films reflect attitudes and fashion opinions, and sometimes influence events in the real world. As I write, a mild comedy about assassinating the dictator of North Korea has sparked a small-scale international flurry, which may yet escalate into something large scale. *Kingdom of Heaven* highlights Crusader brutalities and prejudices, which tap into public antipathy towards the US-led invasion of Iraq and Afghanistan, easily seen in the world of Islam as an anti-Muslim 'crusade'. The original Crusaders came up against Saladin, played in the movie by the Syrian actor Ghassan

Massoud. It certainly mattered to him that his part had some authenticity. As he says in one interview, 'Everything in Saladin's own life is also my philosophy. My culture is that of Saladin. He has been a role model for us since our youth. Saladin was an example of a Muslim hero who returned to Arabs and Muslims their pride and their dignity. He is an example for our people, our leaders, our society.'

And more. He was an example, it seems, for all times and all seasons both in Europe and across the Muslim world. An exemplar of Islam, Christianity, both, and then in the eighteenth century neither, but of revolution, conservatism, refinement, even the noble savagery of pre-Islamic tribesmen or Highland Scottish tribes. He is a mirror in which we can all see ourselves.

Where now are his ideals – of Arab and Islamic unity, of freedom from outside interference, of a peaceful life under Islam? Never realized by him, and today more tattered than ever, torn by all the elements Saladin despised: sectarianism, civil war, exploitation, foreign intervention. The parallels between then and now are obvious, ripe for comment. London's Globe Theatre staged David Eldridge's *Holy Warriors* in 2014, in which the past, in the form of Richard I and Saladin, informs the present – Bush, Blair and other foreign meddlers.

It goes on. Islam tears at its own flanks, offering openings for foreign alliances here and extremism there, with all hope shattered by civil war, bombs and the grotesque barbarities of the so-called Islamic State, destroying the ideals of Islam in the name of Islam. They even blew up the citadel of Tikrit, birthplace of Islam's greatest hero.

There is no sign of a new Saladin, nor any vision of what he might achieve, let alone how. Saladin's dream is for the past, or a very distant future.

Bibliography

Abu Shama, see *Receuil des historiens*

Armstrong, Karen, *Islam: A Short History*, Weidenfeld & Nicolson, London, 2000

Baha al-Din ibn Shaddad, *The rare and excellent history of Saladin, or, al-Nawādir al-Sultāniyya wa'l-Mahāsin al-Yūsufiyya*, trans. D. S. Richards, Ashgate, Aldershot, 2002

Bradbury, Jim, *The Medieval Siege*, Boydell Press, Woodbridge, 1992

Burns, Ross, *Damascus: A History*, Routledge, Abingdon, 2005

Collins, Jim, *Good to Great*, Random House, London, 2001

Coutu, Diane L., 'Putting Leaders on the Couch: A Conversation with Manfred F. R. Kets de Vries', *Harvard Business Review*, January 2004. Reprinted in *On the Mind of the Leader*, HBR, 2005

Edbury, Peter W., *The Conquest of Jerusalem and the Third Crusade: Sources in Translation*, Ashgate, Aldershot, 1998 (an English version of the *Continuation de Guillaume de Tyr*)

Eddé, Ann-Marie, *Saladin*, trans. Jane Marie Todd, Harvard University Press, Cambridge, Mass., 2011

Ehrenkreuz, Andrew, *Saladin*, State University of New York Press, Albany, 1972

Ehrenkreuz, Andrew, 'The Place of Saladin in the Naval History of the Mediterranean Sea in the Middle Ages', *Journal of the American Oriental Society*, 75, 2 (1955)

Ellenblum, Ronnie, *Crusader Castles and Modern Histories,* Cambridge University Press, 2007

Ellenblum, Ronnie, references in Bibliography to Vadum Iacob Research Project, Hebrew University of Jerusalem, online, 2007

France, John, *The Crusades and the Expansion of Catholic Christendom, 1000–1714*, Ashgate, Aldershot, 1998

Gabrieli, Francesco, *Arab Historians of the Crusades*, University of California Press, Oakland, 1991

Goleman, Daniel, Richard Boyatzis and Annie McKee, *The New Leaders: Transforming the Art of Leadership into the Science of Results*, Time Warner, London, 2002; published in the USA as *Primal Leadership*, Harvard Business School Press, Boston, Mass., 2002

Hamilton, Bernard, 'Knowing the Enemy: Western Understanding of Islam at the Time of the Crusades', *Journal of the Royal Asiatic Society*, Third Series, 7, 3 (1997)

Hamilton, Bernard, *The Leper King and His Heirs: Baldwin IV and the Kingdom of Jerusalem*, Cambridge University Press, Cambridge, 2005

Hasan, Haytham, *The Citadel of Masyaf*, Aga Khan Trust for Culture and the Syrian Directorate General, 2008

Hill, George Francis, *A History of Cyprus*, ACLS Humanities e-book, no date

Hillenbrand, Carole, *The Crusades: Islamic Perspectives*, Edinburgh University Press, 1999

Hitti, Philip, *A History of the Arabs*, Macmillan, Basingstoke, 1937 (and many later editions)

Hurd, Russell, 'A teenager revisits her father's death during childhood: a study in resilience and healthy mourning', *Adolescence* (San Diego, 2004), Vol. 39, No. 154

Ibn Jubayr, *The Travels of ibn Jubayr*, trans. Ronald Broadhurst, Aris & Phillips, Warminster, 2001

Jubb, Margaret, *The Legend of Saladin in Western Literature and Historiography*, Edwin Mellen Press, Lewiston, NY, 2000

Kedar, Benjamin Z., 'The Battle of Hattin Revisited', from *The Horns of Hattin: Proceedings of the Second Conference of the Society of the Crusades and the Latin East*, London, 1992

Kennedy, Hugh, *Crusader Castles*, Cambridge University Press, 1994

Kinnamos, John, *Deeds of John and Manuel Comnenus*, trans. Charles M. Brand, Columbia University Press, New York, 1976

La Viere Leiser, Gary, 'The Crusader Raid in the Red Sea in 578/1182–83', *Journal of the American Research Center in Egypt*, 14 (1977)

Lewis, Bernard, 'Saladin and the Assassins', *Bulletin of SOAS*, London, 15, 2 (1953)

Lyons, Malcolm Cameron and D. E. P. Jackson, *Saladin: The Politics of Holy War*, Cambridge University Press, 1982

Maalouf, Amin, *The Crusades Through Arab Eyes*, Saqi, London, 2006

Mallett, Alex, 'A trip down the Red Sea with Reynald of Châtillon', *Journal of the Royal Asiatic Society*, 3, 18, 2 (2008)

Mayer, Hans, 'Henry II of England and the Holy Land', *English Historical Review*, 97, No. 385, 1982

Nicholson, Helen, 'Women on the Third Crusade', *Journal of Medieval History*, 23, 4 (1997)

Nicolle, David, *The Crusades*, Osprey, Oxford, 2001

Nicolle, David, *Hattin 1187: Saladin's Greatest Victory*, Osprey, Oxford, no date

Nicolle, David, *Saladin and the Saracens*, Osprey, Oxford, 1986

Paris, Gaston, '*La Légende de Saladin*', *Journal des Savants*, 215, 1893

Phillips, Christopher, *Everyday Arab Identity: The Daily Reproduction of the Arab World*, Routledge, London, 2012

Receuil des historiens des croisades (Collection of the Historians of the Crusades), Paris, 1844–1906. Thousands of documents in 5 vols. Vol. 4 contains excerpts from Abu Shama's *Book of the Two Gardens* (i.e. Nur al-Din and Saladin) in Arabic and French

Richards, D. S. (trans.), *The chronicle of Ibn al-Athīr for the crusading period from al-Kāmil fī'l-ta'rīkh*, Ashgate, Aldershot, 2006

Runciman, Steven, *A History of the Crusades* (3 vols), Cambridge University Press and Penguin, London, 1951 (many reprints)

Saunders, J. J., *A History of Medieval Islam*, Routledge, London, 1965

Shagrir, Iris, 'The parable of the Three Rings: a revision of its history', *Journal of Medieval History*, 23, 2 (1997)

Usamah ibn Munqidh, *An Arab-Syrian gentleman and warrior in the period of the Crusades: memoirs of Usāmah ibn-Munqidh (Kitāb al-I'tibār)*, trans. Philip Hitti, Columbia University Press, New York, 2000

William, Archbishop of Tyre, *A History of Deeds Done Beyond the Sea*, trans. and annotated by Emily Babcock and A. C. Krey, Columbia University Press, New York, 1943

Photographic
Acknowledgements

Credits read clockwise from top left

Saladin, *c.* 1180: drawing after a contemporary miniature: Print Collector/Getty Images; bronze equestrian stature of Saladin and his warriors by Abdullah al-Sayed, 1993: © Corbis

Nur al-Din, pursued by Godfrey Martel and Hugh de Lusignan, miniature from *Histoire d'Outremer* by William of Tyre, 1232–1261, British Library, Yates Thompson 12 f.132: © The British Library Board; castle, Eilat, gulf of Aqaba: © Kim Briers/ Shutterstock; Kerak castle, Jordan: © dbimages/Alamy; the citadel, Cairo, aerial view: © AGF Srl/Alamy

The citadel, Aleppo: © Anton Ivanov/Shutterstock; siege of Belina, miniature from *Gran conquista de ultramar*, 13th century, Biblioteca Nacional, Madrid: Bridgeman Images; crusaders besieging a city, miniature from *Histoire d'Outremer* by William

Index

INDEX

INDEX

INDEX

INDEX

John Man is a historian with a special interest in the Islamic world and the Far East. His books, published in over twenty languages, include bestselling biographies of Genghis Khan, Kublai Khan and Attila the Hun, as well as histories of the Great Wall of China and the Mongol Empire.